**My
Basilian
Priesthood
1961–1967**

Life Writing Series

In the Life Writing Series, Wilfrid Laurier University Press publishes life writing and new life-writing criticism and theory in order to promote auto-biographical accounts, diaries, letters, memoirs, and testimonials written and/or told by women and men whose political, literary, or philosophical purposes are central to their lives. The Series features accounts written in English, or translated into English from French or the languages of the First Nations, or any of the languages of immigration to Canada.

The audience for the series includes scholars, youth, and avid general readers both in Canada and abroad. The Series hopes to continue its work as a leading publisher of life writing of all kinds, as an imprint that aims for scholarly excellence and represents lived experience as a tool for both historical and autobiographical research.

We publish original life writing that represents the widest range of experiences of lives lived with integrity. Life Writing also publishes original theoretical investigations about life writing, as long as they are not limited to one author or text.

Series Editor
Marlene Kadar
Humanities, York University

My
Basilian
Priesthood
1961–1967

Michael Quealey

WILFRID LAURIER
UNIVERSITY PRESS

Wilfrid Laurier University Press acknowledges the support of the Canada Council for the Arts for our publishing program. We acknowledge the financial support of the Government of Canada through the Canada Book Fund for our publishing activities. This work was supported by the Research Support Fund.

Library and Archives Canada Cataloguing in Publication

Quealey, Michael, 1934–2013, author
    My Basilian priesthood, 1961–1967 / Michael Quealey.

(Life writing)
Issued in print and electronic formats.
ISBN 978-1-77112-242-9 (softcover).—ISBN 978-1-77112-268-9 (EPUB).—
ISBN 978-1-77112-267-2 (PDF)

    1. Quealey, Michael, 1934–2013. 2. Quealey, Michael, 1943–2013—Religion.
3. Basilian Fathers. 4. Catholic Church—Clergy—Biography. 5. Catholic Church—
Ontario—Toronto—History—20th century. 6. Priests—Ontario—Toronto—
Biography. 7. Catholic ex-priests—Ontario—Toronto—Biography. I. Title.
II. Series: Life writing series

BX4705.Q34A3 2019   282.092   C2018-902180-2

Cover design and interior design by Angela Booth Malleau, designbooth.ca

© 2019 Wilfrid Laurier University Press
Waterloo, Ontario, Canada
www.wlupress.wlu.ca

This book is printed on FSC® certified paper and is certified Ecologo. It contains post-consumer fibre, is processed chlorine free, and is manufactured using biogas energy.

Printed in Canada

Every reasonable effort has been made to acquire permission for copyright material used in this text, and to acknowledge all such indebtedness accurately. Any errors and omissions called to the publisher's attention will be corrected in future printings.

To Mary Lou

Contents

The photo section appears on pages 122–137.

Part I
The Thomas More Society
1963–1965

❖

1. An Appointment with an Archbishop, March 1965

What happened on that balmy early-spring evening over thirty years ago? Around March 2, 1965, I received a phone call in the morning from Father Joseph Wey, the Superior General of the Basilian Fathers. He asked me if I would be free that evening to go with himself and Father John Kelly, the President of St. Michael's College, to a meeting requested by Philip Pocock, the Archbishop of Toronto. That was one of the occasions when I "made myself free." Many individual moments surrounding that event still seem to stand out with crystal clarity, while many other factors, events, and faces have been lost through the confusions, rationalizations, discomfitures, painful memories, and clear satisfactions that have survived those years.

Back in the late 1940s, when I had been in high school at Clover Hill, Father John Kelly became a legend with his chaplaincy work at the Don Jail with the Souchan-Jackson Gang, who were to be the last people hung in that jail. Kelly stuck with them to the end and, when I began thinking of joining the Basilians, he was one of the men whose personality and activity attracted me. As a college freshman in 1952–1953, the year after my novitiate, I had taken Kelly's "Introduction to Philosophy" course. Along with a solid introduction to Greek and Thomistic thought, he provided my first exposure to the art of critical thinking. For that I have always been grateful to him.

In the later 1950s his lustre as a fighter and a teacher faded as he became more deeply immersed in administration. My first post-seminary appointment in August 1962 was to St. Michael's College, in order to pursue my graduate studies at the Department of History at the University of Toronto. At that point, Kelly and I were confreres, supposedly living in the same local religious community. We were aware of each other, but I cannot remember having a single significant, straightforward discussion with him either before or after the following events.

My chief contact with Father Wey had been through our mutual friends the MacNeils. I was in grade school at St. Vincent de Paul School in Toronto with some of the children of that family. I had also co-chaired a youth club in the late 1940s with the MacNeil's oldest daughter. Her father, Hector MacNeil, was still the director of the Columbus Boys Camp through most of the 1950s when I had happened to be the Basilian Head Counsellor in charge of the camp program as well as the fifteen to eighteen Basilian scholastics who served as its counsellors. I would see Father Wey when he visited the MacNeils long before he was made Superior General. I mention this background because I had always felt personally comfortable with Father Wey. Because of that I asked him what this meeting with Pocock was all about. He said he was not free to say because the Archbishop wanted to speak to me directly.

My immediate Basilian superior at St. Michael's was Father Donny MacNeil, but it was John Kelly, the President of St. Michael's, not Donny MacNeil, my religious superior, who would come along that evening with Wey and myself. For me, going with Wey and Kelly to meet Pocock had to mean that I was finally being called on the carpet and that I was to be properly chastised for the "public scandal" that I had become. I was not surprised. I had no reason to be surprised. I had made a series of choices going back to January of 1963, if not earlier. The risks I had taken in the two intervening years had been taken with as much clarity and determination as I could muster. I was not only not surprised, I was even somewhat relieved that the overdue axe was finally going to fall.

2. Surgery at St. Joseph's Hospital, January 1963

For me, that March meeting in 1965 was directly connected with the first week of January 1963, when I was scheduled for abdominal surgery at St. Joseph's Hospital. In the spring of 1962, while finishing my fourth year of theology at St. Basil's Seminary, and less than a year after my ordination to the priesthood, I had been hospitalized for three weeks and pumped full of antibiotics to knock back the poison that had filled my abdomen. All the available tests failed to determine the source of the poison, but the drugs stabilized me enough that I was released.

Six months later, early in November, I went again to Emergency at St. Joe's with waves of violent pain that drove me to stay in motion and bounce off walls, rather than sit down or lie still. This time the specific source of the disturbance quickly became apparent as jaundice turned my complexion a definite yellowish-brown. I was in the middle of a gall-bladder attack and it lasted for twenty-seven hours. Eventually it was determined that my gallbladder had been malfunctioning throughout my twenties and had been popping stones throughout the abdomen.

That night in November one of the larger stones had become lodged in the main bile duct and all the poison in my system had backed up. After twenty-seven hours that stone finally moved over and my relief was instant. I was told that, despite the grave risks, they had been on the verge of operating because fighting the attack had been wearing me down too far. They went on to explain that I definitely needed surgery but my insides were still too inflamed for them to proceed safely. I was to go on straight fluids for about a week and then go home and allow my system to calm down for six months, at which point they would operate and take out my gallbladder.

I remember being in a strangely indifferent mood. I had been to St. Joseph's Hospital for several surgical stays through the 1950s, and so far the sheer joy and pleasure of the social contacts with doctors, nurses, and patients had far outweighed the various physical inconveniences. That November I went on my "week of fluids," but I didn't last for more than a couple of days. Fluids or not, something triggered another gallstone attack. This second attack lasted forty-three hours. No one could predict how much longer the attack would persist, and because my stamina was dropping rapidly they were giving me only about four more hours before they would have to take me to the operating room, regardless of the risk. For whatever reason the blockage cleared again.

The following day I was informed that under no circumstances would I be allowed to leave the hospital until they had completed the required surgery. They would keep me on fluids and hope that my inflamed and severely strained system would calm down as quickly as possible. This meant I stayed at St. Joe's over Christmas and New Year's. I don't remember that bothering me, nor my missing any of the holiday festivities on my first Christmas out of the seminary. I was somewhat puzzled as to whether this medical crisis was a sign of divine approval or disapproval of my publication the month before of "Quo Vadimus?" (See Appendix 4.)

What happened the night before that operation remains probably the single most pivotal event in my life. My doctor was Dr. Allan Borowy,

protegé of Dr. Charlie Knowlton. Knowlton had been Chief of Staff at
St. Joe's for many years. His only son, Mickey, was a Basilian, but even
before that the Basilians had always received the best treatment possible,
both at Charlie's office on St. Clair Avenue and at St. Joseph's. I had always
liked Knowlton and during the six weeks of this hospital stay I also came
to like and trust his protegé. Borowy was to succeed Knowlton as Chief
of Staff and would serve in that post until the 1990s. He was never to be
as gregarious or flamboyant as his mentor and only that January did he
complete his residency. I remember him as having an awkward but quietly
straightforward bedside manner. Above all, I did trust him.

I was in one of the private rooms reserved for priests and I had been
prepared as thoroughly as possible for the next morning. It was around
eight o'clock in the evening that Borowy came to my room and pulled
up a chair beside my bed. He then told me that, while I definitely had to
have the operation, my system was still very weak and worn out. He went
on to say that I had a right to know that, in his judgment, I had a less than
a 50–50 chance of surviving the surgery the next day.

What occurred next remains perhaps the single most powerful of any
of my personal realizations. My first reaction to what Borowy was telling
me was that it didn't really matter which way it went. Almost immediately,
my second reaction came. What had I been doing with my life that the
question of whether I lived or died the very next day "didn't matter"? I
was so shocked by these realizations that while I remained calm and collected on the outside it never even occurred to me to give those reactions
to Borowy. He promised to give the operation his best shot, wished me
luck, and left the room. By then I felt a kind of calm that I have rarely
experienced. I knew that there was nothing I could do to affect the out-
come the next day.

I remember trying to pray because that was what the situation seemed
to call for. That didn't go anywhere and that fact irritated me. In the ensu-
ing quiet I had no desire to talk to anyone except myself. I was still only
twenty-eight years old and I was convinced that overall I had tried hard,
sometimes too hard, to do what was right. I do not remember wanting to
blame anyone, including God. As I lay there beginning to doze off from
my sleeping pill, what I was clearest about was that I had not been living
properly and, without realizing how, I had in fact brought myself to this
strange moment in time when even life itself seemed to lack adequate
importance. The last thing I remember saying to myself that night was that

I did want to go on living. My reasons for such a decision were anything but clear. At the very least I was certain of one thing. If it happened that I did survive that operation I was definitely going to live differently. I did not know what I meant by that, but I did realize very, very profoundly that I was going to try to find out.

I still have the scar, over a foot long. They told me that when they got inside they kept finding stones that I "had popped all over the place." The incision was larger than usual because they had to do a full abdominal exploratory, since I still had symptoms that didn't make sense. The main fact is that I survived that day and within about sixty hours I began feeling physically better than I had felt for many years. They told me they had difficulty believing how quickly I recuperated. I was out of the hospital in two weeks instead of the projected four.

3. Graduate Studies, Spring 1961–1963

By the end of January I was back at my assigned task as the assistant prefect of the second floor in Elmsley Hall. I went back to my classes in the Department of History at the U of T, where I was carrying four full graduate courses for the first year of their Ph.D. program. What few people realized was that I had spent most of the first third of that academic year, my first year out of the seminary, searching out pastoral and social contacts. I especially loved to drop into The Coop, the St. Michael's College coffee shop.

What most people did realize was that the second third of that academic year, from early November until late January, I had spent in the hospital. Without my even having to suggest it, several spoke of how no one could reasonably expect that I would be able successfully to complete my graduate year—and they didn't even seem to know or take into consideration how I had spent the first third of that year.

The question of my graduate studies goes back several years. As an extra, I had completed one graduate History course in each of my first two years of formal theological studies. During my third year of theology, on completion of which I was scheduled to be ordained to the priesthood, I did my French-language tests, which was a standard requirement for all graduate studies at U of T. I also began looking for a suitable thesis topic to finish off my M.A. requirements in the U of T's Department of History.

I was ordained on June 29, 1961, the feast of Sts. Peter and Paul, six weeks short of a full ten years since I had entered the Basilians.

After a couple of weeks of holidays with my family I went to Columbus Boys Camp as its chaplain. Next, I asked and received permission to go to Notre Dame University in South Bend, Indiana, to work in their library and archives. I wanted to look into their Orestes Brownson papers and other holdings on the nature of nineteenth-century American-Irish Catholicism. On the way to Notre Dame I made stops for my first visits to Assumption College in Windsor, Catholic Central in Detroit, and Andrean High in Gary before settling in to live and work on the South Bend campus. It was a good summer, but I didn't find enough of the academic resources I had been looking for.

I was back at St. Basil's Seminary for the 1961–1962 academic year. It was the first year of my priesthood, and aside from the three-week hospital stay following my first gallbladder attack it was indeed a full academic year. I was finishing off the final credits for my S.T.B. (Bachelor of Sacred Theology) from the University of St. Michael's College. These credits were difficult because they relied so heavily on regurgitation and I was finding it increasingly stressful to learn without employing some form of open critical analysis. Continuing to work on *The Basilian Teacher* [a journal published by the Basilian fathers at St. Mike's from 1956 to 1968] and on projects such as skit nights was far more satisfying.

During that same year I explored three possible topics to complete my M.A. thesis requirements for History. For various reasons none of the three topics panned out. Then I hit on something that definitely did not "make my heart soar like a hawk" but that just might allow me to complete that M.A. I found a body of papers in the Ontario Archives dealing with a British general who turned back Napoleon's last charge at Waterloo and who, after the Napoleonic Wars, landed a job as the Lieutenant-Governor of Upper Canada in the 1820s. Now, from what I knew, not much very stimulating was happening anywhere in the Eurocentric world during the 1820s, let alone in Upper Canada. Even so, I dove in and for about six weeks actually became quite enthusiastic about this admittedly obscure topic.

I even began wondering if I had latched onto something larger than a M.A. thesis. I worked up a proposal for a five-section doctoral thesis and asked the History department to allow me to skip over the rest of my M.A. and permit me to proceed immediately to the doctoral program. I enclosed a sample draft of one section. They asked for another section and I quickly whipped into reasonable shape what I knew would be my best and most attractive final section. The History department approved my proposal with the understanding that I would have to backtrack and do the required courses and comprehensives of the doctoral program before submitting my thesis. I agreed, and that is why I never received an M.A.

I had until the autumn of 1962 before I could begin my courses, so I asked for permission to spend several weeks living with the Oblates at the Université d'Ottawa while I spent my days at the National Archives. By the end of that summer I had gathered the bulk of the raw material for my thesis. In August I finally left the seminary and moved over to St. Michael's College. This flashback fills in the first year of my priesthood, when pastoral contacts were minimal and were actively discouraged by my superiors so that I could concentrate on my studies. Especially while in Ottawa I was fortunate to have accomplished so much because of the extra time it would allow me later.

In February of 1963, after my surgery at St. Joe's, two things happened inside me. In the first place, I had a surge of energy that was almost uncontainable. I came to realize that the increasing sluggishness that I had felt during my twenties had not been the natural consequence of what I thought aging was all about but had in fact been the by-product of my pathology. Secondly, I thought that if I could focus all this new-found energy on my graduate courses during the final eight weeks of the spring term and if, contrary to general expectations, I was able to do well, then in the future people might remain uncertain as to how much I might really be able to accomplish when under pressure. That was one of the first moments when I realized how arrogant and independent I was becoming. But that realization didn't bother me, because I was liking the way it felt. I was also not aware of my attitude harming anyone else.

It was the intensity of a new-found creativity that surprised me most. I had never been very excited about learning things formally. I had often proclaimed that I had learned far more about human nature during my summers at Columbus Boys Camp than in all my four years of my Honours Modern History program at the U of T, let alone my so-called theological formation at St. Basil's Seminary. In 1963, during those final eight weeks of the academic term, I discovered how passionate I could become over academic questions.

I caught up on the work I had missed and poured myself into the final term papers and exams for all four courses. I became so involved in one paper that it ran to 257 pages plus illustrations. That paper happened to be on "Archbishop John Walsh and the Manitoba School Question: Clerical Intervention in Canadian Politics, 1891 to 1898." Four years later John Saywell, the professor for whom I did that paper, was Dean of Arts at York University. I've always believed that it was the quality of that paper that influenced him to offer me a full-time professorship at York after an interview of only twelve minutes.

There were nine of us doing the "course-work year" in History's doctoral program that year. Without any prior notification the administration at Sidney Smith Hall [home of the Department of History] had decided to clean house, and only three of the nine of us would be allowed to proceed. I was one of the three chosen to continue. It was an enormous boost to my self-confidence. Perhaps there was a lot more that I could accomplish if I simply put my mind to it. It is not that others had not believed in me. Some important people did and other important people did not. I suppose the difficulty was that I had considerable difficulty believing any of them. Now I was at least beginning to believe in myself. It felt strange, frightful, and wonderful.

Looking back now I believe that what happened that night in January at St. Joe's was that I decided to take the lid off all the repression and conformity that I had accepted and/or imposed on myself. What first surged to the surface and wrought wonders I had never known to be possible were waves of creativity, courage, and determination. Later on I would come to realize that these were only the top layers of Pandora's box.

4. A Walk with Mad Mac McCarthy, May 1963

At the end of that term, in the early summer of 1963, two important events occurred that would seriously influence my journey to Newman. In the first place, before we scattered for the summer Father Don McCarthy, who had been on faculty at St. Mike's for several years, took me for a long walk. Don, along with Paul Glynn, had been my mentor at Boys Camp and they had personally chosen me to replace them as head counsellor. Don and I had also worked together in study groups at the seminary on issues of social justice, had done skits together, and tended to share the same outrage towards various dimensions of the Basilian ethos as well as the state of the world generally. I knew him affectionately as Mad Mac and he always called me Big Mike.

We both knew by that spring that he was to be appointed to St. John Fisher College in Rochester for the following year and that I was to remain at St. Mike's as full prefect of the third floor of Elmsley Hall and to work full-time on my doctoral comprehensives. On that walk Don asked me if I would consider replacing him as the Basilian responsible for the Thomas More Sodality, which he had been running for some time at St. Mike's. He said that several of the students in that group who had met me in various contexts, including The Coop, had asked him to approach me. He was also asking for himself, since he dreaded what might happen if certain of our fellow Basilians were to be his replacement. I had enjoyed the few students that I had met from this group and, despite the insecurities I always experience before doing something for the first time, I agreed to take it on.

5. St. Helena's and Columbia University, New York City, June 1963

The second happening of the early summer of 1963 involved how I had chosen to spend those summer months. Restlessness, agitation, and curiosity were driving me to look for opportunities to expand my horizons: academic, spiritual, and personal. I had heard of a priest who had managed to stay at St. Helena's parish in the Bronx to cover for the summer holidays of its large staff of priests. I had also learned that Columbia University offered graduate history courses in the summer months by offering positions to top scholars from across the US. I applied to be a "Special Student," which meant I could audit these courses and not have to produce term papers. I was accepted and ended up taking lecture courses from people like Margaret Meade. I was also accepted into a small seminar group with John Higham, whose work on American nativism I had long admired.

St. Helena's also welcomed me. There I encountered and thoroughly enjoyed the pastoral challenges of a big city parish. It could and did mean doing three weddings on a Saturday, three to four Masses on a Sunday, confessional shifts every other day, eight to fifteen baptisms on a Sunday afternoon, and two to three funeral parlour wakes and as many sick calls on nights when I was on duty. It also meant steak and eggs every morning with the legendary Monsignor Scanlon, who was then in his eighties. Then there were the heated yet rewarding discussions with his staff of five priests and monsignors who were terrific on social justice but definitely disliked this John XXIII and all the "trouble" he had stirred up.

I also made fast friends with several of the parishioners. An Irish cop and his family, the Reddens, adopted me and within two weeks we had weekly discussion groups at their apartment on the edge of Parkchester. My second-floor bedroom was only thirty yards from the elevated Pelham Bay Line. Within days my nervous system adjusted to the enormous rattle of the subway trains and after that I never missed a wink.

6. Grade School Eucharists, 1939–1945

The Mass or Sacred Eucharist had been central to my history, even though it had been a fact of life rather than a dynamic force. Family stories claim that by the time I was five years old I would be discovered "playing" Mass. All through grade school it seemed that I was always the altar boy designated for the 7 a.m. Mass, even though I often fainted or had to leave the sanctuary on the verge of throwing up. These physical reactions seemed to have been mainly because of simple hunger combined with the requirement that altar boys were expected to abstain from food and drink so they could receive daily Communion. Insofar as my mother acknowledged it, she dismissed it as my "growing too fast," so that I could feel guilty even about that. My Dad said nothing so as not to upset my mother. For various reasons I was very prone to having my guilt manipulated, but to this day I have no memory of any priest or parent even noticing let alone doing anything about the price I was paying.

Up until grade 8 at St. Vincent de Paul's Separate School, attendance at daily Mass, especially during Lent, was made the highlight of daily class competition on a row-by-row basis. I hope I never forget a classmate named Jock MacDonald. He came from a large family, all of whom seemed hungry for many things, but he was very quiet and widely respected for his unassuming physical strength and rough-hewn self-confidence. One day, during the daily roll call on who had attended Mass that morning, Jock once more stated quite simply that he had not and that it was nobody's business why he had not been to Mass.

At recess that morning it seemed that all the boys in our row, including myself, were determined to force Jock to change his ways. Unless he gave us his solemn word that he would go to Mass and stop ruining our points total we were going to beat the dickens out of him. The girls from the class had a separate schoolyard, and I have sometimes wondered whether their presence would have helped or worsened this scene. Anyway, the girls were not there.

Jock quietly but firmly told us that we were all stupid and that we could all stay in the hell of the Church if that was what we wanted but to mind our own business and leave him alone. I cannot remember ever before hearing such sacrilegious language. It was enough to inflame still further everyone's righteous indignation. By this point Jock had manoeuvred himself quite deliberately into a corner of the schoolyard with a twelve-foot chain-link fence on his right and the ten-foot board fence at the back of the parish rectory on his left. We unleashed our full fury on him, but because of his choice of the field of battle only two of us could get at him at a time. Well, we had known he was tough even though he had never gone out of his way to prove it. That was why no one had ever previously dared to challenge him one-on-one on this or any other matter.

Then, with that peculiar bravado that only a mob can muster, we laid into him. Jock proceeded to demonstrate that he was a far better street fighter than anyone had imagined. It took only four or five bloody noses, split lips, and swollen eyes before our little crusading mob dissolved. Jock never seemed to hold it against us and we never bothered him again. Along with my shame at having joined in I knew I had participated in something very important that day. It was one of those moments that made me question a lot of things, including even what the Eucharist itself was really all about.

7. Demigods and Tenebrae

The pastor of St. Vincent de Paul was known first as the Duke and then, after he was made a monsignor, as the Monz. He went unchallenged in his repeated proclamations that, as in the Old Testament, the Lord still expected to receive the best fruits from his believers. This meant that the "best boys" were supposed to be altar boys and the "best altar boys" were supposed to become candidates for the priesthood. It was not mentioned nearly as often, but he said the same about the "best young women," who should all be in convents. On several occasions that I witnessed he went so far as to say, "Those who are not good enough to go to the seminary or the convent may as well get married."

In retrospect, what I found most upsetting about these incidents was that I never heard anyone, cleric or layman, in public or in private, ever object to, let alone openly oppose, these kinds of statements. In the 1940s and early 50s the Monz was reported to have "produced" more priests than the rest of Toronto put together. It was in this atmosphere that there occurred what for me were the two most important parish events of each year.

First, most of the seminarians would be home for the holidays and they would all be on the altar at Christmas and during Holy Week along with those of us still in school. This systematic elitism would mean that our own regular altar boys were augmented by at least twenty seminarians. They were aged mainly eighteen to twenty-eight and had a stature in our entire parish culture that was far above that of any athletic, musical, or political star.

This parish was overwhelmingly a working-class Irish ghetto in which seminarians were demigods. Their ordinations and First Masses were held up and celebrated as the pinnacles of possible achievement. Compared to them, according to the unchallenged ideology of that parish, even doctors and lawyers were second-rate because they were "only" laymen. Seminarians and priests were set up as the most truly valid models for success, sanctity, and manhood.

The other most memorable, somewhat liturgical, annual event was Tenebrae, which was held on Monday, Tuesday, and Wednesday evenings in Holy Week. I realize that a ceremony by that name is still an annual occurrence at the Cathedral and that its chief focus is on the blessing of the sacred oils for the coming year.

Our parish goings-on had nothing to do with sacred oils and we never heard of anyone else who celebrated those nights the way we did. I am also not clear on the origins of our parish custom except that the Monz always insisted on it as an essential part of Holy Week. What did happen on those three nights, in our parish at least, was that the parish priests, visiting dignitaries and seminarians on holidays would sit in the rows of pews on each side of the sanctuary reciting and chanting Vespers and Compline from their breviaries. Special soloists were featured, especially the favourite of the younger set, a certain Machine-Gun Burke, the regular choirmaster whose bellow matched his bulk.

For us the real highlight of these evenings occurred towards the end of the ceremony when the lights throughout the church were slowly turned out one by one. This was supposedly to simulate the darkness into which Jerusalem sank as Christ's Passion proceeded. Six to eight altar boys would have already been designated to arrange this climax. It was an assignment that was always far more coveted than that of being selected as any Master of Ceremonies.

For at least a week ahead of time those of us so designated would collect old sheets of corrugated tin and metal trash cans, which we would partially fill with broken bottles and anything else with potential for massive noisemaking. We always had many suggestions and help from willing assistants. The chief criterion for the required material was that it was to be used to create the loudest, most obstreperous cacophony possible. On Monday afternoon of Holy Week we would bring in our collected wonders and situate them appropriately in the six-foot-wide passageway between the back of the main marble altar and the back wall of the sanctuary.

The chosen noise-masters had to sit patiently back there through all the psalms and solos until our moment of glory was signalled with the extinction of the last light in the church. At that point we did try our hardest in the complete darkness to make all pandemonium tear loose. Tin cans with broken glass were shaken, sheets of tin were kicked against the marble walls, strings of soup cans were shaken violently, oscillating flashlights shot rays of light up onto the stained-glass windows and sculptured ceiling, and the largest firecrackers we could afford were set off in garbage cans. A prearranged signal from the Monz told us when enough was enough. It was traditional that we observed that signal on the first two nights and then pretended not to notice it on the third and final night. We would stop on that night only when they turned all the regular lights back on.

Little children were never allowed to be present at these liturgical events because even some of the adults, who came from far and near, claimed to find the above carryings-on to be somewhat frightening. We were never quite clear as to what we were supposed to be signifying. Was it the forces of nature mourning over Christ's death or was it the demons of hell celebrating Christ's apparent defeat? The far greater mystery was why on earth did that miserly, misanthropic, doom-monger of a Jansenist

Irish pastor/ward boss allow such Mardi Gras nonsense year after year? What I have come to realize is that for me personally Tenebrae remained the chief chunk of pre-Grail experience that felt strangely inspirational when I began at Grailville [in the summer of 1963] to wonder about all the things that liturgy might be able to accomplish.

8. Disappointing Eucharists, 1946–1962

Throughout my high-school years, while I struggled with whether or not I was blessed and/or cursed with a "true vocation," I cannot remember the Eucharist having much if anything to do with it. The Eucharist was simply part of the package you bought into, something that priests did, and by attending it or actually doing it you received at least minimal acceptance in the tribe. During the ten years of training to become a Basilian I do not remember a single Mass that in itself seemed very important, let alone salvific. I do remember special events of which a Eucharist was the apparent focal point. But, upon examination, it was the quality of the music, the vigour of the communal singing, and the general camaraderie of special feast days and celebrations that really made those events special.

The emphasis on learning how to say Mass was exclusively on proper form. Very sincere and respected Basilians, like Père Bondy, made powerful connections between the Mass and private spirituality in his homilies on "the Master." But those connections all made the Mass the focus of the personal sanctity and devotional life of the individual priest. The Eucharist never seemed to have any significant communal dimension beyond giving the faithful an opportunity to fulfill their obligations.

The reality of daily Mass at the seminary during those same years was not usually conducive even to simple personal devotion, let alone to profound edification. At the end of morning meditation, that day's first platoon of designated Mass servers proceeded to the "stables" behind the main altar of the seminary chapel. That term refers to the two clean, well-appointed rooms, roughly 30 feet by 20 feet, one behind the main chapel, and the other downstairs behind the south end of the refectory wall. Each room had four cubicles on each side for saying Mass. That meant that, including the two floors, there were spaces for sixteen Masses to go on simultaneously. Even at that it usually took two shifts to accommodate everyone. Irritations at the peculiar noises coming from the neighbouring stalls were all that broke the total isolation of each Mass.

Scholastics considered it a bonus if they didn't have to do the second shift or if you were fortunate enough to be assigned one of the "quickie" priests, whose form usually lacked dignity and whose possible substance seemed highly dubious. Certain priests would become seriously upset by a fallen Eucharistic crumb or if the wine was not warm enough, but never, never would they reveal any sign that they had been excited about a fresh spiritual experience or realization that had happened at their Eucharist that morning. I am now convinced that such Eucharists actually did considerable harm by reinforcing and spiritualizing the obviously self-involved narcissistic inclinations of many of those priests. No wonder there was such resistance when the practice of concelebration was first introduced!

As part of my Basilian training I served as a scholastic prefect in House "2 and 96" at St. Michael's College in 1955–1956 and in Tweedsmuir House at St. Michael's College School in 1956–1957 and 1958–1959. In each of these assignments part of my job was to get the boarders up for daily Mass by any means necessary, except on Saturdays, of course. In each of these situations uncooperative boarders were docked late leaves and weekend passes or given detentions if they eluded my dawn patrols or failed to report at my checkpoint at the rear of the chapel. I would occasionally regale my confreres with my tales of rolling out literally onto the floor, mattress and all, some of the more recalcitrant boarders. I must admit that I took these attitudes with me to Boys Camp when I became its Head Counsellor and insisted on daily head counts at Mass as one of the methods for cabins to score points in their Huron/Iroquois rivalry.

Despite all this nonsense there were occasional moments, especially at Boys Camp, when strange, funny, and even wonderful things would seem to happen during Mass and immediately afterwards. In general, though, I accepted that the communal nature of the Eucharist was primarily in the department of obligation, captive audiences, and propagandic control of the faithful. Along with the compulsory daily readings from the breviary, especially before the transition to the vernacular, the Eucharist was primarily a priest's private act that he occasionally had to allow the faithful to witness.

The Eucharist was supposed to be a sacrament, a sacred sign, something that was in and of itself efficacious and salvific. Increasingly, it seemed to me in its actual performance to be no better than a bad magic show performed by professional incompetents who lacked even the elementary skills of a reasonably capable snake-oil salesman. I have indulged this rather lengthy flashback to indicate the restless state of mind I took with me to Grailville.

9. Loveland, Ohio, the Grail, and New York City, Summer 1963

While I was an undergraduate at the U of T one of the most likeable students in our History classes was a wonderful pixie-like free spirit by the name of Loretta Matura. She later changed her first name back to the original Polish of Nusia and she continued to correspond with myself, Dick Schiefen, and Sam Femiano. At some point, around 1958, she had become involved with the Grail Movement and her letters were more and more filled with her excitement at both the inner peace and passionate involvement that she was gaining there.

She had repeatedly invited me to come and see what was happening at Grailville, which was located at Loveland, Ohio, not far from Cincinnati. I decided to give it a try, especially early in the summer of 1963 when I was already planning a rather circuitous bus trip by way of Washington as my way of getting to New York City. Well, I got to Grailville and that one weekend there profoundly changed my sense of the priesthood, of what liturgy could be all about, of who I was and what I wanted to do.

Nusia met me at the bus depot and drove me out to Grailville. Physically the buildings were not particularly memorable. The accommodations were clean, simple, and comfortable, and there was at least one large space that encouraged multiple usage. The little decorative touches included wildflower arrangements and colourful burlap banners with unusual scriptural and secular quotations. These helped create an open, slightly offbeat, yet stimulating environment.

The overall atmosphere was relaxed yet vibrant. As I remember it, the meals consisted of soups, stews, and salads done in a pickup style with individuals composing their own clusters for eating together. There seemed to be upwards of a hundred present for this particular weekend, many of them permanent residents, others from various Grail locations, and invited guests like myself.

I had already learned that this group was very loosely structured and had, up until that point in time, successfully resisted efforts to make itself into a more canonically recognizable form. They insisted on identifying themselves as "a community of lay women exploring the implications of the Christian message." In that setting I can remember at least two major liturgies, a few discussion groups on set topics, and wonderful bull sessions of various sizes on an astounding range of questions.

They seemed to relish the richness of their individual diversity while at the same time revelling in the sheer strength, delicacy, and vibrancy of what they were creating together. I met a wide range of interesting characters, including Mary Carpenter from my home parish, Mary Anne Weber from Leaside, who actually made catechetics exciting, and Mary Barton, already an established actress at the Shaw Festival.

Another visitor dropped in to preside at the Saturday-evening liturgy. His name was Father Clarence Rivers, an Afro-American priest from a downtown parish in Cincinnati. I was impressed. His chief area of interest was the role of music in the liturgy and he was continuing to compose an alternative which he called "The American Mass." It contained elements of the Misa Luba from the Congo mixed with aspects of American gospel singing, folk songs, and jazz. I got a taste of its possibilities at that evening's liturgy. I had come to Grailville to encourage Nusia, to observe from my usually hypercritical stance, and just maybe to pick up a few useful pastoral tips. All of that quickly became secondary as I became enthralled, enchanted, absorbed, and deeply moved. I wanted to be a participant and not merely a bystander.

As far as I remember, Clarence and I were the only males present. Women did all the readings, the offertory procession, the intentions, the guitars and drums, and the singing. The homily was a warm and brilliant synthesis of that day's liturgical selections from Scripture. The intentions, aside from a few pump-primers, were improvisations on possible connections between those scriptural passages and current issues and concerns, whether they be global, national, diocesan, Grail, or strictly personal.

I felt that the Word was taking on flesh right before my eyes and within me. In a very profound sense that I had never before witnessed or even conceived of the possibility of, I saw that that old repository of revelation, inspiration, and accumulated wisdom called the Scriptures could be wrestled with so enjoyably and so fruitfully. The end result of this mélange of traditional texts, banners, guitars, drums, diverse voices, and mixed dramatic forms was that all present indeed did "receive and enjoy life more abundantly."

I didn't have any idea of what I was going to do with it, but I left Grail-ville profoundly shaken. At that point I could not see any obvious way in which I could apply it. Before leaving I had asked: "How do you get away with it?" My basic pragmatism had long dictated as an essential guiding principle that "by its fruits it will be known, since a good tree cannot give bad fruit and vice versa." Because of that I had no personal difficulty with their many technical deviations from the standing regulations on liturgical forms. This was definitely not a bad tree. Even so, the existing political culture of the North American Church made it truly wondrous that what I had witnessed and participated in had not already been crushed for all the "correct" canonical reasons.

Grailville's answer to my question was that the Archbishop of Cincin-nati was very supportive of their efforts at experimentation and actively shielded them against unwarranted forms of criticism. I found that in itself to be amazing, but my quick mental check of the current roster of Canadian bishops drew a blank on anyone with the self-confidence and the understanding of scripture and liturgy, let alone the political courage, to take a similar stance. Dealing with the possible transportation of the Grail experience back to Canada would need more time and clarity. In the meantime I slept overnight on the bus, spent the entire next day getting my first direct taste of Washington's version of American triumphalism, and then took another overnight bus to New York City.

As already indicated, I will always be grateful to New York City for those two magnificent summers of 1963 and 1964. St. Helena's, on the east side of the Bronx, included the White Castle Diner, where a significant civil-rights action took place that first summer. The parish also embraced Parkchester, a remarkable postwar example of the city's communal-living projects. In the parish, at Columbia, at the chaplaincy at NYU, and with Maryknollers in Harlem I searched for Grail-like signs of awakening and renewal. They were not there. There were pockets of excitement and curiosity, but most obviously there was deep turmoil, anxiety, and even despair over the directions being supported by "the peasant Pope."

I was invited to some discussion groups where even the most elemen-tary aspects of recent biblical criticism remained highly suspect. I tended to concentrate on various historical dimensions and encouraged others to imagine how they would like to see the Word made flesh in their time. Meanwhile, I fell in love with the city and ever since have regarded it as embodying the best and the worst of the human condition, with an enormously rich diversity in between. This wide range of experience confirmed my concentration on the pastoral dimensions and I returned to Toronto deeply enriched by the summer and eager to do something with it.

10. A Sodality Reborn as a Society, September 1963

The "something" quickly revealed itself. I called an inaugural meeting of the veterans of the Thomas More Sodality, introduced myself as Father Don McCarthy's replacement, and asked them what they wanted to do with the year. A wide-ranging discussion ensued, whose underlying purpose seemed to be to give both them and myself an opportunity to get some measure of each other. Only two matters of clear consensus emerged from that initial meeting. The first was to set a time for a follow-up meeting, to which they would invite whomever they thought might be interested.

The second consensus arose over the title of the organization. By 1963, at St. Mike's especially, students were already well into that "sixties thing," which was against belonging rigidly to anything, especially not to anything that sounded old. I had no difficulty agreeing that the term "Sodality" definitely sounded old and probably triggered for prospective participants a range of not always pleasant associations. A discussion followed on an appropriate name replacement.

Most seemed to feel that Thomas More was still an acceptable saint but that "Sodality" should be replaced with the far more neutral and welcoming term "Society." I remain convinced that this apparently simple name change was a sign that effected a metamorphosis. The title was soon shortened in student parlance to the TMS and things began to happen.

Within two weeks a delegation of four students asked to see me. We met, and slowly but with admirable courage they said that they and many in the larger group were deeply troubled by their experience with the Catholic Church and were on the verge of dismissing all of its trappings. They declared that they remained at St. Mike's only to please their parents and to pick up a solid secular education through their courses at the U of T. I asked why they had not already left the Eucharist or even the Church itself.

It emerged that while most had definitely cut back on their Mass attendance, they had not yet found an adequate replacement. They were surprisingly clear in their analysis of why it was that the Mass "really bugged them." At the same time they said they wanted if possible to give it one more try, but the focus had to be on making the Mass make more sense to them. They had come to ask me if I would be willing to help them in this because they were not aware of anyone else they were willing to work with. They were not politically naive and knew that what they wanted could be quickly shot down. They also acknowledged I would have to take some very real political risks. I said I wanted some time to think about this, and we agreed to meet again in a few days.

It did not take me long to come to a decision. I needed the couple of days mainly to double-check a few things. If I had been approached with this challenge even a few months earlier, I am certain I would not have been ready to take the risk. But by now I had been to Grailville and had a much clearer sense of what could be done and of the potential rewards that could outweigh the risks.

Secondly, this particular group of students was bright, intelligent, talented, and wonderful to do anything with. They came from the cream of that St. Mike's tradition that drew gifted American students from Massachusetts to Delaware. Often they were the offspring of St. Mike's alumni, ready and eager to leave the US for a less expensive yet solid liberal education under the protective Catholic umbrella of St. Michael's. This particular grouping was the best I have seen either before or since. They constituted about seventy per cent of TMS. The rest were Canucks, mainly from Toronto, spiced with some remarkable young people from the farms and towns of northern and southwestern Ontario.

Thirdly, that September I had met two new students on campus, Dorothy Thomas from the West Indies and Pat Uhl from Cincinnati, both of whom had spent two whole years at Grailville. Furthermore, Pat Uhl was an expert with the guitar and had already composed and introduced her own religious folk songs at Grailville. Between them they had a wealth of practical experience in liturgy, catechetics, and scripture-study techniques. They were eager to share what they had learned. Whether it was the stars of the zodiac, Jungian synchronicity, or old-fashioned divine providence, it really did seem that the times were ready for something to happen.

The final checkpoint was what all this had to do with the principle of the Church's authority as well as my Basilian vow of obedience. I do not remember having any urge to talk to anyone about this except to myself and to "the Carpenter." It was partly because I did not want to implicate anyone else in my risks. I also saw no sense in alerting or disturbing others in advance. I could be derailed from doing what I was convinced needed to be done by having to clear obstacles that could be put in my way before I even got started. I was not aware at the time, but in retrospect I can see that by this point I had already lost most if not all of my faith in the Basilian community, especially in any matter with pastoral considerations. The last question was "Did I feel bound by any dimension of the Church's authority?" Well, I did and I didn't.

I was officially a doctoral student in Modern History, majoring in Pre-Confederation Canada. In 1962 I had also received an S.T.B. from the University of St. Michael's College. It was supposed to count as a graduate degree. I had long been fascinated by the twists and turns of earthly experience chalked up at all levels by members of Christ's kingdom on earth. Years before, for example, I had been struck by the widely divergent attitudes towards authority between the Church in Italy, as well as in Europe generally, and the Church in North America.

Italian Catholics seemed to take it for granted that their loyalty to the Pope had little or nothing to do with whether or not they accepted his teachings and regulations. To these Italian Catholics and many other European Catholics, the slavish literalness of most of the North American Jansenist hierarchy and their well-trained followers was simply ridiculous. It had long seemed to me that individuals in the European Church were expected to be personally responsible for what they did with their unique "gift of the spirit." Those vested with authority by the institutional Church were to stand back and observe these workings of the Spirit, and step in only to admonish, cajole, or cancel when they had solid evidence that these workings were harmful to the well-being of the faithful, especially those most directly involved in these workings.

In North America, on the other hand, the exercise of authority seemed determined by feudal or divine-right ideologies where the faithful were expected to ask for permission first and to implement only what they were told to do by those higher up. I had long felt that these North American attitudes were highly dehumanizing and derived from secular rather than theological, let alone scriptural, sources. If anything, my own personal Basilian experience in attempting to do my best as Head Counsellor of Columbus Boys Camp and as editor of *The Basilian Teacher* had reinforced these convictions. At the same time, this was one of those moments when the decision I had supposedly made that night in St. Joseph's Hospital in

January of 1963 came back to me. Here it was only eight months later and
I was up against whether or not I would honour my own word to myself.

I spent a final gentle autumn evening wandering around the grounds
of the college and decided that I would choose for now, on the basis of the
supposed catholicity and universality of the Church, to act in this matter
as a European Catholic. I had no doubts whatsoever that the authorities
would very soon know exactly what I was doing. What they might decide
to do about it was their business. What I might do in response to their
reaction was too far down the journey for me to anticipate, let alone come
to any conclusion as to what to do then.

I called in the students, gave them the bare bones of my process and
decision, and we got down to business. I presented certain conditions, all
of which they accepted. I insisted that there was to be no formal membership of any kind and that any student on campus who wished to participate was welcome on a one-time or all-time basis. I insisted that if we
were seriously to explore what the Eucharist might mean for us, then we
must attempt to avoid any deliberate sensationalism.

To give concrete form to this, I strongly recommended that we do our
experimental Eucharist in St. Michael's College Chapel under St. Basil's
Church at nine o'clock on Saturday mornings. I could not come up with
any tougher time in the student week whereby they could prove whether
or not they really wanted this. Finally, I made it clear that if and when the
authorities stepped in and shut us down that I would honour that decision no matter how much I might disagree with it. I attempted to assure
them that if it did come to that I alone would take the responsibility for
this present decision and that I would neither expect nor welcome their
support at that point. I did have to expend a certain amount of energy
fending off the eagerness of a few who were inclined to join me in any
and every possible *auto-da-fé*.

So, we began. We were all a little tentative. I had seen the value of
the guitar at Grailville, and especially with Pat Uhl on the scene and
eager to participate I suggested that we try it. They agreed. Pat knew what
she could do based on her experience at Grailville and in Cincinnati. It
proved to be very, very dramatic and caught even the folk-music fans off-
guard because this stuff was never supposed to cross back into the realms
of traditional religion. That first TMS Eucharist happened, as close as
I can remember, on the first Saturday of October, 1963. I have never

gotten around to check it, and we were oblivious to it at the time, but I now believe that it was also the first time a guitar was used at any public or semi-public Catholic Eucharist anywhere in Canada.

We tried to proceed tentatively, but the truth was that we became more and more excited. We turned the altar around so the students were not facing my back. That was a surprise for me because despite all my insights and convictions I still had to handle the necessary shock of eye-ball-to-eyeball contact while attempting to continue performing a tradi-tionally loaded action. It would later give me a certain amount of sympathy for those priests who never chose to change in the first place. The natural reaction for all of us clerics, given our priestly training and experience, had to be something primitive like: "You mean the laity are supposed to be involved in this too?"

11. Specifics of Liturgical Change, October 1963–April 1964

To begin our experiment without quickly switching to English from Latin seemed ridiculous. That switch was also long, long before it was to be approved for Canada. At the same time, at least as an option available to those faithful who claimed to need it, such a change was ridiculously over-due. The students at first felt liberated being able to understand what they and the priest were actually saying. Almost immediately, however, they had to cope with the loss of all that quiet fantasy and/or reflective time they had become so accustomed to through all their years of attending Mass. Using English meant that we had to surrender a certain comfortable self-involvement and actually acknowledge that someone else and in fact God knows who else was actually in this same boat with us.

For some, an even more profound question was stirred, namely: "Was what was in the approved format and especially in the Canon what they could agree with or what they really wanted to say at all?" So too, being asked to participate in an Offertory procession or being invited to join the priest in a circle around the altar from the "Holy, Holy" onwards assaulted the usual sense of individual comfort and security afforded by those nice solid oak pews. Getting what you thought you wanted was not necessarily a joyride. Some students acknowledged they were getting more than they had bargained for and would openly say that. Because they were not in that much of a hurry to grow up, they would return to the more traditional Mass until they might happen to change their mind and try the TMS approach later.

Most of those participating wanted more. Mind you, we are not yet talking about large numbers. From October of 1963 until April of 1964 the average Saturday morning turnout was between twelve and twenty. I have always been glad that it stayed that small during that first year. It gave us more time to try different things, time to evaluate whatever would happen, and time to decide collectively what we wanted to do step by step. We had the use of a wonderfully solid yet portable altar table that we could situate in the chapel's sanctuary according to our needs. Each Saturday morning volunteers would carry it out from the sacristy of the College Chapel and replace it later, when we were finished.

We discarded the use of servers as an unnecessary and unwelcome distraction. The cruets were placed directly on the altar along with any and all objects from the Offertory procession. The altar table would occasionally seem crowded, but the effect was one of rich bounty and overflowing generosity. Burlap banners were occasionally improvised, and sometimes we would have special dress-ups, which ran counter to the dominant counterculture of the 1960s. On such occasions, Emmanuel Ayoade, a prince's son from Nigeria, would come in the grand flowing robes of his people, and thereby inspired others to dress for those liturgies. It gave us the confidence to choose means and methods even if they challenged the culture of the time.

Not everything worked to our satisfaction. For example, we loved drums but came to use them less and less, simply because they always needed to be played by someone who could keep them well integrated with the rest of the action. The tendency was for a certain natural enthusiasm to take over, which was fine for occasional solos but which could all too easily become a distraction from the focal action of the communal liturgical drama. Piccolos, banjos, regular flutes, tambourines, and even spoons were easily integrated and enriched the end results. Cymbals, saxophones, and trumpets all shared the same hazards as drums, but occasionally we were able to make them work for us. The emphasis was always on participation. The quality of performance was important, but it was always to be judged primarily by its contribution to the total collective action of the liturgy.

In those little Saturday-morning dramas we repeatedly emphasized that we were searching for more and more effective ways for even small groupings of His people, such as ours, consistently and meaningfully to renew our covenant with Him and with each other. The emphasis was on the unique gifts that each individual had to bring so as to enhance the total action. Singing was the great unifier, and even our finest musical accompaniment had to serve the singing.

That singing might be gentle or intense, but it always had to be simple. This was to maximize the possibilities of involving everyone. We used some familiar hymns and some folk and popular music, but increasingly we created our own words and lyrics. The latter option tended to work the best and proved to be the most satisfying. Fortunately, besides Pat Uhl from Grail we had several other very creative people who kept contributing more and more material for us to try. By Christmastime we were receiving feedback that what we were concocting was being labelled the Hootenany Mass, the Jazz Mass, or the Underground Mass. The sense of these remarks was always derogatory. There was never any evidence that those using such phrases had ever been near anything we were actually doing. Those actually involved never used those terms. We referred to what we were doing as the TMS Mass or the Saturday Morning Eucharist.

We continued to insist on the principle of no fixed membership. Some weeks we would become a little anxious about whether or not we would end up having a guitarist. A couple of times it did happen that way, but by then so many were so accustomed to a wide range of our best music that we would quickly agree on someone with true pitch and simply plunge ahead. While the specific participants would vary each week, the overall mix was usually about sixty per cent female and forty per cent male. Gradually individuals would bring friends and guests or parents visiting from out of town who wanted to participate.

At Grailville I had witnessed the potential profundity of a valid "Kiss of Peace." It was one of the first changes we made and it always seemed to work wonders. Especially when the group numbered only a dozen or so, everyone was expected to greet everyone else. We refused to formalize it. We decided that the form could be a single or double handshake, or a quick hug, or even a simple touch. Some word or words were to be used to reinforce the affirmation of the other's presence and importance. We refused to prescribe any specific greeting and most chose individualized personal remarks, especially as we came to know each other better and better. When the official changes finally arrived from Rome, I was greatly relieved that at least a modified version of this practice had been incorporated.

We found a source for whole-wheat communion wafers and we had those who wished to receive communion put their own wafer on the paten at the Offertory. On special occasions we might use a whole loaf of crusty bread from which each person would tear off a chunk and place it on the paten, knowing they would receive a different chunk at communion time. Both of these alternatives emphasized the actual act of chewing, thereby strengthening the sign and function of eating. We found this far more effective than the more familiar white wafers that many of us had been taught must never be touched with our teeth. That had never struck me as much of a sign for solid nourishment.

We substituted special silences and bowed heads at moments usually reserved for bells. We also substituted bows for genuflections and found them far more culturally appropriate. We considered communion "under both species" as more faithful to the text and the commemorative action. We held back from having communion bread distributed by non-clerics as probably unproductively inflammatory at that time. However, I stressed and the students agreed that the traditional practice of the priest placing the host directly on the communicant's tongue definitely needed rethinking.

This was especially true when everyone was lined up like starving baby birds with their mouths gaping while huddled behind a communion rail. That sign seemed more connected to signs of infantilism and abject subservience rather than to the participation of friends at a feast being provided by their mentor and friend from Nazareth. We decided that the consecrated bread was to be placed in the hand of the communicant or the communicant could pick up their own piece of consecrated bread from the paten. What we did regard as essential was that everyone would hold their bread in front of themselves and wait until everyone else had a piece. Then and only then everyone, including myself, would eat together. Next I would pass the chalice to my right or left and not partake of it until it had completed the full circle and was handed back.

At the conclusion of the liturgy we usually carried on with some activity or other. In good weather we would take French bread, cheese, and wine and go over to Queen's Park for a picnic. Of course, the weather during most of the academic year did not allow for such outings. What was more usual was for us to gather at someone's "pad" near campus and over a light lunch vigorously discuss scriptural texts, questions of moral theology, and issues of social justice.

12. Kennedy's Assassination, November 22, 1963

The single most dramatic and indeed traumatic event of that fall term of 1963 was the assassination of US President John F. Kennedy on November 22. That year there were Student Masses in St. Basil's Church on Monday, Wednesday, and Friday afternoons. These were regular parish Eucharists with no experimental intent. A roster of Basilians, including Kutz, Madden, and myself, took turns doing those services. It happened that it was my turn on the day the assassination occurred.

I first heard about it around two in the afternoon, as I was walking across Queen's Park on my way back from the Provincial Archives. As the first Catholic President, Kennedy was already a hero for Canadian as well as American students. Lee Gallery, a TMS original, went to Ethiopia that same year with the Peace Corps and others would soon follow. It would not be until years later that a much fuller picture of Kennedy would emerge. At St. Michael's he was still very much a role model for those attempting to be liberal and progressive in the new style of the sixties. St. Michael's was also the home for the largest and most vibrant community of American students anywhere in Canada. That grouping included an outspoken contingent from Kennedy's home state.

I had barely begun to face the shock that this event had on me personally when I began to realize its probable impact on that afternoon's Student Mass. I had less than two hours to prepare for that Mass, so I immediately buried myself in my room at Clover Hill. For some time before this I had found that the best way for me to prepare a homily was to think about it a lot, to reread material as it occurred to me, and to do a brief outline on a file card. I had not written out in full any homily, sermon, lecture, or talk for many months. I had found that that approach had caused me far too much worry as to whether or not I was repeating accurately what I had put on paper. I did not enjoy the results and I felt I was inhibiting my own response to the group as well as their reaction to what I'd said.

In my room that afternoon my first challenge was simply to let myself cry. Those tears came very easily and very powerfully. They were tears of homage, of rage, of personal loss, of helplessness, and of profound grief. I would have many more tears to cry later, but I knew I had to release some pressure or I would be too supercharged to do justice to the Eucharist that was needed that afternoon. I also realized that it was going to be a major struggle for me not to break down emotionally.

I knew that I had no right to do that and that it would be disastrous for the others who were present. So, in the time remaining, I sat down and wrote out a brief homily attempting to connect this horrendous event to that "other sacrifice." I kept it to a single page and knew that to complete that liturgy with any dignity I would have to stick to what I had written. As I walked into the sanctuary that afternoon I could feel a dense tension that filled every nook and cranny all the way to the top rafters. St. Basil's was jammed, with standing room only.

There were few skeptics on campus that afternoon. They knew they needed to be together and they came to what they had never fully realized before was the one place on campus that had always been intended for that very purpose. I chose not to use a server but had left a message for Kutz to join me to help with the communions, which I sensed would be many but which I was certain should not be unduly prolonged. I found all of it very, very difficult to do. At the same time, I felt enormously privileged to have been given this opportunity.

Two things were especially difficult. The first was the homily. I still do not remember what the assigned scriptural texts were for that day. I realized that the enormity of events had overridden the specific. Even at graduations and ordinations, St. Basil's had never been as charged as it was that afternoon. In a way it was all those tortured faces out there that had to be my text and I had to attempt to relate *their* text with *the* text. I had already written out an interconnection between Dallas and Golgotha and what both meant to each of us. A couple of times my voice cracked but it never broke. I stuck to what I had written. I have always held on to a copy of that homily.

The second most difficult thing was the distribution of Communion. It was their eyes that were most eloquent. Some were calm, glazed over, or in shock. They had not been able to let the full impact sink in as yet. Others, including burly football players, had given up trying to hide or even wipe away the tears that washed their cheeks. Still others were already down deep enough to resolve that neither this tragedy nor any other would ever stop them from going on. And there were so many of them. Stan Kutz had arrived to help, but even then it seemed that they must have been lined up outside, unable to get in, but they still stayed for Communion. They kept coming and coming and coming.

I have never personally witnessed nor been part of a scene where so many were experiencing so much upset and grief. It was one of those times when it wasn't "I and they" but "we" that were there. I had to resist the urge to turn my eyes away from the intensity of so much rawness and undisguised emotion. Yet despite our individual agonies there seemed to be a togetherness, an experience of the commonality of even the worst moments of the human condition. Some had come by clear choice, while others seemed to have simply followed others wherever they were going so that they could at least be together.

Some told me later that they had not been to any church for a long time but they were there that day. St. Basil's was there when we needed it most and the Eucharist was a focus, a way station, a refuge, a resting place where we could dig deep within and also reach out enough to someone else so that we all ended up being better for having been there.

Presiding at that liturgy was one of the most difficult things I have ever had to do. At the same time it has also seemed to be one of the most important things I have ever done.

13. TMS Weekends in the Caledon Hills

Besides Saturday-morning Eucharists there were two other kinds of activity that TMS sponsored. Early in November and again in March we organized TMS Weekends. I suppose they were really only attempts to upgrade traditional retreats. Hart House, at the U of T, owned a small farm property in the Caledon Hills that had a farmhouse and a kind of bunkhouse on it. The accommodations were simple, even somewhat primitive, but wonderfully inexpensive. Oh yes, I should mention that all TMS activities were completely self-supporting. We never asked for nor were we offered any outside financial assistance. We wanted it that way and we kept it that way.

At our weekends we could crowd in about thirty students. Being crowded was part of what made it all work. We had to bring our own sleeping bags and food. We did our own cooking and cleaning up. A sunrise scriptural service on a nearby hilltop was probably our most innovative and successful experiment. Walks, small and large talks, various Bible

Vigils and Eucharists, some of them outdoors on the hilltops, easily filled all the time available. Conditions were somewhat primitive so we returned to the city in a rather grungy, exhausted state, but the dynamics of those weekends dissolved barriers and generated fresh reservoirs of hope that lasted and became crucial touchstones of our collective memory.

14. TMS Bible Vigils in Elmsley Hall

The other format we explored was the use of TMS Bible Vigils. In this area we deliberately borrowed from the Grail approach. This mechanism was especially valuable for reaching out across campus to pull together like-minded people from various faiths and persuasions so they could focus their concerns and encourage each other. From the very beginning, which was an Advent Bible Vigil, this format consistently drew 150 to 200 students.

It worked partly because it was not familiar and allowed many students who had already rejected traditional forms such as the Eucharist to explore a possible re-entry point and at least to have temporary communion with a group spiritual experience. The unfamiliar nature of the gathering disarmed even our most chronic critics. The greatest charge that they could muster against these vigils was that they were "too dramatic." We took that as a high compliment and our critics were left with the dilemma of explaining by any and every criterion why these events were so successful, again and again.

The essentially free-form structure of this format was ideal for using a wide range of religious and secular texts focused on a chosen theme. For example, we did one on "Selma and Civil Rights: Courage and Hope." Again, students would be scattered long before Christmas, so in December, towards the end of mid-term exams, we gathered to anticipate the Christmas event by concentrating on "Waiting, Listening, and Searching." Christmas and Easter had traditionally been annual moments when St. Basil's did function as the collegiate church. We encouraged everyone to observe that custom and refused to set up an alternate on those occasions. Instead, for example, we concentrated on a Bible Vigil on the Saturday evening before Palm Sunday on the theme "Moments That Change Things."

Selections from the Old and New Testaments provided the continuity for any of these themes and allowed for the integration of excerpts from the sacred texts of other faiths and cultures. Various kinds of music and collective chants also created an atmosphere where spontaneous intentions were often of the highest quality. We usually did these vigils in the main lounge of Elmsley Hall, although we were sometimes asked to take forms of it to locations across campus. We deliberately set all the seating in concentric circles, usually around a theme table on which were placed flowers, harvest gourds, sculptures, and displays of photos and newspaper clippings appropriate to the theme. The theme table was always at coffee-table height or lower, so as to provide a focus but not a distraction for the participants seeing each other across and around the circle.

That circular format was a deliberate attempt to break down individual isolation and to evoke the richer resonances of campfire gatherings going all the way back to the primitively tribal. We kept the lighting as soft as possible, with dramatic spots on the theme table as well as on the speaker's podium when it was in use.

Candlelight was always an essential feature and often provided the only source of illumination. We used it in various ways. For example, a squat, bulky, central candle would be the focal point of the theme table and towards the conclusion it would be extinguished as soon as a male and a female student had simultaneously lit their hand-held candles from it. Those two students would then begin spreading the candlelight to those candles held by all the other students in the room. At that point we might suggest that as a group we all face in unison the four directions of the compass.

This would drive in even deeper the multiple dimensions of our contacts and surroundings while emphasizing our individual empowerment and responsibility. The final total effect would declare the hope, strength, and triumph of our collective solidarity. The use of scripture was crucial, but the primary purpose was to stress "the receptacle of the received Word," namely, "the coming together of His people." What did it mean for an individual simultaneously to retain their radical integrity and yet realize that they belonged to a people? What was involved in sustaining the vitality of a purposeful people? And when, where, and how did the Word made Flesh celebrate and proclaim itself?

❖

15. Spinoffs and Escapes from Shutdowns

That first year of TMS, from September 1963 to April 1964, was almost idyllic in many ways. The above activities were the main focus of my energies, but they also generated a large number of spinoffs. I spent many hours each week on individual counselling. I discovered a very small room, really an overgrown broom closet, beside Petro Belaniuk's office in Windle House on Elmsley Place, and asked if I could use it as a counselling office. The college agreed because my quite spacious office as prefect of the third floor in Elmsley Hall was accessible only to the male students in residence.

I was also listed as one of the chaplains for Loretto College and at the end of the year did a retreat for their student sisters at their summer home at Roche's Point. I also did my share of Sunday work in the city's parishes and convents, where I conveyed through homilies many of the principles indicated above but where I was extra-careful not to surprise them with any of my liturgical "experiments."

On March 1, the day after my thirtieth birthday, my father died, less than three weeks after his sixty-fifth birthday. Several years of circulatory degeneration had robbed him of his playfulness and good humour. Approximately a dozen of the TMS regulars kindly came out to Our Lady of Sorrows to pay their respects. For some reason that I still do not understand, that event, although difficult, stiffened my resolve to push forward. By then, besides other things, I was concentrating on my written and oral doctoral comprehensives for the Department of History at the U of T.

The greatest single surprise of the year was that TMS had not been stopped. I knew from my own sources that by the end of our first month of activities both the Chancery Office and the Basilian General Curia were receiving regular reports on our "liturgical aberrations." I have already explained the reasoning I had evolved to justify my behaviour. I was still quite willing to answer any questions and to accept the judgment of the proper authorities. But nothing was said, at least not to me directly either in public or in private.

On the other hand, I was called in at one point by the Basilian from the General Council who was responsible for all Basilians on graduate studies. He expressed his serious concern and said that it was also the concern of the entire Council. He asserted that many confreres had informed them that I had become far too involved in student affairs and that my primary responsibilities for that year—namely, my graduate studies at the U of T—must be suffering. He did everything but order me to cease and desist from any and all pastoral involvements.

I replied that I disagreed with his conclusions and that if any of my confreres were really so concerned with my welfare why was it that not a single one of them had come to me personally and, in fraternal charity, expressed that concern? Furthermore, why was the Curia concluding that such remarks were valid without either checking with me or insisting that their informants come to see me. I added that these questions would apply especially to any Basilians at my own local community at St. Michael's who had indeed generally become more distant, but none of them had ever said anything directly to me.

This interview did nothing to enhance or heal my existing attitudes as to the quality of the community's composition or leadership. I told him that I would report to him as soon as the academic results of my year's work were publicized. Then, if he was still dissatisfied, we could resume our discussion. He was obviously not pleased, but I was already beyond giving any respect to this kind of nonsense. It must be obvious, from what I have reported above, that I had indeed been having a very busy year and that it definitely had not all been academic. I had deliberately gambled that I could stretch far enough to do justice to all of it. And all of it was what I had wanted to do and had chosen to do.

Approximately six weeks after the above interview I wrote to that same Basilian superior informing him that I had passed both my written and oral doctoral comprehensives with first-class honours. I informed him that my Ontario scholarship to continue my doctoral program had been renewed for another year. I also informed him that in response to an application I had made I had won a $5,000 award from the Canada Council that included travel money to go to England and Europe to pursue certain thesis-related "lost papers." The superior in question sent a simple acknowledgement of receipt of my letter with no suggestion that any further discussion was either necessary or desirable.

❖

16. New York City, Part II, Summer 1964

For the summer of 1964 I returned to New York City and did another version of blending my pastoral work at St. Helena's with my Special Student status in the graduate History program at Columbia. There were signs that those of us from TMS were missing each other over the long summer break, especially when so many had gone back to parishes that were badly mired somewhere before John XXIII. I put together a little five- or six-page news sheet that I entitled "Notes to the Diaspora" and ended up sending out three or maybe four issues over the summer. Since there were also clusters of TMS students whose homes were in the general area surrounding New York City, I ended up doing mini-vigils with small groups of them, including their families and friends, at Rye in Westchester, at Ocean City on the Jersey Shore, at Montauk on Long Island, and at St. Helena's in the Bronx.

Early one morning I borrowed a car, picked up a couple of St. Mike's students in New Jersey and proceeded by way of the Cape May Ferry to Annapolis, where we were put up by the family of another St. Mike's student. The next morning we went to Kennedy's grave in Arlington National Cemetery, in Virginia. The flame was there by then, but the rest was mud with a few planks to walk on. It was raining steadily with only a handful of people defying the elements. Even now both the grave and the experience of standing there in silence with those students still seem very raw yet fresh.

I met some interesting young Maryknollers at Columbia and tried a little parish work in Harlem until I got jumped by a gang of five young men two nights before the Harlem Riots of that year. I lost a good pipe, but I survived and continued my romance with the city. Around this time I was especially enthralled by the implications of Harvey Cox's book *Feast of Fools*, on the role of ritual and festivity, as well as his *The Secular City*, on the sacramental dimensions of the secular. In addition I was very excited by Andrew M. Greeley's seminal article, "The Temptation of the New Breed," which contained a most cogent analysis of generation gaps in the sixties.

17. Montauk and the Walshes, Summer 1964

The most rewarding discovery of that summer was spending time at Montauk, at the easternmost tip of Long Island, and getting to know Doc Walsh and his family. Katie Walsh had been one of the TMS originals. At her graduation in June I had met her parents. Kate, her mother, was the embodiment of Irish-American confidence, wit, and warmth. Katie's father, Professor John Walsh, had been teaching for many years at Pace College in NYC. I have seldom if ever met anyone who was so genuinely curious about what, how, and why other people saw things the way they did.

I was especially intrigued by his approach to drinking scotch. He liked his scotch with water but no ice. That was not unusual, but the way he handled it definitely was. We first met at a garden party reception for St. Mike's graduates. He simply asked the bartender for his scotch and water in separate glasses. Then, with a deftness that I have never seen before or since, he continued with our conversation while holding both glasses in the same hand, one above the other. When he would quite casually imbibe, he would sip scotch from the top glass held by his thumb and forefinger. Then, with the dexterity of a consummate juggler, he would use his other hand to hold the scotch glass while shifting the bottom glass of water to the delivery position and returning the scotch glass to the bottom position. He would then sip from the water glass and proceed with his free hand to return the glasses to their natural order. I was not the only one in awe of such fancy handiwork, so he gently explained that it was his method for "not spoiling the taste of either of the liquids." This was my introduction to one of the most amazing characters I have ever encountered. Upon learning that I would be in NYC again that summer, Kate and John gave me an obviously heartfelt invitation to visit them out at Montauk.

I went to Montauk several times that summer. More than once I would break off our seemingly endless bull sessions around midnight to drive back on the Long Island Expressway for about five hours so I could arrive at St. Helena's in time to say the early-morning masses before going to bed. Those jaunts to that particular land's end were always enormously worthwhile. Montauk's resorts, lighthouse, and grand beach were rewarding enough in themselves. The highlight, however, was always what would happen at the Walshes. Their place was a New England–style cottage on the outside and pure Dickensian clutter on the inside. Every nook and cranny was stashed with books and magazines to the point where, because you could scarcely see any walls at all, it really did seem that books held the place together. There was a circular table in a corner of the crowded kitchen that could seat six or eight.

I would drive two or three of Katie's schoolmates out from NYC and we would sprawl overnight on various cots and couches, gradually emerging in the morning to gather at that kitchen table. In his own good time John Walsh would appear and invariably he began the morning with "My greetings to the assembled multitude." Then we would start a day of discussion, wit, and heated discourse, faltering only slightly over food and broken only by walks on that wonderful beach. Kate would usually be in the background concocting a soup, salad, or fish stew, while adding her own astute asides and always wise interjections to the discussion.

We learned that John Walsh would teach his undergraduate courses at Pace in philosophy, logic, ethics, and modern history by insisting that the required reading was to be the daily *New York Times*. Probably his most passionate area of expertise was literature. On several occasions we would try to stump him by raising a topic that at least one of us was up on to see what he could do with it. Always, and I do mean always, he would launch into something that he had read recently on that very topic.

However, even more remarkable than the depth and range of his erudition was his desire and ability to listen. He really wanted to know what anybody and everybody thought about. He would mine gems from our half-cocked mutterings. Hours sped by at that kitchen table. I cannot remember ever learning so much nor enjoying so much the learning of it. From that summer of 1964 John Walsh became my major mentor and a great friend.

18. TMS Becomes "The Student Mass," September 1964–April 1965

Upon returning to St. Mike's in September I was asked by John Kelly and my superior, Donny MacNeil, to allow TMS to expand and become an official student Mass for the entire College. This would mean moving it from Saturday morning to a more accessible Thursday afternoon, as well as to a regular slot on Sunday mornings. It would also probably mean the challenge of accommodating significantly larger numbers. I checked with the returning students and we agreed we couldn't freeze the life of what we had discovered, been blessed with, and/or had co-created. It was time to accept the challenge and our Eucharist's feasibility with larger numbers. In retrospect, I realize that without that second year of TMS I would not have been ready to do what was needed at the Newman Centre.

Neither before nor after this point did we ever do any promotion or advertising of our Eucharists. We didn't have to. Word of mouth was more than sufficient. If there was any surprise it was in the number and diversity of people from off-campus who began to appear. Attendance always kept that College Chapel in the basement of St. Basil's at least half to two-thirds full. Students from the professional faculties and from graduate programs, including priests and nuns, began to come. A contingent from the entertainment industry, visiting members of the Grail, and high-school teachers who brought their more venturesome students as a day trip definitely broadened our constituency. Perhaps most moving of all was a small group of senior citizens who, once they discovered us, never missed a Thursday.

It was never again a strictly student Mass nor even an exclusively campus event. It even transcended the city boundaries when parents from the north or the States would time their weekend visits so they could be there for Thursday afternoons. Without anyone foreseeing it, it had become something quite richly diverse and universal. It was turning out that what we had was something far more truly catholic than I had anticipated.

Most of the characteristics of what we had co-created handled the transition very well. We added a second and sometimes even a third guitar to ensure adequate sound projection for the full chapel. We never used any microphones. We began exploring possible enhancements of the Offertory processions and had to sacrifice some of the intimacy of the earlier forms. We still asked that everyone who wished to should come into the sanctuary and stand around the altar from the Canon onwards, even if that might mean they were cheek by jowl and four or even five deep. For various reasons many were only one-time or occasional visitors, which put serious strains on the hosting done by more regular participants. It was sometimes quite stressful, but all who worked to make it happen agreed that it was repaid a thousandfold by the looks and expressions of sheer joy and hope that so many seemed able to experience and take away with them.

The downside was that many participants took that enthusiasm back to their parish priests and began pressuring them to provide something comparable. Although I had not intended this, I was not that surprised when I realized what was happening. Some parish priests, in various degrees of upset or excitement, came to see for themselves. Of those who came I never met a single one who didn't go away favourably impressed. How I knew was from their subsequent thank-you notes and phone calls as well as from the personal reactions they gave me at the back of the chapel after the Eucharist.

At that time in Toronto it was, to the best of my knowledge, only non-Catholic ministers who greeted their congregations at the door of the church, either before or after services. Whether or not other priests were doing it, I realized very quickly that I had to do it. It was an absolutely essential means of counteracting the natural increase in isolation and anonymity that could so easily accompany our increase in numbers, diversity, and "occasional users."

There was another aspect that continued and, if anything, intensified during that second year of TMS. In the early sixties there was still what seemed like an ancient custom of total silence from the moment one entered a church or place of worship until one was once more outside. No library had it so good! After a couple of TMS liturgies I noticed that there was a mounting buzz from the moment people began to arrive for the Eucharist. And afterwards they wouldn't leave! The business beforehand was like the opening bars of a mounting crescendo. My instinct was not to quell it in any way. I quickly realized that this "noisiness" only enhanced the impact of the silences we had built into the liturgy. Every Eucharist became like a one-of-a-kind reunion where they all had so very, very much to say to each other.

After the Eucharist the noise intensified, simply because the participants were so opened up that they had all these responses to the Eucharist itself, in addition to what they had brought with them. They simply could not contain all their emotion. They had to share at least some of it with one, if not several, kindred spirits. Some of my confreres objected to what they called the "noise," "confusion," and "disorderly mayhem" of all of this. It was especially a problem at the conclusion of the liturgy. If other events had been scheduled to follow us in the college chapel, I often experienced real pressure around "moving our gang out" so the subsequent event could happen on schedule.

I was not always successful in containing and dispersing this exuberance resulting from the Eucharist, and it became a peg upon which my confreres could and sometimes did hang their envies and general objections. This had begun during the first year of operations. It was worse during the second year, when there was no follow-up activity like picnics or bull sessions that I could improvise to deal with the much larger numbers. It is one of the reasons I would insist so strongly on coffee in the house as an essential activity as soon as I arrived at Newman.

A few Basilians also came from time to time to our TMS Eucharists. They were mainly long-standing friends who had worked with me at Boys Camp or on producing *The Basilian Teacher*. They were not always in agreement and let me know why if they were not, but generally they were supportive. One visitor who left a very strong impression on me personally was Father Terry Forrestal from the Seminary. I had been fortunate enough to take his classes in Sacred Scripture when he first returned from the Holy Land. Those classes, along with those of Gregory Baum, were the only islands of valuable theological reflection that I had encountered in my four full years of formal, supposedly professional, training for the priesthood.

Well, Terry came to a TMS Eucharist. Afterwards he told me that he had come partly out of curiosity at what all the excitement was about. We had always gotten along, but, as he told me later, on the basis of what he had been hearing from several other Basilian priests he had fully expected to witness some form of bizarre, sensationalist behaviour. After that Eucharist he made a strong point of informing me personally that he had witnessed and participated in something quite different. He had been pleasantly surprised that I had managed to ground all the enthusiasm in a homily whose successful popularization of the scriptural texts had proclaimed loud and clear that the core of Christ's call, while humane, was indeed also very tough. I never received as clear and strong an affirmation of my efforts from any other Basilian.

Because I was going to be leaving for England before the end of the school year, it was decided in September of 1964 that I would not be a prefect that year in the student residences. Instead, I had a room on the south side, second floor, the first room west of the entrance to St. Basil's parish offices. I was working on my doctoral thesis and wanted to get everything possible done on its research while still in Toronto so that while I was abroad I could concentrate on other things.

I still had my cubbyhole in Windle House for counselling sessions and I was appointed as one of the chaplains for the resident students and nuns at St. Joseph's College until I actually left for England. It was during this second season of the TMS that Father Stan Kutz became involved as my backup. Stan and I had always worked very well together and he agreed to take over the TMS activities and finish off that school year after I had left.

19. Encounters with Counselling

There is one other area that evolved out of my counselling activities that would affect quite significantly what I moved into both during and after Newman. Even before TMS I had encountered students and adults who had to be hospitalized because of the severity of their personal disturbances. I quickly became quite appalled at the "state-of-the-art" treatment that otherwise very gifted and courageous people were subjected to. It seemed that even the best of the mental "healers" were primarily interested in arriving at the correct balance of medication that would make such patients quiet and no trouble to themselves and especially not to others. The worst practitioners of this so-called "art of healing" seemed far too eager to use electric shock as the most efficient means of controlling the behaviour of such troublesome individuals.

In the period before Newman this was the pastoral area that I found the most disturbing. After seeing on two distinct occasions magnificent individuals who had encountered so-called "breakdowns" and had ended up little better than zombies after the "best" medical attention, I decided that I would cease to send such gifted but troubled people on for so-called "professional" help. I would rather take on the pressure of counselling them and being available for them to the best of my ability, rather than abuse their trust by recommending them to "experts," no matter how carefully I had researched who were the best professionals available. I found this strategy to be increasingly onerous because of my considerable ignorance and lack of training in this delicate area.

Since I had been born in Toronto and had spent almost all the intervening time in this city, I did and still do have a wide range of contacts and acquaintances. During the late spring of 1964 I happened to encounter in quite separate instances three individuals I had known off and on for many years but whom I had not seen for a while. In each of these instances I was struck by how different they were from the ways in which I remembered them. In attempting to describe the difference to myself it did not seem that they had adopted new mannerisms, let alone some brand-new personality. Rather, it was as if what was best in them and had always been there somewhere was now front and centre. It really was as if they had blossomed or flowered and were more fully and truly themselves. In each instance my curiosity drove me to tell them that I seemed to notice a significant change in them, that I very much liked that change and that I was curious as to whether they had been doing something to bring about these changes.

Each of them thanked me for my compliment, acknowledged that they also liked the changes, and said that it was probably because of what they had been learning about themselves by doing some therapy with Mrs. Smith up on Admiral Road. In those days I thought therapy was something you did to your leg, or whatever, to get it back into shape after an accident. Admiral Road I knew was a street in the Annex where Lester Pearson had lived. This Mrs. Smith, however, I had never heard of before. Soon after these incidents I went back to New York City for the summer of 1964, but I remained puzzled by these encounters.

20. Variations on Suicide, November 1964

In the autumn of 1964, a pastoral problem that I had never met before erupted on my doorstep. First one student and then another and finally small groups of two or three came to me for advice on a common problem. A third-year undergraduate whom I happened to know was living in one of the many apartments and flats in old houses near the campus, each of which were shared by three or four students. That autumn something had happened to this young man and he had ended up making the rounds of all his student acquaintances at all hours of the day and night pouring out his tale of woe, consuming a great deal of alcohol and talking endlessly of his suicidal fantasies.

When not drinking this student was very gifted and had genuinely endeared himself to many of his fellow students. Those were the students who had now approached me for advice because they felt at their wits' end and were afraid they were going to be unable to hold him back from an actual suicide. One of these students happened to mention that there seemed to be a therapist in the picture, and when I asked who it was they said it was "a certain Mrs. Smith."

Personally I did not feel confident about how to handle this situation, so I decided to phone this Mrs. Smith. After adjusting to her strong, melodious English accent on the other end of the line, I explained the situation, indicated that I had no intention of interfering with whatever was going on in this student's therapy, but asked for her advice so that I might be able through the students around him to support rather than undermine her efforts.

What ensued was an amazing talk on "true" versus "false" suicide, suicide as power play, and the differences between genuine support and false sympathy for someone in this state. I was astounded by how quickly this woman sliced through to the core of the issues and how simple, clear, and solid was her analysis of this student and of what might assist the situation. When I got off the phone I called one of his concerned flatmates and told him to spread the word to anyone and everyone involved in this situation that they meet with me at Windle House that evening. Over a dozen showed up, about half of whom were regulars at TMS. I conveyed as best I could my new-found but still shaky understanding of the situation, and after fielding their questions as well as possible suggested a common strategy that we all could agree to and support each other in. Partly out of desperation and partly because of their trust in my judgment, they all agreed.

We did not withdraw from the student in question, but we did establish much clearer boundaries and supported each other in what we would and would not put up with. The results were almost immediate. Unable to perpetrate successfully his usual appeals for sympathy, yet faced with the fairness and firmness of everyone who did not abandon him but rather remained there as friends, the student in question quickly became very, very upset about what was really bothering him and had to take that upset to his therapist for real help. Right up until the results began pouring in, I remained with some lingering doubts about being so hard on him. Ever since that episode the question of suicide has never disturbed me—even when it has periodically saddened me a great deal.

By the spring of 1965 I had been approached on more than one occasion and been invited to join a support therapy group made up almost exclusively of priests and nuns. They had approached this same Mrs. Smith to act as their presiding therapist, even though she had had no previous experience with priests or nuns and very little with Catholics generally. By that time, based on the above incidents, I was curious as to what such a group might involve.

My rugged isolationism and arrogance limited my chances of finding a fresh method to improve my pastoral skills. Heaven and hell forbid that I acknowledge even the possibility that I might actually need such a program for myself personally! At any rate, such an involvement required a long-term commitment and I was already scheduled to leave in April for several months in England and Europe. So I put the entire question off until I returned from my trip.

Meanwhile, despite the endless rumours of entreaties by various disgruntled pastors and certain kinds of laymen to shut us down, the TMS simply kept going. All student movements have a built-in attrition factor simply because students are on campus for only a few brief years. Even by the summer of 1964 several originals had graduated, dropped out, or transferred. Others moved on to more explicitly secularist movements for social justice. From the beginning I had hoped that for those who had already been moving away from the structured church, even a brief sojourn with something like TMS might allow them to proceed with less crippling bitterness. In that sense I had hoped that TMS might function as a healthy halfway house for those already on their way out.

21. The Meeting with Pocock, March 1965

So by the time Joe Wey's call came on that day early in March of 1965, I had packed in a lot of experience and perhaps had been lulled into a certain complacency by the absence of any official condemnation. As I remember, Kelly was driving and he had Wey with him when they picked me up at the doorway to the Parish offices. There was only small chit-chat on the way over to the archbishop's palace in Rosedale.

Pocock received us casually enough and when he offered me a scotch I took it because I could at least have that much control over my court martial. All four of us settled into the plush leather chairs in his office and he quietly stated something like: "The Newman Club on the campus at U of T has been very inactive for several years now, and after consulting with Fathers Wey and Kelly I have decided to ask you to go over there and see what you can do to get things moving again."

I'm not sure if I spilled my scotch or not, but I was genuinely surprised. I had arrived braced and resigned to my execution and instead I was being offered a promotion. I agreed with his assessment of Newman. The way he said it had, in fact, been common knowledge for many years. The authorities had seemed content to let Newman drift and my contacts had stopped even spreading rumours about the place. I realized that I was currently on my last full year of graduate studies and I had occasionally mused as to where I might be posted next. But I had never even considered Newman simply because it seemed to be the permanent fiefdom of T.A. McDonald and his cronies.

Wey and Kelly had not reined me in during the previous year and a half, but they had also shown little if any awareness—let alone approval—of what I was trying to do down there in the basement of St. Basil's. The only possible exception was when Donny MacNeil had approached me and suggested that the TMS Mass become the College's actual Student Mass. That probably required his clearing it with Kelly. Now all they seemed to do was smile their consent to the Archbishop's proposal. The action all seemed very much between Pocock and myself. I do not remember outwardly registering any surprise or satisfaction, let alone gratitude. That was because of all that was not being said.

After a moment of silence, I said quietly to Pocock: "You do know who you are asking to take this on, don't you?" He nodded and simply said yes. I couldn't leave it like that, so I came back with: "You don't expect me to change how I have been behaving, do you?" To this he replied something like: "No, I hope that you will continue to do what you do best." This is the closest Pocock ever got to endorsing what I was trying to do.

Before accepting his offer I attempted to set two conditions. The first was that each of them arrange to come to Newman to witness personally what I was doing so that they would have some point of comparison when they began receiving the inevitable complaints. They agreed. Then I requested that Pocock assure me that I could have direct access to him personally if and when I felt it was necessary. Again Pocock agreed.

I was by no means entirely pleased with the evening's strange turn of events, but Newman did seem a logical place for me to situate myself for the immediate future. I was scheduled to leave in a few weeks on my Canada Council travel grant, so we agreed that I would take up the appointment at Newman sometime in September, before university classes began. I do not remember anything that Wey or Kelly might have said on the ride home. My personal turmoils of that period undercut any pleasure or sense of satisfaction about this appointment. It postponed things rather than resolved them. I went to bed heavy-hearted but determined to make the most I could out of Newman.

22. Kutz Replaces Lee, April 1965

The formal appointment to Newman from Wey was dated March 10, 1965. A few days later I learned that in the same round of appointments Fr. Owen Lee had been appointed to Newman as my assistant. I of course had not been consulted. Owen and I had spent several years together at the seminary and I vaguely remembered that he had been a counsellor on a couple of occasions under me at Boys Camp. Above all we had worked closely together on many skit nights at the seminary. We had always gotten along very well.

Although I was not aware of Owen being particularly interested in the kind of liturgical and pastoral issues with which I had become associated, I concluded that the General Council had assumed it would be wise to have him at Newman either to help me with the musical dimensions of the liturgy or to soften at least some of my riskier enthusiasms. I remember feeling a little strange about what this indicated concerning the quality of support I could expect from that Council, but I do not remember being particularly disturbed.

A few days later I did begin to be disturbed. My sources informed me that Owen was deeply upset by this appointment. He was a different kind of community man than I would ever be and, upon reflection, I could see that he might well be frightened at being cooped up with me in the relative isolation of the Newman Club on St. George Street. It dawned on me that he might be beside himself with how he was supposed to help me, slow me down, or even survive personally. What disturbed me most was that as the days went by stories of Owen's upset intensified and there was no response at all from the General Council, which must have known of Owen's upset. Only then did I write a letter directly to Wey.

I tried very hard to make it clear that in no way did I find Owen's reaction personally offensive but that even with the best of intentions the Council had created a situation that might severely jeopardize any possible success of the changeover they were attempting at Newman. I acknowledged that part of the problem was that there were fewer and fewer Basilians that I was prepared to take seriously, let alone listen to for advice in the areas of my concerns.

I pointed out that while the Council would probably regard my appointment as risky, the track record showed that Stan Kutz was one of the few Basilians that I still took seriously and whose advice I had even acted on against certain of my own inclinations. Incidentally, I had already checked with Stan whether he would be interested in the course of action I was suggesting. I did not want another Owen situation on my hands. As I suspected, he loved the idea. The truth was that we had already been in cahoots for several years on a wide range of issues. We were definitely different from each other, but we had also developed a deep respect and trust in each other's expertise.

I suppose it was typical of those days, but Wey never even acknowledged the receipt of my letter, let alone call to discuss it with me or inform me personally of the new decision. Before I flew to London I learned through my own grapevine that Owen had been appointed elsewhere and that Stan Kutz had been designated as his substitute.

23. T.A. McDonald as Bursar, April 1965

Sometime in late March or early April Wey and I did have one discussion which would affect the subsequent dynamic at Newman. Wey stated that of course he would move T.A. away from Newman before I arrived there. I immediately objected, which certainly took Wey by surprise. It has never been clear to me how strong a motive it was that at least one of the Curia's reasons for this whole exercise was to dislodge T.A. from his cozy sinecure as Director of the Newman Club.

I explained to Wey that my understanding was that there was one area at Newman where T.A. was very competent. That was in his steady acquisition of operating funds from his contacts dating back to and even before his Holy Rosary days with the city's "Irish Murphia." I told Wey that I had no interest in the challenge of finding alternate sources of funds and that such an effort would seriously undermine what I might be able to do otherwise.

Wey accepted that reasoning but also expressed some concern about McDonald's strong tendencies to intimidate those he lived with and, to make things worse, this was a situation where I was dislodging him. I acknowledged that there were certain risks but that I did feel that McDonald and I could find a mutual accommodation. Besides, by then I felt I knew how to turn Irish bluster into a nuisance rather than allow it to become a full-grown problem. Wey agreed to leave McDonald at Newman as its bursar.

I then informed T.A. that he could stay in his prime suite at the east end of the second floor, and I told Stan that I wanted him to have the large room on the north side. I myself deliberately took a windowless cubbyhole next to the small TV room, not out of any generosity or self-denial but simply because that was the simplest way to increase the odds that we might all get off to a good start.

24. London and Europe, April to September 1965

On April 21, 1965, I flew to London. I would not return to Toronto until September 14. That meant almost five months away from my home base. It was also a crucial break between the TMS and Newman. I still surprise myself when moments from that summer resurface either painfully or pleasantly. It was indeed for me personally the best of times and the worst of times. I settled in at the Knights of St. Columba Club on Lansdowne Road in the Notting Hill district. That club would remain one of my rest stops for the coming months.

That first night in London I went pub-hopping with Gerry McGuigan, a Basilian studying at the London School of Economics, and during one of our stops he suggested that I keep a journal of my summer. I was intrigued by his suggestion and the very next day began to write. I am convinced that writing regularly in that journal saved my life at certain moments during that summer. Even routinely it enabled me to capture and commit to paper enough of what I was absorbing that I could risk exposing myself to even more.

By the way, and it often seemed very much to be by the way, my doctoral thesis was actually coming along rather well. As an indication of how diverse or disparate my life had become, I hereby note that the formal title of my thesis was "The Administration of Sir Peregrine Maitland,

Lieutenant-Governor of Upper Canada, 1818–1828." I did my research at the British Museum and at the Imperial War Museum and tracked down and interviewed descendants of Sir Peregrine Maitland. In my research I ran into more dead ends than I had expected, but I was convinced that there were many other ways that I could repay the Canada Council's investment.

I completed as much research as was feasible and then began to travel and seek out other learning experiences. Besides Gerry McGuigan I met up at various times and places with other Basilians such as Jim Howard, Michel Deglene, Charlie Principe, Paul Broadhurst, "Swamper" LaLonde, Sam Femiano, and Bud Pare. I spent time at the Basilian house of studies in the suburbs of Paris and at Annonay in the Ardeche. I visited Taize, Lourdes, and Fatima, as well as Rome, Naples, Florence, Berlin, Madrid, Oslo, Stockholm, and many other big and small places.

I had a Eurail Pass and, carrying a small overnight bag, used that pass to catch uncrowded trains around midnight. Then I would wash out my drip-dry shirt, get six to seven hours of sleep stretched out in a compartment, shave with cold water on a bumpy train, get off in a strange town or city in the early morning, check my bag in the train station, and would have the entire day to explore that place before returning to catch another train in the late evening. In one particular stretch I kept going like that, without an actual bed, for eighteen straight days and nights.

I got into terrific shape and absorbed a lot of Europe. Besides confreres I would hook up with various students from St. Mike's, contacts recommended from back in Toronto, and people I would meet along the way. I learned more and more about myself and that seemed to open up an ever-broadening and deepening spectrum. It is still difficult to say all this had to do with Newman. A lot of it seemed far more immediate or long-term, but all of it did seem interrelated. Through all of this I spoke most of all to my journal.

25. A Pilgrimage to Chartres, May 1965

I have decided to include in this present narrative the journal entry covering my participation in the annual pilgrimage to Chartres organized by the university students of Paris.

May 8, 1965: Maison Ste. Basile, Paris

I got up in time to have breakfast with the scholastics, Frs. Prince and McCann, as well as Archbishop Flahiff, who is staying here for the weekend. We got into a good bull session, which lasted for most of the morning. The Archbishop had obviously heard some rough hearsay versions concerning what was going on with my Thomas More Society Mass. His impressions seemed to be universally negative and were a hodgepodge of distortion and accuracy. He said he was very disappointed with me, and certainly he had never before spoken to me so harshly.

I asked him if he had challenged any of his informants to come and speak to me directly, especially if they pretended to be my confreres as well as his. He admitted that he had not, so I challenged him as to why he seemed so quick to agree with their bad reports on something that none of them had ever personally witnessed. He didn't have an answer for that, but at least he admitted that he didn't. I then pushed harder and pointed out that I had made no secret of what I had been doing with the liturgy. I had now been doing it for two full academic years, and from the beginning the proper authorities had been given detailed accounts and/or conjectures from many sources. I had been rather fatalistic about my chances of being able to continue, yet somehow the axe had never fallen.

I asked him if he had been informed that, back in March, without any prior consultation, Joe Wey and John Kelly had taken me to Archbishop Pocock's Rosedale residence, where I was asked if I would be willing to take over the Newman Club on St. George Street and try to do something with it. Flahiff said he was aware of that. Then I pushed him for his understanding as to why those three men, by far my most important religious superiors, had deliberately made no mention of what I had already been doing, though that was what had led them to ask me in the first place.

I had come to this meeting expecting to be executed and instead was being offered a promotion! In fact, in an attempt to get further clarification, I had to press them with the remark: "You must realize that, since you have chosen to ask me, that I am very much a known quantity. So your invitation must mean that you want me to take over to St. George the experience I have already gained in the basement of St. Basil's. Is that a fair and accurate assumption?" After a pause Pocock nodded his assent, and only then did Wey and Kelly also add their nods.

I then asked Flahiff how he could account for my having received that kind of treatment from them and why was it so different from the manner in which he was presently treating the question. He was definitely not happy that I was not simply swallowing his unsupported criticisms. At that point I wondered if perhaps, despite his fine reputation in many areas, he had been in a position of authority for too long and had not had to respond to any straight talk for a very long time. He certainly had no clear responses to the obvious discrepancies that I had put to him.

Finally, I added something that I have found myself repeating more and more frequently in recent months—namely that, as far as I could discern, the greatest single evil currently affecting the Basilian community was the quantity and quality of its vicious and unchallenged gossip. I'll swear he squirmed at that remark, because anyone with ears to hear could recognize that what I had emphasized was exactly what he had been doing to me. I then proceeded to invite him to come and see for himself what I was trying to do.

By that point he was only able to mutter that he couldn't commit himself to something like that because he had to consider the implications of such a visit. I realized, at least to some extent, that I was feeling very reckless, but I was also very sick and very, very tired of this sort of nonsense, so I simply concluded by saying: "Don't you mean wouldn't rather than couldn't"? He made no reply. That morning my respect for him took a nosedive.

Meanwhile, the scholastics have been great in getting me all the stuff I need for the pilgrimage to Chartres. I was assigned to group P109. As an English-speaking chaplain, I was assigned to one of the few English groups. There were about forty in each group, with a chaplain and, in our case, Werner, a German boy, and Lena, a Puerto Rican girl, as leaders. We took the train from Paris to Epernon, and then, after some general instructions (including no smoking), we started off.

The theme for this year's pilgrimage was "Dieu est Amour" and we were divided into walking groups for at least an hour of walking discussion, then a rest and food break, another hour or so of walking in silence, then a stop where summations and general discussion among the entire forty took place. We did this Saturday afternoon and Sunday morning and afternoon. Oddly enough, Leon Trechakovitch and Rosie from the RCAF base at Fountainbleau were there in my group, and another girl, Malle Zimmers from Marquette, knows Tom Draine, who is now at PIMS [Pontifical Institute of Mediaeval Studies, in Toronto].

At one point, during our first silent period, a whole flock of real sheep trotted up to the fence and baaed so loudly that we couldn't help but laugh back. It was a dull, overcast day but cool enough for good walking. Altogether that afternoon we covered between twenty-five and thirty kilometres on our zigzag route to Chartres. Most of it was on back roads over gently rolling farmland and through small innocuous villages whose inhabitants showed mixed reactions.

After our supper break we went the last leg of the day to a château in the countryside. After going through the gatehouse and courtyard we went through the building itself and crossed a bridge to climb a grassy slope. Here were two platforms, at different levels, for the celebration of the Word and of the Eucharist. About eleven priests concelebrated and the homily was by a Jewish convert who is now national chaplain of these student movements. The students from several, but by no means all, of the routes had converged for this Night Mass, with the illuminated château in the background.

They were arranged in a huge circle with an inner circle of scholastics, priests, and seminarians. Everyone was holding burning torches. It was a beautiful Eucharist for many reasons and it looked for a while as if even Chartres would have a difficult time topping it. After Mass we were reassembled by groups and then split so that the girls had only a couple of hundred yards to go to their barn whereas the boys were off on a "little" four-kilometre hike to our barn. As it turned out, the girls slept on dirty pavement in stuffy barns, while we had straw under our sleeping bags in open sheds. I went to sleep with a Polish boy at my feet, a Kenyan on one side, a German on the other, and a young French atheist at my head. I was tired enough and, after a slug of *vin rouge* from the neat Spanish drinking skin that Sammy had dug up for me, I was off to somewhere else.

May 9, 1965: Chartres

I have seldom been moved as I was by what happened at Chartres today. We began by crawling out of our sleeping bags at 7:30 this morning and walking the four kilometres back to the château just to get warmed up. Then we started off for our morning discussion-walk. The weather wasn't so good and the glamour had diminished considerably, so now it was mainly just hard work. Around eleven that morning we caught our first glimpse of the spires of the cathedral at Chartres and we stopped all together and sang a Salve Regina—but, oh, did it look like a long way off.

We started off again and it was brought vividly home to me where I had first even heard about the students' pilgrimage to Chartres. It had been through Gerald Trottier's paintings of this famous student pilgrimage that had been begun by Charles Péguy. I could see now why he used so many crosses in his paintings. Each group of forty had their own handmade cross. They were of every possible size, shape, and composition. Joined together, they made the segments of a solid stream of humanity, five or six abreast, winding their way inexorably over the hills and around the bends. We stopped in a grove of elm saplings for lunch.

By mid-afternoon I ached as I have seldom ached. The straps of my packsack bit into my shoulders. The soles of my feet became more and more tender but never blistered. I developed some terrific aches on the tops of my arches and I was really afraid my calf muscles would cramp or seize and I would not be able to keep up. It's amazing, though, especially when you are in a large group that develops a rhythm of its own, that you somehow keep going no matter how much you want to stop. Then too I saw blisters bigger than silver dollars on students' feet and many of them had far less strength than I.

A wonderful sharing had developed by this time and the camaraderie in our group was tangible. The worst low was late on Sunday afternoon. We had temporarily lost sight of the steeples of Chartres and when we pulled into our last stop we knew it was still seven kilometres away.

Then two things happened. The sun came out for the first time and stayed out. Secondly, at this last stop we met a large group of students in wheelchairs who had been brought out to make this last stage of the pilgrimage. Without any hesitation, students who were already down to their last reserves of raw energy doubled up on shoulder packs so that others would be free to push those students for the last seven kilometres.

Also, at this last stop, all the group chaplains and priests had to leave our groups so we could get to Chartres in time to practise our own concelebration. We even had a ride partway but then had to walk across the town of Chartres itself. It was quite a sight. Groups of clerics with packs that had almost grown into their backs were staggering and stumbling along the side streets and alleys. Even so, we hit the cathedral square just as they began to turn the bells loose. A fantastic crescendo of sound criss-crossed the square and crashed into us from all directions at once.

We limped up the steps and down one of the long passageways into the basement of the cathedral. We ditched our packs and quickly donned albs, amices, and cinctures. Then we were ushered into a long room with four rows of chairs, each with a set of vestments. When vested we simply sat there until we were given our general instructions. I must admit that, along with their railways, the French can sure run their liturgies well.

While we were waiting, we could look out a window and see students streaming in one of the entrances. Besides those I have already mentioned who were in wheelchairs there were many more who probably should have been. For many, it was obvious that every step was sheer torture, but they simply would not give up. Some were being physically carried up those last stone steps because by then they all wanted each other to make it. They came in chanting that haunting melody "Je vous salue Marie," which had kept morale up on the tough stretches on the road.

When they were an inside we began our procession. I have not yet heard any official account, but it was said that there were approximately 150 priests, led by the Coadjutor Archbishop of Paris, who were to concelebrate that Mass. As we came into the end of the nave for our procession down to the sanctuary, it was obvious that, despite its large size, the cathedral really was packed to the doors with students. There could easily have been the estimated 15,000.

As we passed through them with that measured movement that clerics seem able to muster no matter how they feel, it was obvious that the congregation was very, very tired but also very, very ready to do what they had come so far for. The late-afternoon sun was still pouring gloriously through those fantastic stained-glass windows, spraying spots of all sorts of strange colours no matter where or how you looked.

We did the Celebration of the Word with the priests all in the choir. This was one of those times when I really enjoyed the full richness and power of a pipe organ. However, what really sent shivers up the spine was when those golden trumpets turned loose on the Alleluias. For the Gloria and Creed all the students alternated with the clerics and even that huge space had difficulty holding the sound. The altar of the Eucharist was beautifully set up at the *croix* of the cathedral on a large platform with plenty of room for lots of liturgy. From the Offertory on it was on that platform that those of us who were concelebrating gathered in a large ring two and three deep.

It was very powerful to be part of something that big and to blend with all those priests who were saying, or rather chanting, with a quiet but determined strength the words of the consecration. I had to watch like a hawk because I wasn't certain I had caught all the instructions in French.

At Communion the priests communicated themselves, advancing to the altar five by five. The archbishop, after communicating himself, skipped everyone else and made his way through the crowd so that he himself could give communion to the students in wheelchairs. Before that with mitre and crozier he had preached a twelve- or fifteen-minute homily. From where I was sitting in the choir I could see him in a spotlight, and past him I could see the nave jammed with students still holding aloft their crude crosses and liturgical banners. I suddenly realized that this was the first time I was seeing such a cathedral actually being used for its intended purpose.

Here was a structure dating back many, many centuries, which architecturally and aesthetically is a piece of carved poetry, yet here, on this evening, it was transcending all the museums of the world by the intensity of its living witness.

I was fortunate to be among the first sixty or so priests to receive communion and who were then given small golden cups that were serving as ciboria. I relieved at several communion stations and this simple action has seldom meant so much to me. At one point there appeared before me a squad of young soldiers in dirty, full-battle fatigues who had obviously come directly from their military training. Then I moved up to give the hosts to some of the choir and also to those students who had pushed the wheelchairs. There were tears, and seldom have I cried so well.

There were so many things happening. An archbishop who clearly cared about these young people. Priests of every colour and nationality who had emphatically wanted to be on this freedom march. Students who skipped the celebrations back in Paris for the twentieth anniversary of VE Day so they could go to Chartres to pray that there would be no more wars.

Throughout the day I had been increasingly impressed by the militancy and proficiency of this student movement as well as by something more profound. In so many of them the faith rediscovered or consistently sought had given them a quiet self-confidence and genuine sympathy and openness to goodness and truth wherever it might be found. Yet, at the same time, they seemed really proud to be Christians. It was reassuring and I might even say magnificent.

After Mass, the students regrouped outside the cathedral, which was now resplendent in spotlights. These students were so exhilarated that they couldn't and wouldn't stop singing. And oh, what they sang! From Latin American rumbas and German drinking songs to English WW II songs and African chants. These were the students of the world determined to do what they could to leave the world a better place than they had found it.

About half of us had to stand on the train on the way back to Paris, but that really was irrelevant. It was amazing that after a day and a half together it seemed as if we had known each other for months. Someone passed out special commemorative cards, and quickly everyone was signing everyone else's. I even picked up a few addresses, just in case.

Some will always stand out from those two days. Yvonne, the aristocrat from Montevideo in Uruguay, who kept walking the last dozen kilometres on so many open blisters; Elana from Puerto Rico, who was the great morale booster, always calling on Carlos, a Spanish student, to get the sack for the garbage; Werner Knobl from Frankfurt, who eventually is going on for the priesthood; Leon and Rosie, who grew even closer together during those two days; Isabelle, the little lass with a twinkle in her smile; Malli from Marquette, with her openness and generosity; the quiet strength of Michel; the mischief of Jean; the delightful cynicism of Pauline; and the flirting of Françoise.

It was difficult to leave them at the station. I went past other groups singing in big circles outside the station and in nearby sidewalk cafés. I finally dragged into Maison Ste. Basile at about midnight. Sam was up, but we didn't talk too long. We didn't need to, because he had been on that pilgrimage the previous year. I was very, very tired, but also very, very happy.

26. The Liturgical Commission's Report, May 1965

While I was in England and Europe, a letter from Father John Madden finally caught up with me. It informed me that a formal Liturgical Commission had been assigned by Pocock to investigate the Student Mass at St. Michael's. Madden was on that group and asked me to reply to several questions, which I did by return mail. Madden also remarked that it was unfortunate that I was not back in Toronto to assist the commission with its work. To that I replied that I had absolutely no advance notice that this enquiry was going to be appointed, that I had explicitly informed Pocock, Wey, and Kelly of my Canada Council travel grant, and that I would be away from approximately mid-April until the week before university classes in September. I stated that I was willing to respond to any further questions of the commission but saw no extra benefit to be achieved by my returning to Toronto at that point. I received no further questions.

I was more puzzled than upset at this turn of affairs. I had absolutely no doubt that Pocock had been informed for a long time now, with great accuracy, of exactly what I was and was not doing with the liturgy. His silence on those matters for the previous year and a half clearly indicated that he did not want to have to make a public decision. In addition, his request that I take over Newman had occurred only a few weeks before I left for overseas. Could this commission business mean that he wanted to back off on his offer to me and would use a commission report as the pretext for his finally having been informed of what was really going on? I could see that as a possibility, but when I considered that hypothesis I was amazingly undisturbed. I already felt at a personal crossroads and Pocock's possible reversal seemed only to change my next option, not where I was already at.

There was a different possible explanation, which from my very first reading of Madden's letter I had considered to be far more likely. That was that word had probably gotten around the archdiocese that I was to be promoted instead of punished, and that Pocock had reaped a whirlwind of renewed objections. Appointing a commission to investigate could give him the flexibility to cover any reversal he might choose to make, or it might be used to mollify those pests who obviously were still refusing to come to me directly. I never did learn what Pocock thought of the commission's report. What I did learn from this incident was that here, only a few weeks after he explicitly promised me direct access, and before I had even arrived at Newman, Pocock already had not even had the courtesy to inform me that a commission was in the works.

Several weeks later Madden did send me a copy of the seven-page report of the commission. Even though I had not been offered any say in the selection of the commission's members I was quite pleased with the names of those who had served. I was also pleasantly surprised with the fairness of their proceedings, the accuracy of their findings, and the balance of their recommendations. In the last analysis, the commission accurately detailed many of the activities that had not received prior authorization, but it urged that this form of liturgy not be cancelled. In fact it urged that a way be found for appropriate future authorization and reporting. The ball had been put into Pocock's court.

As I remember, I even liked the business of authorization and reporting. The time had come for that, and, it would put the entire matter on a much solider footing. If Pocock were to insist on unacceptable terms for such authorization and reporting, I could always withdraw my acceptance of the posting on the grounds that the original arrangement was not being honoured. I rather surprised myself with this, but it all served to highlight that I had not staked everything on becoming Newman's director. It would depend on what Pocock did with the commission's report. I strongly suspected that he would not do anything, in the same way he had managed to avoid taking any action over the previous year and a half. On the other hand, if he did refuse to decide, then that in itself would mean that if I did go to Newman I would very definitely be on my own. Rightly or wrongly, I had by then been living like that for some time and did not find it too frightening or distasteful.

Part II
The Newman Centre
1965–1967

✤

27. My Introduction to Newman, September 1965

I arrived back in Toronto on September 14, 1965. I had already arranged with Stan to have my things moved over to Newman. My last week away had been spent in the Bronx with the Reddens and at Montauk with the Walshes. One long talk with John Walsh in an upstairs bedroom was the wisest single move I made to capsulize the summer months. In retrospect, my long absence from Toronto seemed to have allowed certain things to calm down. It was as if very few even noticed when I finally slid back into town. That was fine because I felt certain that the relative calm, as in the eye of a hurricane, would not last very long.

At Newman that first night I sat down to a good meal with Stan Kutz and T.A. McDonald in Newman's private dining room. I had previously made it clear that I would use as my office the panelled room on the ground floor, first on the right from the front door. I had spent the afternoon setting up that office the way I wanted it. Stan and T.A. would have their offices on the St. George Street end of the second floor. Supper was pleasant enough, and afterwards Stan and I spent the evening getting caught up.

At breakfast the next morning T.A. and I had our first encounter. His anxiety got the better of him. It became clear that he definitely wanted to know what I intended to do to his beloved Newman Club. I replied that aside from trying out some of the liturgical things I had already learned with TMS over at St. Michael's College, I was going to wait and see what the situation needed.

He was not satisfied with that and proceeded to state quite bluntly that as far as he was concerned my biggest job should be to get out there and sign up as many as possible new student memberships in the Newman Club. As calmly as I could I asked what his analysis was for the apparently drastic drop-off in such memberships in recent years. He blustered in various directions, all of which placed the blame on "what was happening to modern youth." I asked him if he had considered that the very notion of "club" might unnecessarily be putting students off.

He said that was ridiculous and that all I had to do was look at how successfully this place had functioned as a club through the 1930s and 40s. Since he was insisting, I then pushed him to explain why that same ethos did not seem to be working anymore. He obviously didn't like the way this conversation was going. I saw no point in delaying the conclusion.

I told him I had been thinking about it a lot while I was away in Europe and I was convinced that by having the TMS change the "S" in its title from "Sodality" to "Society," that group at SMC had discovered a whole new existence. I then told him I wanted him to arrange for new signs to be placed on the front lawn at the entrances, on St. George Street and on Hoskin Avenue outside the St. Thomas Aquinas Chapel that identified this place as the Newman Centre. I said I did not see why there should be any fuss about this, as all the legal documents could remain the same. And if there was not a significant turnaround in numbers within a few months, then I promised that I would return to the club concept.

Well, I cannot pretend that he liked this at all and he protested vehemently that we couldn't take the financial loss from having no memberships. I asked to see the list of paid-up members and he had to admit that there were few if any. In fact it seemed that the only signed-up members were the students in Newman's two student residences. They were members because it was a compulsory condition for them to remain in residence.

Incidentally, another reason I had pushed Father Wey to leave T.A. at Newman was because his traditional post had included looking after processing student applications for residence and subsequent physical repairs, discipline, and ministrations for the eighteen slots on the male third floor of 89 St. Joseph Street and the twenty-two slots for female students in our separate residence eight doors further up St. George.

Most but not all of those Newman residents clamored for those positions not because of any apostolic fervour but because T.A. made it very attractive financially. I welcomed those who did participate in our liturgies and I did set up bull sessions with each contingent both individually and in combination, but I left the everyday workings of those two student groups to T.A.

Returning to my inaugural discussion with the same T. A., I tried to point out that by generating more traffic to make use of our existing properties we should be able to offset quite easily any loss from unrenewed club memberships. He still did not like this, but those new signs were in place outside within two weeks. Incidentally, this was the first action I took at Newman without seeking prior authorization from anyone. Among other things, I did see it as the simplest way to send a clear signal as to what was likely to be my modus operandi. Thus ended Toronto's Newman Club, and to the best of my knowledge there has never been any attempt to reverse the above decision.

On all levels my most solid and consistent anchor during my mere twenty-three months at Newman was Stan Kutz. Stan and I had come to realize that we were kindred spirits back in the days of Columbus Boys Camp and *The Basilian Teacher*. When Stan was appointed to Munich for his graduate studies in Moral Theology I kept up consistent correspondence with him concerning theological questions and dilemmas of Basiliana. Wey's approval of Kutz's appointment to Newman was the single most helpful decision he made for us.

On a quite elementary economical level, our liaison turned out to prove a crucial factor in making those two years at Newman functional for both of us. Stan's parents donated the funds for a Volkswagen Beetle for the exclusive use of Stan and myself. It was approved by the General Council of the Basilian Fathers. This left T.A. free to continue using the behemoth of a Detroit tank previously given to him by the grateful parishioners of Holy Rosary and/or his friends in the Newman Foundation. Above all, what made Newman work between September 1965 and August 1967 was a particular dynamic between Stan and myself concerning pastoral situations.

When I would be asked to give a particular talk on a specific topic I would go to Stan and ask him about the current state of the question from a theological perspective. I always had a profound respect for Stan's current knowledge on the rapidly evolving theological issues of the 60s and for his ability to capsulize issues and include clear summaries of the pros and cons of each. Armed with that kind of a briefing and continuing to trust my own instincts, I seemed able to handle a wide range of audiences.

Similarly, when Stan was invited to various gatherings or speaking engagements he would often come to me, give me his breakdown of the issues at stake and of the composition of the group in question, and then would ask which angles or dialogue approaches I would use in such a situation. Even off the top and with little time for serious reflection, I seemed able to give him enough feedback that he always found the process useful and always came back for more. In several ways we were quite different in our approaches to people and issues. Those who knew us well enough realized that we never had any serious disagreements, even if we did approach and deal with things differently. One parishioner even dubbed us the "Hit 'em High, Hit 'em Low" team, because of our ability to complement each other's skills.

There were three other people on staff at Newman when I arrived and they remained there while I was its director. There was Manuel, a quiet, unassuming Portuguese-Canadian whose insecurity with English seemed to make him unnecessarily diffident. He produced very fine meals, looked after the outside grounds, made certain that the laundry and altar linens were done well and on time, and did the cleaning in the chapel and the residence. T.A. looked after him and stayed on top of all the related necessities. Personally, Manuel and I had a cordial but not close relationship that never seemed to be a problem.

Margaret, at least that is what I remember her name as, was already on staff as the phone receptionist, but her main assignment was to satisfy the secretarial assignments connected to the mounting of the Newman Tours and the annual production of *The Ontario Catholic Directory*. In both of these tasks she was always under the direction of Father Frank Mallon.

Once *The Canticle of the Gift*—a record we made of the guitar music and singing of the hymns used in the Student Mass—was ready for sale and mailing, she took on that task as well. Aside from that and having to handle my phone messages, we had little else between us. Again, during my sojourn I am not aware of any difficulties. Both of these employees were very loyal to Newman, but their contacts were primarily with T.A. and Mallon and I saw no need to interfere with that.

Besides Stan, T.A., and myself, Father Frank Mallon was the fourth Basilian assigned to Newman. He had never been assigned to any pastoral dimension at Newman, but his consistent efforts had sustained the Newman Tours and *The Ontario Catholic Directory* for many years. I was never certain as to whether those activities made or lost money for Newman, but it always seemed part of my truce with T.A. that I not challenge or disrupt these activities of his sidekick. Mallon had lived for several of the previous years on-site at Newman, and the arrival of Kutz and myself did mean that he had to move back to St. Michael's and come over to work at Newman only during the day.

Mallon continued to use his collection of three or four offices on the second floor for the admittedly complex paperwork involved in soliciting advertisers and annually upgrading the material for the Directory. He also needed space to plan his Tours and solicit fresh people for the annual groups that he conducted personally to various parts of England, Europe, or the Holy Land. It became clear that a significant number of his most committed customers had taken previous tours with him. They tended to be an older set and I was never aware of any of them who attended our liturgies, but I still felt that what he was doing was a genuine apostolate.

I soon realized that his *Ontario Catholic Directory* was a much more complicated activity than I had realized. It provided for all of Ontario the basic information on locations, parish priests and assistants, times of Masses, and various activities for the entire province. As the Director of Newman I quickly realized that in terms of the *Ontario Catholic Directory* my responsibility each spring was to coordinate teams of students from our male and female Newman residences on St. George Street along with other volunteers from the parish congregation and the Newman Foundation alumni and membership. These teams would be assigned for two or three weeks to the front doors of the Catholic churches of Toronto, where they would promote and send copies of the Directory to parishioners as they left their parish churches on those designated Sundays. It was not something that I enjoyed, but I did manage to get the volunteers and set up the schedules so that the results for 1966 and 1967 were at least as good as any in comparable years.

The closest Mallon and I ever came to having words was during the first couple of weeks. He too asked me what I intended to do with my new appointment. As with T.A., I told him that I did not have any master plan but that I would try to respond as best I could to matters as they unfolded. He asked if he could make a suggestion and I replied, "Of course." He then stated rather passionately that what Newman really needed was someone to catalogue the books in its Library and perhaps I could and should do that.

I replied as calmly and clearly as I could that the so-called Newman Library showed no signs of having been used at all for many years, except possibly as a study area by our resident students, that the books were very few with little breadth or depth of coverage, that after a quick perusal I could find none that had been published in the previous fifteen years, that I had no training in library cataloguing, and, finally, that my chief areas of concern were with liturgical and pastoral matters. He really did appear stunned that I had not seized immediately on his suggestion.

Mallon and T.A. had lunch together on a regular basis and for the rest of our time together neither of them brought their discontent to me personally, but they obviously remained unhappy about what was happening. They were also tale-tellers and at least some of what got back to me was clear exaggeration, if not deliberately false. For example, even though I invited both of them to participate or at least come and see for themselves what we were doing with the liturgy, neither of them ever made an appearance at anything. That apparently did not prevent them from pontificating to others on Stan's and my goings-on. I occasionally wondered if I had not made a serious error in not insisting that they both be removed from the premises before I arrived.

28. First Weeks of Liturgy, September 15–October 10, 1965

St. Michael's College had already indicated that they wanted to continue with the Student Mass on that campus. I spoke directly to my first team of musicians and asked them to continue their service at St. Mike's so as to minimize the difficulties of the transition. I also spoke to Stan Kutz, and he was open to returning there as often as necessary when he was asked by St. Mike's. The college did ask Stan because there was no rush of Basilian volunteers to step into the arena I had created. I then brought my second-string musicians over to Newman to get started. Even more than in September of 1964, the necessary absence of graduated students and the shifting concerns and demands on the surviving veterans required some serious juggling.

The first challenge was to stabilize the Sunday liturgy, so we postponed renewing the time slot of Thursday afternoons for more explicit experimentation with liturgical forms. The first and second Sundays seemed to bear out expectations. Rumours had persisted that attendance on Sundays at Newman had dwindled to thirty to forty people. Approximately that many faculty members, their families, a few of the professional students, and a few neighbours were there. In addition, there were another thirty or so who were familiar faces from our activities on the St. Mike's campus. At the beginning we simply replicated what had been working successfully on Sundays in the basement of St. Basil's.

The change in program, which I did insist on from the first Sunday, was the inauguration of Coffee in the House immediately after the Sunday liturgy. I used it to forestall any feelings of a St. Mike's invasion, to provide a mixer for the students that in itself would attract more of their friends to the liturgy, to provide a forum for immediate feedback on what they perceived as their greatest needs at Newman, and generally to give the increasingly diverse components of those attending the liturgy an opportunity to get to know one another.

Hopefully these liturgical coffee follow-ups would be an essential technique for creating the multiple interrelationships that I regarded as a prerequisite for a valid worshipping community. A few graduate students stepped forward to ensure that the coffee was ready each week, T.A. came up with the funds, and the Coffee and Cleanup Crew became our first and most enduring committee.

29. Debastardizing the Gothic, October 1965

T.A. had been using a quite simple yet beautiful wooden altar table that he had placed at the lip of the existing sanctuary. It had probably served the small worshipping group quite well before the turnover. What I realized immediately was that the existing space was physically ridiculous for what we had come to value. For example, in those first two weeks when I invited those present to approach and gather at the altar, it physically could not work. The pews were in the way and most people had to stand crowded into the two side aisles, which negated any possible gathering together.

I had been informed that the basic architectural style of the St. Thomas Aquinas Chapel was called English Bastard Gothic. This was not a derogatory term but referred to the presence of one side gallery and the absence of a second counterbalancing gallery. I have always felt that it was a creative use of the lot of land available, given the time of its construction.

But the period that built it was also focused on personal piety embodied in an attitude that you could best follow the Mass in your missal because that way it didn't matter that no one understood the Latin. Besides, the missal meant it didn't matter that the so-called sacred parts of the Mass couldn't even be seen because you were facing the priest's back up there at the end of an isolated alcove known as the sanctuary. So the fact that you might also be parked behind a Gothic pillar only added one more block to an environment that was already seriously visually impaired.

As much as I had always loved the grace, delicacy, and beauty of the Gothic style, I had by the mid-sixties begun to question why the institutional Church had moved so decisively to architectural forms of worship that were modelled on those in Greek and Roman worshipping communities rather than the more circular forms of tribal campfires. Was the table at the Last Supper really a head table, and did it really face a blank wall? I remain convinced that there are serious and automatic consequences as soon as one chooses a rectangle over a circle as the basic forum in which to perform any communal act.

By the end of the second week at Newman I knew I was on the verge of an emergency. As the numbers attending the Sunday liturgies would increase, and I was absolutely certain that they would, it would become impossible to continue the liturgical forms I had come to believe in. We already couldn't do what we required as essential with numbers far smaller than those we had been accustomed to in the basement of St. Basil's.

We were heading for disaster if the numbers were to grow so that they spilled over into that side gallery. There they could conveniently opt out or, even worse, be condemned to a frustrated ghetto of limited possible participation. I was beyond being reconciled to the older usages of this space. On a quiet October afternoon I went into the chapel and stared at that space from every vantage point I could imagine. After a couple of hours I was convinced as to exactly how I could make this space work properly.

On the second Sunday in October I made an announcement at the end of the liturgy. I stated that I wanted to spatially rearrange the chapel so as to upgrade it to our present needs. I asked for any volunteers who could come on Wednesday and Thursday evenings of the coming week. The volunteers must bring their own hammers, screwdrivers, and crowbars. People did seem a little stunned but were definitely excited.

As I remember that Wednesday evening, about twenty-four Catholics, four Anglicans, three Jews, and four or five would-be agnostics or atheists arrived with their tools. The first task was simply to unscrew the hinges that attached the pews to the floor. Eight or nine of the pews at the back, those at the south end of the present altar, did not have to be touched at all. The detached pews were then stacked on the side while we cleared the space for a new altar platform halfway down the east wall.

I had already calculated the numbers and relative sizes of all the existing pews and worked out various configurations that would provide for the same total seating without the construction of any new pews or the destruction of any existing ones. A member of the community had approached me on Monday of that week and volunteered to get and pay for two Portuguese carpenters who had the skill to do any actual carpentry we might need. I was greatly relieved by this offer. I had been willing to use the bare floor as the location for the altar table for at least a few weeks because I was convinced that the top priority was to get the basic realignments accomplished first. I pried about $150–200 out of T.A. for the raw lumber and we set about that first night to build a three-step platform against that east wall. That platform was replaced in the intervening years by one that is larger and more substantial but does lack the versatility of our stage of modification.

That October I set the dimensions for that platform according to two main determinants. Firstly, I wanted it high enough to maximize the sightlines for Sunday liturgies and special occasions that might require standing-room-only situations. Secondly, I wanted it to be a minimal size in terms of its occupation of floor space between that east wall and the line of pillars on the west. That was because I had decided that we required a different space configuration if we were to continue the intimacy of our student Eucharist experiments.

I had already seen the potential uses for T.A.'s new altar. In its simplicity it resembled the one we had used back in the chapel at St. Mike's and was eminently portable. That meant we could leave it on the platform for the Sunday liturgies but then lift it down to the floor immediately in front of the platform when we wanted to use full circles and gatherings around the altar that would be more appropriate for smaller groups. Overall I hoped that this experiment in architectural revisionism would thereby create an essentially dual-purpose sanctuary space.

By around midnight of that Wednesday evening all the necessary pews had been detached and stacked, the prototype pews had been fastened down in their new homes, and the substructure of the altar platform was complete. I invited those who could to return the following evening. Most of them did, along with a few fresh recruits. There was not a single serious hitch, and by the end of that Thursday all our objectives were achieved. Those who had participated enjoyed an enormous sense of satisfaction. Even given my tendency to overdramatize it seemed to me, without my having anticipated it, that what we had gained for ourselves was a taste of a very old experience, a taste of what those workmen and ordinary members of the community might have experienced when they completed the various stages of the first great Gothic structures. What had doubtless been new for them was now rendered doubly new for us by doing it for ourselves.

When the Newman community gathered the following Sunday I'll swear that you could touch the change in their mood. Partially that was because the new configuration forced and/or enabled them to see each other. The focus of communal activity shifted from something that might be happening at the end of the room to an open space in their very midst. The new platform was still raw lumber and the old floor in front of the platform still showed the scars from where some of the pews had been. Somehow that added to the atmosphere. When attempting to verbalize it people most often spoke of their amazement that so much had been accomplished so quickly, so tastefully, and with so little fuss.

It wasn't until then that I realized what a blessing it had been not to have had the funds to hire professional architects. For quite different reasons I would not have hired them anyway. But what had resulted from listening to my own instincts on the nature and timing of this remodelling was that a significant portion of this little community had experienced a kind of mini-crossing-of-the-new-Red-Sea. It did turn out to be a founding experience for this community whose concrete sharing had produced a bonding that was never to be seriously shaken by anything during the next two years. I still regard hope as the greatest of the nonverbal gifts. For a significant number of people, hope happened that week and, once ignited, it could not be dimmed.

The altar platform remained as raw timber until just before Christmas, when T.A., bothered by its crude looks but somewhat grudgingly accepting the reality of the increasing usage of the chapel, lined up one of his friends from the Newman Foundation to donate the cost of a carpet to cover the platform and the open area in front of it. We had left the northwest corner intact. It had always been a side altar and was where T.A. continued to say his daily private Mass, with Manuel as his server.

The foregoing narrative does not account for the factor of obtaining permission for these changes. I quite simply did not ask anyone for permission. I felt that I had been made the Director of this place and, arrogant or not, I simply knew of no one, certainly not in the Toronto area, who had as good a sense of what was needed spatially at Newman. I felt that what needed to be done contained a strong urgency factor if our attempts to rebirth Newman were to have a decent chance. Pocock's handling of the recent Liturgical Commission report had certainly not convinced me of his ongoing support. I could conceive of lots of correct reasons for his delaying and even possibly refusing any request for prior approval. I did not want to take that risk. I did not make a big deal of it, and I even deliberately softened or dodged this permission dimension when questioned about it by individuals.

Later, in March of 1966, I unexpectedly received a notification from Pocock that his Archdiocesan Architectural Committee had investigated the physical changes at Newman and had found them "not injurious for purposes of worship." I had not been looking for any such approval and was especially not pleased that this committee had been given this mandate without my even being notified and that its so-called investigation had neither informed me of its existence nor even bothered in the name of due process to ask me a single question.

30. An Evolving Mandate: Newman, 1920s to 1960s

From the beginning, Newman's original mandate had seemed to me to be both very clear and yet somewhat complicated. I realized that its original intent had been to serve those Catholic students in the professional faculties at the U of T. Apparently this was especially necessary in the early days, when faculty and students at St. Michael's looked suspiciously on any Catholic students who endangered their immortal souls at the U of T by directly pursuing the secular sciences without the guiding light of Thomism.

Over the years there were persistent stories of this alienation and mutual isolation and perhaps even distrust and lack of respect. In other words, some of Newman's origins were from ideological necessity. Otherwise, why couldn't the then relatively abundant resources of the Basilians have been adequate to embrace this obvious pastoral need? It was also often stated that certain elements of Toronto's Irish nouveau riche retained considerable anticlericalism as well as suspicion of the all-embracing ethos that the Basilians maintained over on St. Joseph Street. Even liberal arts students registered at St. Mike's would experience some of this tension if they happened to be majoring in math, physics, or chemistry simply because those subjects were being taught exclusively across campus. They were seen as not receiving enough of their education on campus—meaning St. Michael's, of course. It was no accident that the first Newman chaplains were Diocesan priests or Paulist Fathers.

The original mandate assumed that Newman would provide a safe haven where anxious Catholic parents could have some assurance of proper dating and mating for their offspring while they were attending the big, bad university. This type of endorsement produced a sexual pressure cooker that did in fact produce memorable dates, dances, and a large number of marriages. While Newman was regarded as successful in its early years, which were seen by many as the glory years, it has always seemed to me that the workings of the original mandate had far more to do with ethnic purity and class preservation than with any scriptural, theological, or liturgical formation, let alone inspiration. I have yet to hear a single reminiscence from that period that focuses on a particularly important liturgical, theological, or sacral moment.

That original mandate quickly evolved from the exclusive focus on Catholic students in the professional faculties. It evolved initially for two reasons. In the first place, some of the students who graduated preferred to keep coming back to Newman, especially after their children were born, rather than settle in their assigned parishes. Secondly, Catholic faculty members at U of T, especially if they lived nearby, looked to Newman for a higher level of intellectual parish activity, where their efforts to contribute were not as easily swamped by a clerical overclass as at St. Michael's. Next, the mandate was broadened by including the friends of existing Newmanites and graduates from other Newman clubs.

By 1965, when I arrived at Newman, it was my clear understanding that its primary focus was still on serving the Catholic students at U of T that were not at St. Michael's. At the same time, the term "extraterritorial" was attached to the mandate to indicate a specific kind of canonical parish status that was determined not by the usual geographical boundaries but by the common bonding of its members. I remember its mandate being explicitly declared by T.A. McDonald as analogous to that of a military chaplaincy.

Almost immediately after Kutz and I arrived at Newman that mandate evolved again in two new ways. First of all, the old tension between

Newman and St. Michael's had virtually disappeared, almost exclusively because of the steady decline of Newman's influence. When word got out that Kutz and I were to replace T.A., a sizable contingent of St. Michael's students and lay faculty migrated across campus to Newman. Some of it was simply a question of style. We never did anything to explicitly encourage this migration, but the fact was that enough people had become familiar with our approach to things and some of them simply wanted to come to wherever we were doing it. This seemed to be especially true of many of the new graduate students, both lay and religious, who were enrolled in St. Michael's new Graduate Program in Theology.

Secondly, the same ferment that preceded Vatican II and continued into its early phases was also abroad in the parishes of Toronto, where more and more lay people, while not necessarily ex-Newmanites, were usually university-educated and deeply concerned with the new issues. Again, without any deliberate provocation on our part, Newman became a magnet for many of the disaffected who had recently left the Church as well as for refugees from parishes that by any criterion were indeed hopeless.

I never had any difficulty in insisting on the mandate's primary focus as being the Catholic students at U of T who were not at St. Michael's, but in fact the active worshipping community had become much more multifaceted. I not only did not see that as a problem; I remember welcoming the complexity. As far as I was concerned, all of these were complementary and mutually enriching components. I never doubted the quality of the results as manifested especially in the Sunday Liturgies and the coffee mixers afterwards.

31. Using the New Space, 1965–1967

Most of what we had learned with TMS and the Student Mass proved very exportable and easily adapted to the Newman scene. We soon settled into a steady rhythm that featured the same balance of a Thursday late-afternoon students' Experimental Liturgy along with a Sunday liturgy tuned to the much more complex general community. The Thursday afternoons gave us an opportunity for a kind of revival of the first year of TMS in terms of the intimacy and innovation possible with twelve to thirty participants. For example, it was in this context that some experienced Dance students began to inject that art into our Offertories. On Sundays we had at least two liturgies that steadily increased their numbers from each of the constituencies.

Someone gave us a Calder-style mobile and I approved suspending it from the rafters directly above the open space in front of the altar platform with its lowest point approximately ten feet off the floor. It worked far better than I had expected. You could stand on the side and watch as the chapel filled up for an occasion. Especially for newcomers, the physics of dominant perspective would force people to notice it as they first came through the entrance to the chapel. Its flat geometric planes of solid colour constantly but slowly changed their relationships to each other. For those with eyes to see, it signalled that they were entering a space where whatever was going to happen would probably not fit their habitual expectations of what was "supposed" to happen here. Similarly, like any well-balanced Calder mobile it was designed to capture and use the slightest air currents. Soundlessly it never stopped moving and therefore served as a non-stop metaphor for the movements of the Spirit.

One of the trickiest decisions was what to do with the blank wall space directly behind the altar platform. I knew I did not want a crucifix of any kind. I was convinced by then and am still convinced that as a cultural symbol it suffers severely from the insensitivity, indifference, and contempt that comes from familiarity and overexposure. One of my more recent fantasies in terms of liturgical adaptation has been of having a permanent large monitor behind the main altar. A different image could be screened for each Eucharist. An entire sequence of images accompanied by appropriate music could serve as an overture to the uniqueness of what was going to happen. In a sense the monitor could function as an updated medieval triptych. These images could be flashbacks, allusions to possible contemporary relevance, or flash-forwards to hopes and future possibles. Above all, I was convinced that for most people the crucifix had at least temporarily if not permanently stopped doing its thing.

I wanted this focal piece of wall space to interact directly with my sense of Christology, but this was quite a challenge. I had welcomed the "God is Dead" movement of the sixties. It shook up individual and collective cosmologies enough that you could get a hearing for such questions as "OK then, let's assume there is no God, at least as we thought we knew Him. Still, how do you account for the enormous historical impact, both positively and negatively, of followers of the 'Carpenter from Nazareth'?"

For several years, during Advent, I would threaten to launch a "Take Christ Out of Christmas Campaign." I would question whether or not most of current Christian practices around "the Babe in the manger' were not highly heretical and old-fashioned heretical at that. Even if believers still refused to accept anything about Midrash, they certainly acted as if they accepted that a little God jumped into a baby's body in a stable and immediately started blessing everything in sight.

I would ask if this wasn't one more way, akin to any standard magic, of our all-too-human attempts to control the sacred. Were the apparently spiritual gushings of Christmas perhaps a defence hiding our reluctance to take on the full-grown Jesus and the full impact of what his life and words might mean to us? Personally, I found the Christology of Teilhard de Chardin far more enthralling. Suppose Jesus was the prototype of the next stage for humanity in the due process of an evolutionary creation! That could mean that he had managed to become so truly human that he did metamorphize into the first "god-man"! Were his life and words really meant as a how-to manual for those interested in following him through into that evolutionary breakthrough?

In the midst of the above a student named Brian Crowe from the Ontario College of Art brought me an oil he had done on a three-by-six-foot piece of brown paper. He said it was mine to use as I saw fit. The painting depicted, crudely but solidly, a Christ who was reaching down with one hand with His own eyes obscured. I found it quite evocative rather than determinative. It also fitted my determination to use student material wherever possible. We decided to try it. It went up on the wall, with no frame, ragged paper edges and all. It seemed to work. Later, after we had moved on to using other things in that space, including a variety of large semi-abstract burlap banners, I asked Brian if I could keep it. He was thrilled with what I had done with it and insisted on giving it to me permanently. I took it with me when I left Newman, later had it framed, and still have it.

An entire new grouping of high-school teachers and their families became one of our strongest and most consistent subcultures. Especially on Thursday evenings we drew more and more Torontonians from the professional schools, including a future federal Member of Parliament and a future high-ranking cabinet minister at Queen's Park. We rented the new Basilian property at Erindale and used it for Weekends, some for students exclusively and others for married couples. We continued exploring new forms of musical expression and included on a regular basis appropriate popular folk songs in their original form.

By the first Christmas we were consistently crowded on Sundays and became accustomed to using a standard three guitarists, who began each liturgy by teaching any new music or helping newcomers catch up with our old faithfuls. Those guitarists remained remarkably loyal and experienced minimal turnover during those two years. Michael Brown, Louis DiRocco, Cot LaFond, Kathi Acton, Basil Harris, Maureen McCabe, and at least two others whose names I cannot recall became our stalwarts. Our first Midnight Mass featured silences and spreadings of the light and proved very rewarding.

One of the failures of that first year was my experiment with what was then still called the Sacrament of Penance. When we arranged the chapel physically I had left the old pipe organ exactly where it had been in the southwest corner. I did that deliberately, to retain it as one option among many. In fact, it ended up being used only a couple of times for weddings. The other thing I left intact in that back corner was the traditional confessional. I did that because I saw it as unproductively provocative to remove it and that corner was already visually dead for our purposes. At the same time, at an early liturgy I explained that I would not be using it for the sacrament of Penance. I proposed an alternate form for that sacrament.

Back in the 1940s, while trading teenage taunts with our non-Catholic peers in and around our west-end Irish ghetto, I remember being reached by those remarks that referred to the confessional as the Catholics' "sin bin." Quite often we would hear remarks such as: "You cat-lickers are phonies when it comes to real sinning. You save up all your bad urges, especially the sexy ones, until Saturday night. Then you do whatever you want, gambling that you'll survive until the morning, when you can dump them all into your sin bins before those Masses of yours. So you really get off scot-free and have a clean slate until the next Saturday night. Us Protestants have to keep living with the consequences of our sins, which just keep piling up. You birds get away with murder and you won't even admit it."

They were both envious of our system that got us off the hook and enraged that we were getting away with something under all our pious posturing. In addition, I personally had a number of quite hideous experiences in the confessional that left me with a perpetual dread of this so-called sacrament of healing and liberation. In the intervening years before and since Newman I have been surprised that a lot more attention has not been focused on the gross abuses of priestly power that are perpetrated behind those curtains.

One other very practical and personal dimension of this question goes back to when I was nine years old. One day I ran out onto the street from between two parked cars while being chased by an older boy with a lasso. I ran smack into the front bumper of a rather large ice truck that was cruising the street looking for those who wanted blocks of ice for their iceboxes. I was knocked unconscious and that night my right ear bled. I seemed to recover, but as the years passed I would get my neck in a kink whenever I concentrated for an extended period on something like a movie or a lecture. That would be because I was straining forward with my good ear to get as much as possible of what was happening. I learned much later that because of my encounter with the ice truck I had lost approximately eighty-five per cent of the hearing in my right ear and fifteen per cent in the left.

When it came to ordination and using the confessional I ran into real trouble. I got a hearing aid, but it was virtually useless for picking up muffled whispers. I got into the habit of carrying with me a small piece of dense cloth that I could drape over the right-hand curtain in the confessional, thereby enabling me to swivel around enough to use my good ear on the right side without the penitent's being able to see what I was doing through the curtain. All of this got mixed up with my pastoral conviction that sin was still being seen far too narcissistically, without nearly enough attention to its communal impact. By the time I arrived at Newman, I believed more fervently than ever in the sacrament of Penance as seen in the context of recent sacramental theology with its stresses on honesty, integrity, healing, reconciliation, communal injury, and collective purpose.

I attempted to explain to the Newman community that I wanted to explore fresh approaches to this area. I proposed that we put renewed importance on those sections of the Eucharist that dealt with our individual, mutual, and collective sense of responsibility as well as attitudes to our failings in those departments. This seemed to get across, and we did get somewhere with it. Secondly, I informed them that those who preferred the traditional forms of individual confession would be able to find suitable confessors in several of the surrounding parishes.

However, I would be spending the time I had available for this activity in exploring new forms for its expression. I shared my conviction that the traditional anonymity of the confessional might mute or undermine the full impact of the sacrament, at least for some penitents. I suggested that those wishing to receive that sacrament at Newman call me and set up an appointment. Then we would discuss—in full confidence, of course— whatever was bothering that individual in those areas traditionally covered by this sacrament. When we had discussed it enough and that person then requested absolution, I would first have them propose a suitable penance with my reserving the right to comment on and approve its suitability. Then I would give absolution.

This approach did not become popular, even though more and more of our constituents were becoming familiar with that mechanism in the truncated and secular forms of their increasingly popular therapeutic counselling sessions of various stripes. My weeks were often swamped with personal counselling sessions where everything except the request for absolution frequently occurred. My proposed experiment was a failure as a revised form for the sacrament, but I still do not understand why.

32. *The Canticle of the Gift*

Even before I arrived at Newman there had been consistent pressure to make the ethos and music of TMS more widely usable. I encountered it especially in the second year of TMS, when the pastoral problem was how to introduce so many well-intentioned "occasional users" to music and liturgical forms that were not familiar to them. We simply could not continually introduce newcomers each and every week to what we were doing. That was not nearly fair enough to the regulars.

At the same time I refused to allow newcomers to be bystanders. Both before and since then, I have regarded personal missals and even hymnals as schizophrenic, in the sense that they greased the participant's split between personal devotion and communal worship. Contrary to the usual conditioning of that time period, my primary goal was as much communal participation as possible.

Finally, we did produce a small hand-printed TMS liturgical booklet. It ran to about forty pages and included a capsule history of our development and attitude towards Liturgy as well as some sets of words without the musical notations for some of the material used most frequently at our liturgies. It also included a "Covenant," which the students and I worked out together and which attempted to crystalize our viewpoint on life. We used that for the 1964–1965 academic session, but it ended up that almost all of the booklets disappeared by the end of the year primarily because of well-intentioned souvenir hunters. When we arrived at Newman we quickly experienced a similar need. A member of the Newman community came forward and volunteered to finance another edition of that same booklet. We had neither the time nor fresh awarenesses to revise that booklet, so we simply ran off another batch and used it at our Sunday liturgies.

But what were we to do with the music? By the time we reached Newman there were already several highly successful pieces that we had stopped using simply because there were so many newer things we wanted to try. A man named Markle approached me in October of 1965 and offered to pay for the studio time and production costs for a vinyl LP of our music. All he asked was that his costs be reimbursed from the initial sales of the record. If those sales were insufficient he would absorb the loss. I had received earlier overtures before Newman, but for some reason I trusted this man. It would be an answer to a growing number of inquiries, it would be a great focus for a significant group of students, and it might even generate a little extra income for Newman. I checked it all out with a lawyer, got releases from those student composers who could be identified, and signed a contract with Markle.

As I remember it, we announced on a couple of Sundays that we would be putting out an LP of our music and called for volunteers for a choral group whose members would be expected to stick together and work on it until its final studio production. We made no attempt at screening as to talent because we were not looking for that kind of a polished production. One of our main points was that this was a sample of what a group of ordinary parishioners had come to value and it was intended to be illustrative instead of determinative. A group of twenty-five or thirty showed up and stuck with it all the way through. Fortunately, some of them did have choral backgrounds and all of them had plenty of enthusiasm. I urged them to stress articulation, passion, and timing. I even ended up doing one spoken line in the final production, but aside from that I left it up to the group. Approximately thirty per cent were from the TMS old guard. All were students because the rehearsal schedule required student timetables. The choral leaders were both SMC graduate theology students.

The choral members had no significant difficulty with attendance at practice sessions. I still believe that it all went so smoothly because they simply enjoyed so much working with each other. In a manner similar to what had happened with the crew renovating the chapel they had their own version of "A Red Sea Crossing." They too bonded, as we say these days, or in those days we simply said that they came to mean a great deal to each other. In some ways the most difficult thing was what to do when it was all over.

That group would have made a great foundation for a traditional choir, but that would have run contrary to our commitment to full participation by everyone in every liturgy. Occasionally we did use a soloist or even a small three- or four-voice group as pump-primers for the fuller vocalization of the general group. Especially at that time, I was convinced that permanent choirs risked placing an unnecessary layer between the individual and the group action.

I had some production difficulties around the album cover, and Markle disappointed me with a few arbitrary decisions towards the conclusion, but overall it came off very well indeed. The LP was released in February, and within a month direct sales and mail orders had cleaned out the original printing. We paid back the production costs, pressed two thousand more copies, and we had a hit on our hands.

This, of course, was in the quite limited category of "religious folk songs." The disc was well reviewed in the appropriate publications and it did produce not a bonanza but enough extra revenue that T.A. was somewhat mollified. By the autumn of 1966 we had close to enough new material that several sources were pressing us to put out a second album. For various reasons we never did get around to repeating our earlier success.

33. The Weddings, the Weddings, the Weddings

The sacrament of Matrimony became enormously more significant to me after I moved to Newman. I had already done several weddings, but one of the consequences of taking on Newman was taking on its extraterritorial parish status. This was one area where I saw the ever-broadening dimensions of the Newman mandate as a definite asset. In my previous three years of the priesthood I had performed several marriages but nothing like what began to happen now. I learned that in certain circles my nickname was Marrying Mike. In fact, at one point I counted up the number I had done both at Newman and elsewhere between January and December of 1966 and discovered that the grand total was eighty-four. I realized that compared to some priests, say at St. Helena's in the Bronx, that was not necessarily that impressive. However, I did find it to be both demanding and satisfying. Many of those weddings were scattered across Canada and the New England states and New York, but most of them were done at Newman.

It seems that the word got around that I was approachable on difficult cases. Sometimes the difficulty was simply the inhumanity and sadism of some of the city's so-called pastors. One of the advantages of extraterritoriality was that I did not have to take on any of the couples that came to me. I would make it clear that I would not assist in any marriage in which I did not believe. It happened in only two instances that I can remember where, after several conversations with the couple in question, I told them that other pastors might consent to marry them but that I was able to find adequate grounds neither to support the use of the sacrament in their instance nor, for myself, to stand as a witness to what they were doing.

Most couples were very believable. Some came because they were hoping to modify the ceremony in certain ways and had been turned down by their territorial pastor. For example, a singer and a violin player from the Canadian Opera Company had four friends from the opera orchestra who had composed an entire liturgy for them to be performed by a string quartet from the same company. They had been turned down on the grounds that it was too fancy. I successfully masked my rage at such unchallengeable viciousness and told them I would be honoured to officiate at such a carefilled ceremony in our chapel. It was one of the richest and most powerful events in which I have participated.

On another occasion, a young Japanese-Canadian man, whose musical specialty was Japanese electronic music, and his fiancée, a young Polish-Canadian woman who did vocal arrangements for symphony orchestras, had each composed original musical material as gifts to each other to symbolize the fullness of their union. They had been unable to find anyone who would allow them to use this material at their wedding. I welcomed it and still cherish the memory of the day they wed.

I suppose the furthest I stretched was on one occasion when a Catholic boy was marrying a Protestant girl whose father was a Protestant minister in town. They definitely wanted to be married in the Catholic Church and she had no difficulty with committing herself to raising the children as Catholics. Their one special request was to have the father of the bride participate in some way as a Protestant minister. Since both he and I had licences from the Ontario government to perform marriages, only one of us could officially preside at the ceremony and sign the official documents as the presiding minister. Since this was to happen in my chapel, that father had no difficulty in agreeing that I should be the official presider.

From there on we worked it out. We stood side by side in our respective ministerial garb. He asked some of the questions and I asked others. The couple devised and delivered their vows without any prompting from either of us, and when it came time for the blessing of the union we intertwined both our stoles around their joined hands. I have never regretted doing it that way, even though a short time later I learned of another Basilian priest who lost his diocesan faculties for doing something similar.

I did all the pre-wedding counselling myself. This is one of the most concrete areas where I would apply my general principle that "if and when the clear needs of the individual conflict or seem to conflict with the legal decrees of the institution, then I will do everything possible on the side of the individual." I found weddings to be one of the most satisfying dimensions of my Newman ministry. It was second only to the Thursday-afternoon and Sunday-morning liturgies. I still experience great difficulty in attending family weddings where the young couple are treated badly by selfish, incompetent priests whose entire manner is anything but life-affirming.

34. The Newman Foundation and National Newman

My understanding as to the legal status of the Newman Club was that Senator Frank O'Connor had either purchased or arranged for the purchase of the Matthews mansion when it came on the market. Either way, he then had the deed to the property transferred to the Newman Foundation, which was entrusted with the property and expected to ensure that the facilities be used to benefit the Catholic students at the University of Toronto who were not at St. Michael's College. This placed the property under lay rather than archdiocesan control.

I've never heard the rationale for that particular arrangement. The Foundation was to consist of a given number of persons, elected annually, who in turn would elect a chairman. The actual programming was to be entrusted to a clerical Director appointed by the presiding Archbishop. I never did know any of the details of how and when the St. Thomas Aquinas chapel was designed and erected, or of how and when a second old mansion on St. George Street half a dozen houses north of the Matthews Mansion was purchased as a residence for Catholic women students.

The Newman Foundation was all but invisible during my tenure at Newman. I never asked to see the legal documents or the finances of the organization past or present. It was the one area where I had complete confidence in T.A. McDonald. None of the programming that Stan and I wanted required extra drains on whatever funds the Foundation controlled. The legally required annual meetings consisted of a bull session over scotch in T.A.'s spacious back room. Three or four men, no women in those days, would be present. They were people like the McNamara brothers and King Clancy, all of them old cronies of T.A.

I would be asked for an oral report in which I sketched in casual noninflammatory language the bare bones of what we had been doing and intended to do. There was never any objection. There were even a few compliments, if my memory still serves me. On very rare occasions, T.A. would inform me that a member of the Board was coming that Sunday to our liturgy. Occasionally someone would identify themselves as such, but never was it a problem.

As I mentioned earlier, T.A. did do a commendable job looking after the staff, overseeing the upkeep of the buildings and grounds, paying the bills, and supervising the male and female resident students. As confreres, we never came close to making it. A sizable chunk of the responsibility for that failure lies with me. My imagination simply never came up with overtures that I might make to add greater humanity to our living together. I did turn down almost all of his invitations to his room to have a drink. God knows, I was drinking almost everywhere else. I could have made the effort and given things a chance to develop. Whether or not he was badmouthing me to the rest of the Basilians, I still could have extended myself. Stan was much better in this department than I was. I still do feel that I let both of us down by my stupid stubbornness in this area. I regret not having at least tried to talk to him before his death. Frank Mallon is a similar story.

The National Federation of Newman Clubs held an annual convention. As I recall, in 1965 it was in Fredericton, and in 1966 it was in Kingston. The National Chairman at that time was Warren Allmand, who went on to become a prominent cabinet minister under Pierre Trudeau and, later, under Jean Chrétien. There was a lot of life in those conventions, mainly because they collected some of the most interesting and committed students from coast to coast. At the same time, it was a quick and rewarding way to tap the mood both of the country on national and regional issues and of the state of the Church in those same areas. This was especially true during those specific years, because the implications of Vatican II were beginning to sink in and the responses and/or backlashes were both exciting and alarming.

For myself personally, the highlight of these gatherings was the opportunity to touch base with the other chaplains working with university students. Over fifty per cent of them had been assigned to the task and had little heart and no passion for the challenge. The rest were magnificent. By then I was cynical enough to think: "Now, if only the Basilians were made up of men like this, what wonders we could produce!" Father Paul Crunican, a diocesan at Western, and Father Marc Gervais, a Jesuit at the Université de Montréal, stand out as two of my favourites, even though they did happen to be Canadian historians as well.

As far as I was concerned, the peak moment of these conventions occurred on Saturday night. It was then, after the conclusion of all formal activities, that the chaplains would gather in a designated hotel room for their own private bull session. More than the Roman collars would come off in that smoke-filled room. Scotch and all its younger sisters flowed freely, as individuals would slowly drop their guards and acknowledge openly where they were at. It was in Kingston in 1966 that I probably went a little too far. I was really sailing that night and I was increasingly uncertain as to how much time I had left at Newman. Finally, I posed a rather rhetorical question: "Gentlemen, what do you do when you wake up one morning and have a sudden realization that Holy Mother the Church is really a bitch?" From their reaction I quickly realized that I was not supposed to have said that. Since lynching suddenly seemed like the next most logical collective action, I decided to ease off for a while.

My favourite National Newman person was Father Louis Raby from the Université d'Ottawa. He was an Oblate, over twenty years older than I was, but still abundantly aware of the human condition and very much in love with his priesthood. He possessed an abundance of Gallic charm in a quiet, steady, determined mode. I'll swear that he was unshockable because he was too interested in life in all its forms. He invited Stan and me to Ottawa with a group of our Newman students. We loaded up two minivans and went gladly for a weekend. It was a way of taking our show on the road, and everyone loved it. He was my best contact for finding out and understanding what was going on in the French-Canadian Church.

What he told us was that despite the history of worker priests and the turmoil of the Cultural Revolution, to the best of his knowledge there was nothing happening liturgically in Quebec that came anywhere near to being as effective as what Stan and I were accomplishing at the U of T. On the one hand that assessment, no matter how much I trusted it, made me feel sad that even in French Canada they had not heard "the Peasant Pope." It also made me feel even further out on the proverbial limb. At the same time, I must admit, it was gratifying. In March of 1967 he was truly saddened when I informed him of my interviews with Wey. He sent me one of the most heartfelt letters that I received from anyone in those months.

35. The Department of History and the U of T

As part of my ongoing doctoral program I was hired as a Teaching Assistant to run seminar groups both in 1965–66 and 1966–67 in a third-year Department of History Honours course called "Problems in Canadian History." Those were teaching treats. I had already done two full years of high-school teaching at St. Michael's College School back in 1956–57 and 1957–58. They were part of my Basilian "on the road" experience as a scholastic. I had thoroughly enjoyed those classroom challenges as well as the Extension courses in Church history that I did at St. Michael's College in the summers of 1962, 1963, and 1964. Most History doctoral students had not had such previous experience, so I quickly did very well in this supposedly secular environment. It meant that during each of my Newman years approximately one day of each week during the academic term was devoted to this arena. Newman's Matthews House, even before its historical restoration, was still a grand place for mid-term and end-of-term gatherings for myself and those History students.

I had not yet finished off my doctoral thesis and while at Newman, despite a few attempts, never did make a big enough chunk of time to bear down on it. That did not hinder my status with the Department. In fact, in 1966 I was selected as one of thirty most promising Canadian historians to go to Vancouver for a week in August for a think tank to consider issues to be highlighted for the country's Centennial in the following year.

A major factor in Newman's reaching out to the larger campus was our involvement in the Sir Robert Falconer Society. This was the name of the council of all campus chaplains. We met monthly for wide-ranging discussions on many issues and both Stan and I became quite fond of several of the ministers and rabbis. Those meetings, as well as a lecture series that we sponsored jointly, were usually held at Newman, mainly because at that time we had by far the most commodious settings of any of the campus ministries. Both Stan and I seemed to do well in that setting, and at the conclusion of the first year each of us was asked to act as chair of the organization for the following year. Both of us declined because of other issues that were looming. When both Stan and I were dismissed from Newman in 1967, that group of chaplains sent an unsolicited, very moving letter of support on our behalf to the Archbishop and all others concerned.

The SCM (Student Christian Movement) has a long and distinguished presence on the U of T campus. Since the 1940s it had been respected for running the finest bookstore in the city. In the sixties it was probably still the chief instigator and supporter of collective action on issues of social justice. I liked students involved in SCM because they were solidly Christian but completely inclusive in their efforts to rally all like-minded people around specific issues. They were crucial in sustaining the Selma civil-rights sit-in at the American consulate. They were the most consistent supporters of various Vietnam protests and ban-the-bomb marches. They also put their resources and talents behind the expansion of campus co-op housing and the eventual building of Rochdale College.

I became involved with SCM members during 1965–1966 by collab- orating with them in organizing and supporting the large International Teach-In at Varsity Stadium. In September of 1966 the local SCM nomi- nated me to join the National Executive of SCM. No other Catholic, let alone priest, had ever been invited to such a position. I accepted and was amazed at the range and depth of characters with whom this put me in touch. Monthly meetings of that executive were always engaging, stirring, and fruitful. At the end of that academic year I had to inform them that I would have to resign because in the fall I would no longer have the clerical status for which I had been selected.

My leaving Newman really did seem a much larger shock to SCM than to many other groups with which I was associated. At the meeting in which I made the announcement there was a brief stunned silence. Then within seconds another member of the executive insisted that they still wanted me to be there. They would change the title of my position and nominate me as a representative of the university faculty members of SCM. This proposal was agreed to unanimously and I served for another year after leaving Newman. Then, in the summer of 1968, SCM selected me to represent all their Canadian faculty members at three world conferences in Finland. I accepted this all-expenses-paid venture and ended up in that summer of 1968 at the same conference table in Turku with student representatives from Czechoslovakia and Russia on the morning that the tanks rumbled into Prague. I still love the soft yet highly relevant and effective works of SCM's version of Christianity.

36. An Appointment with Father Wey, March 1966

Early in March 1966 Father Wey phoned me and asked if I could come up to his office on Russell Hill Road so we could "talk over a few things." We arranged a time and I passed through for the first time those elegant portals. We settled into our discussion rather easily. His agenda, at least the one he spoke to me about, seemed to be exclusively on what I was or was not doing with the liturgy. Most of his questions required only simple factual answers.

I had learned long before that it was much safer to be a dissenting theologian or scripture scholar than a liturgist. That was because the vast majority of clerical administrators, including those of religious communities, were not chosen for those positions because of their familiarity with the intricacies of scholarship, either recent or remote, on theological matters. Such administrators were easily intimidated or confused by the words and/or word games of a competent theologian or scripture scholar. In the case of Father Wey, for example, I was not aware of his having a clear theological opinion on any contemporary issue.

But I was there as a practitioner of liturgy, which was primarily visual and eminently checkable, especially if orthodoxy depended exclusively on objective formalism. Not a single one of his liturgical questions had anything to do with purpose, intent, or relevance of the sign, let alone nature of impact or short and long-term results. At best, his questions were the sad results of his profound liturgical illiteracy. I knew he was an accomplished medieval scholar, but he left me wondering if he had ever reflected on what the Eucharist meant to him personally. The questions included: "Do you use whole-wheat bread at Mass?," "Do you use English in those parts of the Mass where it has not yet been approved?," and "Do you ever distribute communion under both species?" My answers to all of these questions were by now well known to him and to others in the Church. He challenged none of my responses to these questions and simply kept moving down his list. At one point I asked if I could inter-rupt, and when he agreed I stated that I was puzzled because none of the information I was supplying was new. All of it was known to him before he took me to Pocock's meeting the previous year. That meeting with the Archbishop could not be interpreted as anything but at least tacit approval of what I had already been doing for a year and a half with TMS, and it certainly seemed the Archbishop wanted me to continue the same sort of work at Newman. Otherwise, what had that meeting been about?

By this point in the interview Wey was becoming more and more awk-ward. His response to my last question seemed to be that he had received these questions from many sources and had been urged to ask me about them directly. I then asked whether or not he had urged or perhaps even insisted that these persistent complainers come to me directly. He admitted that he had not and that it was difficult because many people were upset with all these new changes. As at the Pocock meeting a year earlier, I again suggested that if he were to come and see for himself what was happening at Newman he might feel far more secure in dealing with these objections. His reply to that was something like "Yes, that's a good idea. I must do that sometime."

Things sputtered after that, and I finally asked if he had any further questions. At first he indicated no, but as I began to rise he hesitantly said: "Well, Mike, there is one other matter, not dealing with the liturgy, which I hesitate to bring up because it may be only idle gossip." By now, I had long abandoned any jitters I was supposed to feel in this situation. I settled back and said something like: "Father, I don't care what it might be. It is obviously on your mind, so why not spell it out and I'll answer it as honestly as I can." He was physically shrugging with embarrassment as he proceeded haltingly: "Well, Mike, it has come to my attention that you have become, shall we say, rather attracted to one of the young ladies on campus."

I'm still not certain whether my immediate response came from defensiveness, contempt for authority, or sheer devilment. I moved forward to the edge of my chair, swelled up with feigned indignation, and replied: "Father Wey, I wish to take complete exception to that remark on the grounds of number." There was a brief pause and then he burst into laughter. There was no follow-up, and my remark served for him as the welcome termination of an encounter that really did seem to have been much more difficult for him than for me.

I maintained a grin, but inside I was torn between the kick from successfully dropping a one-liner and the sadness I felt on noting that his response clearly indicated that he welcomed my remark as an excuse for a way out. As I drove down the hill I thought, "God help me if I had wanted to, or had felt the need to, turn to him for any real help in that area." I was certain he had no idea of the absurdity of his behaviour. His spontaneous response and his failure to add anything to it clearly stated that it was quite acceptable for a priest to have an entire harem as long as he didn't allow any one woman to become too important to him. As far as I'm concerned, Wey got a failing grade for that interview, on all possible counts.

37. The Journalists and I – "Mutual Exploitation"

The question of journalistic coverage of our liturgical changes long preceded our arrival at Newman. Probably the first newspaper item came from a columnist who had been a guest at Loretto College one Sunday when I happened to be taking my turn as its chaplain. The college had adopted some of our TMS techniques, which impressed the journalist simply because they were "not the way the Mass was supposed to be done." Coverage remained light until Stan and I went to Newman. As I have noted, the very visibility factor in what we were doing may have set off alarm bells for traditional formalists, but it was a cornucopia for investigative reporters or those trying to make a name for themselves. We even became the feature article for an issue of *The Weekend Magazine*, and a small photo of Newman Chapel was later included in the magazine's promotional collage page along with Gordie Howe, Princess Grace, and the Queen Mary as notable contemporary newsmakers.

I am not very satisfied with my performance in this arena. I will not blame it on my being misquoted. You take that risk or you don't do interviews. Overall I still believe that I was handled quite fairly. The problem lay more in my department of prudence. I would become seduced by my own word-mongering. And I did find it flattering to be sought out for my opinion on almost everything that moved. Fear of the Lord may indeed be a gift of the Spirit, but I had long replaced my fear of church authorities with sadness, disdain, and even contempt for their levels of competency and courage.

At best I was trying to say to all who would listen: "There are many valid ways of being Christian, and even Catholic. Trust, honour, and nourish the unique gift of the Spirit that is already in you. Each of us remains primarily responsible for ourselves even if official authorities reject that responsibility." At worst, I was venting my spleen at what I considered to be the numerous missed pastoral opportunities and the professional incompetence of too many of its clerical representatives. The expression that tended to be most quoted and in which I did take a real pride, perverse and otherwise, was: "If and when the legal demands of the institution conflict with the legitimate needs of the individual believers, then I choose to fight on the side of the individual."

I could and did preach on the need for legitimate authority but definitely stressed the dangers of unquestioning obedience and focused on the far more difficult challenge of struggling with the demands of our individual consciences and the dimensions of our personal responses to the challenges of our immediate environment. On some level I was probably daring the authorities to stop me, and of course eventually they did. In the meantime I believe I was determined to give them a run for their money. The so-called religious authorities and my religious and clerical colleagues would not even bother to witness the very thing they were so quick to condemn. In that context I found the press a convenient vehicle to use against versions of authority that I was convinced needed to be challenged. In that sense I used the press far more than they ever exploited me.

The one article I still regret is the one in which I was quoted blasting nuns. I regretted soon afterwards my degree of overstatement in that piece. The truth was that even then I personally knew several remarkable women who were choosing to remain inside existing structures yet whose steadfastness, creativity, and equanimity I found truly edifying. Over the years I have remained convinced that while there will always be problems of abusive power and various forms of corruption in every convent, as in every institution, I definitely overdid it and many nuns got lumped in as innocent bystanders in my body count on that day.

Sometimes it was the references in the press that had not originated in an interview that delivered the greatest sense of satisfaction. For example, two months before I left Newman, *Time* magazine did a special issue devoted to Canada's Centennial. The usual two-page *Time* essay attempted to capsulize the current mood of the country and what it was that made Canadians different from Americans. Towards the conclusion of that piece I was quoted as suggesting, in effect, that one of our greatest virtues as a people—one that we did not appreciate adequately—was our ability to muddle forever on issues rather that allow those issues to be absolutized into polarized conflict. It turned out that this had been cited because the *Time* representative for all of Canada had been brought by a friend to a Newman liturgy. I cannot recapture the context in which I would have included that kind of remark in my homily, but, as even my best friends will still tell you, "Quealey did have a pronounced tendency to throw everything into his homilies, including the kitchen sink."

38. Draft Evaders, Quakers, and the CIA

There was another of my Newman contacts with the outside world that even seemed to involve the CIA. This story stems from the reality that Toronto during the mid-sixties became a more and more attractive safe harbour for draft dodgers from the Vietnam War. St. Michael's, with its disproportionately high percentage of American students, was an especially convenient place for those who wished to mask their deeper motives for being in Toronto under the blanket of academic respectability. While still at St. Mike's, Stan and I had already gotten to know and counsel several of these "students." When we came to Newman, more and more of them seemed to be seeking us out. Stan and I had both been opposed to the Vietnam War from its earliest stages. This was widely known and did not endear us to Toronto's "Irish Murphia," who were generally rednecked in their unquestioning support of anything to do with the US Marines.

In the autumn of 1966 a member of our Newman community came forward with a suggestion that might help focus and make creative the frustrations that so many of us felt about this terrible war. The Quakers were raising funds to send medical supplies to Vietnam. They assured any supporters of their program that the funds would be divided equally, one-third each, among North Vietnam, South Vietnam, and the Viet Cong.

On behalf of Newman, Stan and I agreed to participate. We proposed it at our next Sunday liturgy and suggested that it take the form of a second collection. The suggestion was widely received with relief and enthusiasm and many did give until it hurt. They asked if we could continue the collection each week until Christmas, partially to help us ground in reality all the other elements of that season. Every Monday morning, either Stan or I would drop off at the Quakers the results of that second collection. At the same time I began to experience an increase in my hate mail and nasty anonymous phone calls.

One day I received a call from an individual asking me for an appointment. He did identify himself by name and claimed that he had been recently attending our Sunday liturgies. I gave him a time slot and made certain that I was there and on time. I had recognized this individual's name from our draft-dodger friends. They claimed that this individual was widely considered to be the official CIA man on staff at the American consulate on University Avenue. He had collected quite a reputation for his various forms of harassment against any and all members of the draft-dodger subculture. Well, he arrived for our appointment on time and suavely established his credibility by rhyming off each and every Catholic parish, grade school, high school, college, and university that he had attended throughout the New England states.

He then expressed his concerns as a fellow Catholic because of some of the things he had been hearing about my behaviour. I asked him to spell out to what he was referring. He said that, while I was doubtless operating with the best of intentions, did I realize that I was in fact encouraging seditious behaviour among the American students on campus, especially the Catholic ones? I pointed out that it was still not at all clear to me what he was talking about.

He went on to elaborate that "every good Catholic knew that, as terrible as it was, the Vietnam War was nevertheless a 'just war,'" and that

American Catholics risked the loss of their souls by not actively supporting it. According to him, as an ordained Catholic priest I should know better. Furthermore, my counselling of draft dodgers was encouraging them in their delusions and cowardice as well as aiding and abetting the enemy. What he was now suggesting that I do to make up, at least partially, for my transgressions was to tell him the names of those students on campus who were Americans and especially those of them that were evading the draft or sympathetic to that behaviour.

My first response was to make it absolutely clear that I had no intention of giving him any names whatsoever. I also pointed out as gently but firmly as I could that the people of Vietnam were not my enemy, despite some of the highly questionable collusions of my Canadian government in developing weapons of chemical and germ warfare and delivering them directly to his government. He admitted that he was an employee of the American consulate but would not be pinned down further on his specific duties. I explained that I was asking because he was often mentioned as one who harassed American students on campus, whether or not they were avoiding the American draft.

I also emphasized that I did not automatically regard evaders of the draft as cowards and, as far as my counselling was concerned, I stressed with everyone on every issue that their primary duty was to the integrity of their own conscience rather than blind automatic obedience to external directives on any matter above the obeying of traffic lights. By now it was apparent that this appointment was not going the way my guest had intended. He attempted to switch channels by commenting on my public misbehaviour at the Sunday liturgies in supporting the second collections for the Quaker Medical Relief Fund.

He contended that this was particularly disturbing to any congregation of Catholic believers and would foster their rebellion against all authority, including even the leadership of our sacred hierarchy and our Holy Father. I must admit it was a little scary how absolutely he accepted this nonsense. I assured him that my worshipping community was not nearly so feeble-minded as to become that confused.

His final thrust consisted of his deep concern for my immortal soul, because I was so resistant to these insights of Christian charity that he had gone out of his way to share with me. He claimed to regret it, but, because I had been so uncooperative, he might have to—out of his Christian duty, of course—report my activities and opinions to the RCMP, even if they already had a file on me, which, he strongly suspected, might already be true.

That triggered one of my finest belly laughs. When it had subsided enough, I told him: "That would be wonderful. I've always hoped that the RCMP had a file on me, especially for the right reasons." His cultivated charm had long dissolved. I do not remember him even offering to shake my hand as he ejected himself from my office. I never saw him again. It was one of the saddest, most bizarre, and ugliest moments of my stay at Newman.

39. Increasing Internal Pressure, Spring 1966

As winter slowly let go of its grip in the spring of 1966 I became more and more aware of the tensions and stresses I was carrying around with me all the time. I was still attempting to get by on four to five hours of sleep a night and would go through stretches when I would down twelve to fifteen painkillers a day just to keep going. Stan remained my closest confidant, but there were areas of tension that I was reluctant to articulate even to myself, let alone to anyone else. I used a mixture of rationalization, romanticization, denial, and defiance to keep moving forward. I wrote in private journals and even attempted semi-poetic pieces as methods of keeping a grip on what was in front of me. In March of that year I made a quick trip down to Montauk for a huddle with Doc Walsh. As always, it was helpful. While there I also took a long walk on the beach and tried to write about it. It is as typical an example as I can remember of this particular coping mechanism.

> **Montauk Beach, March 1966**
> Spilling surf, sun-kissed spray, and unpicked pebbles
>   call to the child and adult in me
> Canopied by the soft blue of a sky
>   meant to be climbed into,
>   I faced into the sun and wind and walked
>   the line of undulating wet sand
> Making tracks in that sand
>   and not worrying if they be wiped out
>   because that is only where I've been

Past the silly fancy shacks of those
  who can only take the sea
  on their own terms and in due season
Sad that such huts stand
  as the emasculated monuments to all of us
  when we are unable to know and love
  the sea as she is
Traversing the wind-carved contours
  of lightly dusted beach
  I raced the salty wetness
  to pick up a sparkling pebble
  or a tumbled seashell
Turning to retrace my steps
  the wind billows my shimmering shadow
  over crushed and twisted sea debris
I settled for a while amidst dune grass
  defiantly waiting for spring
  and watched the lazy swooping
  of a skeptical seagull
Down the coast I considered cliffs
  scarred by the ravaging sea
  yet quietly awaiting
  the more tender moments
  of its tempestuous lover
Finding a piece of driftwood
  shaped like the baton of a relay runner
  I met a ladybug underneath
  who returned courage for friendship
Above all it was the snow-white crests
  of steel-blue waves
  that absorbed and rewarded
Far out, the big ones seemed to crest too soon
  yet thereby asserted their lordship
  over the horizon
Wind-whipped mist was peeled off the crest
  of giant rollers by offshore gales
On that jousting ground
  where sea battles shore
  fleets of rollers charged in
  for their assault on the beach

The crests curl, the troughs open
  and yet the swells carry those
  that dare to ride them well
Still, one must respect the sea's power
  and love its magnificence
  or suffer its destruction and vengeance
The blustering surf approached
  with the bravado of a preening peacock
  or an inexperienced young lover
Yet ends by gently licking the naked sand
  and retreats to find new strength
  so as to try to love again
It is here that a person can find
  the courage to battle the surf
  face the challenge of the open sea
  and cross over to the other shore
This it is to be alone in the midst of majesty

40. Lea Hindley-Smith and Admiral Road

My own personal internal pressures became increasingly paralleled by what I came to see as a possible resolution, or at least approach, to the deeper needs of many students and adults who were coming to me for counselling. First, the personal part. The summer of 1965 had stirred the depths of whatever innards I was carrying. A great deal of what was stirring in me I simply did not understand and it seemed to be in greater and greater danger of spinning out of control. That autumn I was invited again to join the Catholic group on Admiral Road. I had checked out the composition of the group. It seemed to comprise primarily about a dozen clerics and nuns from various communities who had been stationed at St. Michael's College by their communities to pursue various graduate programs.

In many ways, even before Admiral Road, they had already consti-tuted themselves as a tightly knit group of friends, despite their diverse origins—the New England states, Germany, the Canadian prairies, Aus-tralia, and the American Midwest. They found in each other considerable concurrence on a wide range of issues and had also become accustomed to celebrating their own private Eucharists at the chapel in Elmsley Hall.

Advice from their spiritual directors and word of mouth had resulted in their regrouping in weekly therapy sessions on Admiral Road.

Members of Toronto's own religious communities and the priesthood from various dioceses gradually gravitated to this same group. I had known various members of this group since before I had gone to Europe but had not in fact participated in their gatherings. I did admire them on various grounds, and it appeared increasingly that their therapy vehicle was the most attractive method for my own needs of self-discovery. It was in October of 1965 that I first attended one of their groups. I was desperate in some ways but still very, very defensive in other ways. It was not until the spring of 1966 that I asked to see its therapist, Lea Hindley-Smith, for a few private sessions. What struck me at first in the group sessions was the extent of commonality of many of the confusions that I had assumed were unique to myself.

Secondly, despite our common Catholic background we seemed able to transcend the worst of our so-called religious upbringings and really see each other's unique humanity. Stan and I were able to reserve the Basilians' Erindale property for one of the prototype "marathons" for this group.

These weekends were something like old-fashioned retreats except that there rarely was any direct reference to religious beliefs. The bulk of the time was spent in long group sessions that gave individuals the opportunity to say whatever they wanted to say. That in itself proved to be a remarkable liberation. The therapist, Lea Hindley-Smith, would occasionally interject. Sometimes it was simply in suggestive rather than overtly directive ways. At other times she had a knack of being able to slice through to the core element in the neurotic behaviour being revealed.

I had never been on any Basilian retreat that came anywhere as close to dealing with personal devils, to dealing effectively with long-festering wounds, and to setting free secret aspirations that benefited all concerned. I became increasingly enthralled with this whole new approach to what would have previously been called personal and pastoral needs.

This contact with Mrs. Smith and Admiral Road had a profound influence on my counselling at Newman. In one way it helped to solve my earlier dilemma about what to do with seriously disturbed people. Whatever it was that was happening on Admiral Road had far greater grounds for hope than the then standard medical approach of "medication, medication" or "just one more shock treatment."

This fresh approach was referred to as "Admiral Road" simply because that was the street in Toronto's Annex where Mrs. Smith lived and where she also directed a couple of House Groups for those who wanted a live-in situation for more concentrated, shorter-term sessions to address the blocks that were holding them back from living truer and more productive lives. They retained that nickname until after I left the Basilians and it was that name that was increasingly used with strong derogatory connotations by various Basilians—especially John Kelly, the President of St. Michael's College. Kelly shouted from the rooftops against "this Mrs. Smith" who was stealing away the cream of St. Michael's graduate students, most of whom also happened to be clerics and nuns.

Meanwhile, over at Newman I was increasingly suggesting to individuals whose disturbance and despair was not yielding to the best of what we had to offer at Newman that they explore Admiral Road to see if that might prove helpful. In addition, I was firmly convinced that many people who might never need professional help in the technical sense could still benefit enormously and expand the liberation they had already accomplished by a concentrated stretch with whatever was available on Admiral Road. A lot of individuals at Newman had already come to trust such suggestions from Stan or myself. A few, then a trickle, then a large number found their way to Admiral Road both before and after our sojourn at Newman.

41. Conference of Inter-American Student Projects

We almost always called it by the short form, CIASP. It stood for what I still believe was perhaps the healthiest student movement of the 1960s. It had begun on the Yale campus in 1961. A couple of students brought it to St. Peter's in London and St. Michael's in Toronto. A large contingent of students from St. Mike's went to Mexico in the summer of 1965. Several of our TMS regulars were among the chief organizers in 1964, 1965, and again in 1966 and 1967. When Kutz and I moved to Newman we encouraged this group to use our facilities even if they were not active in the worshipping community.

CIASP was student-run. They covered all the necessary expenses for an eight-week stay in the mountains of Mexico. Each student was responsible for raising their own funds as well as a portion of the total project's cost. They did a wide range of fundraising activities that were generously supported by the student body generally as well as by faculty and friends. Perhaps the simplest reason for the extent of their support was that this group attracted and held the allegiance of many of the best and most natural student leaders on campus. In addition, all those joining the group had to commit time throughout the regular academic year for Spanish classes as well as mini-courses on Mexican history, elementary education, first aid, and community development. We contributed the facilities at Newman for many of these functions.

Each year CIASP invited one or more clerics or seminarians to accompany them with the very clear understanding that their itinerary and specific responsibilities would be under student direction. I was invited to go with them in that capacity in the summer of 1966, at the end of my first year at Newman. It turned out to be one of the most difficult yet worthwhile things I have yet done with life. We left by bus on May 9 to return on July 2 and, except for meals, travelled non-stop for three days and nights to Mexico City. There were eighty-six students in this contingent along with Father Gene Uram from London and myself.

In late June a second contingent would arrive to replace our teams on the same *ranchos*. They too would be giving eight weeks of their summer and return in mid-August. Because most of these students were dependent on summer jobs to earn their expenses for the following year at university, the program deliberately limited their assignment to eight weeks. Almost thirty American campuses would also be sending CIASP students under their own administrators. The Canadians this summer came from universities in Halifax, Montreal, Ottawa, London, Waterloo, Windsor, and Toronto, and one-third of them were French Canadians.

There was a small washroom in the back of each bus and several of the students took turns stretching out in the luggage racks and even on the floor of the aisle for chunks of sleep. After several days of final orientation sessions in Mexico City, we went again by bus almost due north on the old Pan-American Highway back towards Nuevo Laredo to our drop-off points in the Sierra Madre mountains in the northern regions of Hidalgo.

[In May of 1999, while working on this enlarged revision of the writing on CIASP, which I had first done back in 1995, I discovered a set of journal entries covering the first ten days of that journey, from May 9 to May 18, 1966. I had even entitled them tentatively "Listening to the Sierra Madres." They were made originally in a small notebook that I kept in my back pocket. They cease on May 18, probably because I became far too busy to sustain the effort. I realized that the entries were not flowing as smoothly as they had in the previous summer, but I do regret not having been able to keep at it. I have decided to reproduce them with minimal editing because of the crispness of their details, many of which had subsequently slipped away from my memory.]

May 9, 1966: This was my departure day for an adventure I had been looking forward to for years but which events of recent weeks have clouded considerably. Now it has happened. I am actually on my way. The day began at 8 a.m. after about three hours of sleep. Trips to the bank, the barber, St. Mike's, the U of T's Health Service for my last shots, and Sidney Smith to drop off my graded Canadian History final exams somehow all got done. I was back at Newman for breakfast and a two-hour bull session with my brother, Brian, who flew in from Houston just last night. It was the first time I had seen him in over a year and we talked as if we had never talked. It turned out that he was involved in similar areas and he really did understand what I was trying to say.

Rushing back around 2 p.m. to begin my packing, I straightened out with Stan some last-minute details about "The Canticle" and various marriages he was picking up for me. Because of all that has happened in the past week, we have grown very close. At 4:30 p.m. we picked up Kathy Gillespie and various medical supplies. Stan and Brian drove us out to Whitby, where we met up with our two Burley buses. The Toronto group was there and we split up, with one bus headed for Waterloo and London while the other headed back to Toronto to pick up the groups from Halifax, Ottawa, and Montreal at Union Station. Supper was a good pizza on Yonge Street with Kathy Gillespie and Sue Koch.

Our bus was loaded by the time we got back, but I found a seat at the back with Gerry LePine from Timmins, who drills in the mines during the summer and graduates from Ottawa's Minor Sem next year. It was a beautiful evening to be leaving Toronto with the Gardiner and the "Queen E" looking so fresh now that I wouldn't be seeing them for a while. We slipped up Highway 10 and then west on the 401 into a sunset that was *muy, muy bonita*. On the way down to Windsor I had good but brief talks with Kathy, Sue, and especially with Annie Harris. Windsor came up very quickly and there was some of that big-city magic about Detroit's skyline as seen from the Ambassador Bridge. We waited at American customs for our bus from London with some very jovial bridge officials thoroughly enjoying an off-season. Some enthusiastic reunions when the buses met and then off through Detroit, south "down Dayton way," and our first night of bus sleep.

May 10, 1966: This was a full day on the road. I awoke after getting one of my best chunks of eight hours of sleep in many weeks while scrunched up on my back seat in the bus. It was a humid night, and by the end of it several CIASPers were stretched out full length on the floor of the aisle. Mike Cassidy had even managed to slide up into the overhead baggage rack. We hit St. Louis around 11:30 a.m. after a breakfast in Terre Haute, Indiana. From a very long way off we could see the new arch symbolizing St. Louis as the Gateway to the West, but from the little we could see the city seemed modern but rather bland.

I did get my first view of the mighty Mississippi and shortly afterwards we used the Resurrectionist Major Seminary to shower, shave, and have lunch. Then it was a long run down through Missouri with supper at Springhill and then off again for Oklahoma. This was a delightfully lazy kind of day. I worked on my Spanish, talked with a few people, had a good Spanish class with Sue Koch for a few hours, and then a long talk with Kathy Gillespie until late at night. Mainly it had been a long day for a good deal of thinking. I was rather low-key all day and did a lot of daydreaming. The mood of everyone around me seemed to be much the same. Last night, while sliding down the 401, we had been singing together, which began weaving the first threads of unity. It began with Spanish and then went into French and English folk tunes. Today there wasn't as much singing and I found myself unwinding, getting used to the notion that I was actually on my way to another stage, another place.

From this perspective, the period since last September seems as close as real hell gets. It's strange to say that concerning a year so full of excitements and many kinds of apparent achievements. The turmoil of the past week brought so many things to a head. I devoted my energy simply to holding on. I feel that same familiar sense of tumbling through space, but more and more it is without any sense of time, distance, or direction. I do want desperately to believe that I can rebuild or create anew, or perhaps even build something brand new that is worthwhile.

May 11, 1966: This was another long travelling day. We stopped in Pearsall, Texas, for a mid-morning break and had Richard and Michel do a *High Noon*–style gunfighters' draw on the main street. Afterwards it was a straight run though San Antonio (I missed Dallas, which we passed through at 3 a.m.) and down to Laredo on the American border with Mexico. Here we met our first heat and it was truly sweltering. We were a few hours ahead of schedule as we left our Burley bus in the bus terminal. I went to the local bank to get some money changed into Mexican currency. Then I went with Kathy and Sue to shop and eat and soak up the heat and characters of this classic border town.

Back at the bus terminal we had to switch all of our baggage from our old Burley to a Mexican chartered bus because of international regulations. I even managed to work up my first good sweat in a very long time. At Mexican customs we had to unload everything still again for an inspection in which contents didn't actually get inspected at all. Then we were off through the streets of Nuevo Laredo on the Mexican side of the Rio Grande, where the people, colours, and everything else changed radically. It was definitely a cheap, rough border town, but I have seldom been so aware of faces. Before we got out of town our bus actually collided with an automobile, apparently without any great damage, because our brakes failed. Only a few of us realized this as we set off across the desert for Monterrey.

We encountered our first glorious Mexican sunset over the wasteland to our right. It's amazing how truly empty the land is up here in Mexico's north. We hit Monterrey around 10 p.m. There we had supper and our first credenzas (Mexican beer). Then we had to switch again to a bus that had both air-conditioning and brakes. From our stops so far it seems clear that some of our girls are going to have lots of either fun or trouble from their contacts with Mexican men. They simply don't seem to realize what they are really doing. We finally got jammed into our new bus for our last night's run down to Mexico City. For this run I was sitting with Tony White, who regaled me with stories of what happened to him last year at the Rancho Malengo. It really did make me feel that I was in a different land, which in turn triggered musings about "all my tomorrows."

May 12, 1966: Waking up this morning we found our bus sliding down the new Pan-American Highway into Mexico City. We stopped for an early breakfast where the orange juice was truly fresh and then it was back on the buses for the final leg. The dryness, flatness, and desolation were broken only occasionally by patches of green, and the few people we could see working in and around *ranchos* were in rags and withered by the sun and wind.

On the outskirts of Mexico City the contrasts became even more obvious as we saw peons trudging through the gates of giant industrial compounds exchanging their sombreros for steel safety helmets while outside the gates their women trudged by with huge gourds of water balanced precariously on their heads and babies smothered in shawls on their backs and hips to protect them from the omnipresent dust. As we worked our way into and through the length of Mexico City we gained some notion of just how huge and vibrant it really is. With approximately six million people jammed in here, there are far more obvious contrasts between sophistication and poverty. The monuments, the bustling streets, Chapultepec Park, and the chaotic traffic all provided a rather forceful introduction to this other world.

We finally found our way to Tlalpan and the two convents where we were to stay. They were separated by a small park that hosted a massive municipal market. The girls' retreat house had a huge kiosk/minaret in the middle of their courtyard as well as meeting rooms and a chapel for our orientation sessions. I was assigned to a massive room across from the bishop's suite. There was a shower and *bano* next door, which made it rather special by the standards of this area of town. We changed quickly and I even shaved for the first time in a couple of days. Then Eileen, Kathy, Julie, and I headed downtown for an all-too-brief three-hour spree. First we crossed Alameda Central to get something to eat, after which we caught a cab out to the Peralvillo markets, where the stuff is actually made on the spot. It was a lot of fun simply browsing with that threesome.

It began to rain a little, but we were able to get a ride into town where we had tequila sours, which were truly fine. Trouble getting another taxi made us late for Mass and supper, but we did manage to squeeze in our orientation plus a singsong before it was time for closed doors at 10 p.m. A good day, I'd say!

May 13, 1966: This was a full day of orientation. Professor Horeitas from the training centre at Cuernavaca gave us a great talk on the anthropology of Meso-America with connections to and reflections on our contemporary scene. In the afternoon Father Hessler, a semi-retired Dominican, presented a kind of spiritual orientation that was honest enough but somehow didn't really come across. Father Placido, head of all the projects under CIASP in Mexico, presided at the Eucharist, and both Gene Uram and I had to watch like hawks because this was the template for what we would be doing.

Oh yes, I almost forgot that one of the greatest things about yesterday was that I got to see Betty Dwyer again. She drove up in her jeep shortly after we arrived, all browned, full of life and stories, and with plenty of big hugs for everyone. It was very good to see her again. She was an original TMSer and had been down with CIASP in 1965. At the end of that summer CIASP hired her to remain throughout the September-to-May seasons to establish fresh contacts and nourish old ones. During those same months our Canadian students had raised the funds to allow her to stay in Mexico. She truly loved those mountains and its people. Betty and I didn't immediately get a chance to talk very much, but I gave her the bottle of Chivas Regal that I had brought for her from Canada so she could keep it until we could find the right tree to sit under for a long, long bull session.

At suppertime I learned that Bob Powers and Dick Ramirez, two Basilian scholastics, were literally only two blocks away from where I was staying. I knew they were in Mexico City but never dreamt that they would be staying in the same area of the same outskirts. I had given up hope of seeing the Basilians at San Juan de Aragon in Mexico City, but this changed everything. After supper, Uram, Jay Maplee, and I went down to the Grand Seminary. We met Powers and Ramirez, got a tour of the Sem, which is rather imposing, and then settled in their rooms with Cokes for a good long bull session on the Church in Mexico. The situation looks very sad in many ways, with very few new priests, especially from the cities, the drain of sinecures deemed necessary to keep priests' families, the gap between old pastors and a few very capable younger men, and the riots shortly before Christmas, in which eighteen Catholics and ten Protestants were killed just south of Mexico City.

Almost the only bright spot was at Cuernavaca, with its far-sighted Bishop, who was encouraging concelebration with Anglicans possessing valid orders, as well as his seminary, where degrees determine position—as contrasted with the situation here in Mexico City, where the seminarians are consciously fearful of any contact with university students and confused about the strange interplay of doctrinal and devotional levels in the Church's experience in Mexico. It was a good session. It was good to spend time with Bob and Dick again. I borrowed an alarm clock so I could get up on time for what we had planned for the following morning.

May 14, 1966: I was able to get out the back door of the convent so I could meet Bob and Dick. We finally got a cab to take us downtown and then another cab to take us out to our Basilian parish of San Juan de Aragon. Here I met Tom Dugan and Frank Launtrie and was able to fill them in on what was happening up north. I also met the legendary Father Max Murphy for the first time. Bob and Dick borrowed the parish jeep to take me on a tour of the parish. Apparently this is a typical barrio with its mix of new government housing alongside the old hovels and tin shacks of the brickmakers. We visited a cemetery where the cult of the dead was very much in evidence. The previous week a young man had been buried in his father's fresh grave with his bullet-smashed skull clearly visible.

We visited a small chapel that Frank Launtrie had built but which has since been taken over by the Oblates, who immediately saturated it with numerous coin boxes. The church at San Juan itself was interesting mainly for its statues. The principal one was of a suffering Christ bent under a cross. It was handmade, quite hideous, and named *Our Father Jesus*. Apparently this statue is put in a cage in the church's vestibule during Holy Week. There was also a statue dedicated to Martin de Porres, the black Dominican lay brother of Lima, Peru. The statue was named *El Barrendero*, which in English means the Broom Man, which the people would brush with their own brooms and then turn and brush their children.

In some places the priests are crating up this type of statue and leaving them in the sacristy, but in other places that behaviour is enough to have the priests run out of town. Later we drove over to the Basilica of Guadalupe. It was interesting to witness the mixed reactions of Bob and Dick to this shrine. For myself, whatever it is that is here seems much more real than anything I saw at Lourdes, Fatima, and especially Rome. This was just an ordinary Saturday, yet the Basilica was crowded with people from all over the country who had come to pay homage to their Mother.

The sight of families in rags and with children obviously suffering from malnutrition dropping their centavo pieces into the coin boxes was tragic, disconcerting, and yet somehow very moving. Bob told me that the minimal income for this church had been fourteen million pesos for the year, that agnostics call it Mexico's biggest money factory, and that no one seems to know exactly where the money is going. He also informed me that a devout and meticulous Mexican lay brother had been doing research and was puzzled by his own conclusion that the serape with the Virgin's image on it is in fact too large to be worn by any known peasant.

Eventually we had to hustle back to San Juan and try to hail a cab. Bob came back with me, but it was touch and go as I definitely had to be back by noon. On the way we discussed the whole nature of religious communities, vows, a sense of community, commitment, celibacy, etc. I tried to be honest but was persistently aware of my tendencies to projection. He's a good man, though, and he'll be all right. I had to rush to put the finishing touches on the preparation for my first Mass in Spanish. It felt strange to put on a cassock again as I've worn it only for mixed marriages over this past year. I really tried to make it a solid Eucharist and finished the homily with my Korean parable.

Lunch was passable, but in the afternoon we had a terrific conference from a Doctor Cohen on Mexican psychology. He was especially good on the role of mother images, violence, and machismo. I became quite excited at the prospects of applying the same critical apparatus to understanding American and Canadian anthropology. After that session I got into my first really heated discussion with our own students, especially with Monique Lauzon on machismo and related questions such as the Church here in Mexico and at home, the nature of change, and the role of law.

Then Betty and I hopped into her jeep and took off downtown to a quiet little French restaurant, of all things, for a wonderful meal and all kinds of words about friends and things. We got back in time for a good singsong with some CIASPers from Dayton, Ohio. I had some letters to write, but inwardly I was continuing to churn away about many things. Like so much of this stuff called living that I'm only beginning to learn about it looks like I'm just going to have to keep floundering as best I can. You might say it was a rather full day charged with many different emotions.

May 15, 1966: This morning was spent in our specific project groupings, so I split my time between San Nicolas and Pisaflores. It was reemphasized that there was a considerable dichotomy between the poor and middle classes in both towns and that the vast majority of the *campesinos* [i.e., farmers] in the *ranchos* around Pisaflores were tenant farmers while in some areas around San Nicolas up to fifty per cent might own their own land. Even among the latter, with their greater economic resources, there was still serious reluctance to group together to tackle common problems.

We were reminded that we do want them to change, but we can't force them to do so. Our efforts must be based on their own sense of personal dignity. It is an insult to see them as, let alone treat them as, only big children. We are attempting to wake them up to a greater sense of their own needs and of the benefits of working together. We are attacking their passivity and indifference, we are trying to get them to think and talk in very concrete terms with each other, we are trying to reactivate their hopes and get them to try again without any unnecessary dependence on us or anyone else. It will be what they pick up about how we treat each other that may well have the most lasting impact.

The general caliber of our students seems exceptionally high with a minimum of possible problem cases. After lunch we boarded buses. Two groups went out to Guadalupe first, but I went with the veterans directly to the Museo de Antropologia. Rudy, an assistant to Placido and a law student at the University of Mexico, guided us around. This has to be the most beautiful museum I have ever seen anywhere.

Even structurally it is a piece of carved poetry which captures the strength and magnificence of Mexico's many traditions. Rudy was excellent both on ancient and contemporary cultures. We had only about two hours, but it is certainly one of those places that I hope to come back to. We were on a tight schedule now, so we headed back to the convents for a quick meal and to change into dress clothes.

We boarded the buses again at 7 p.m. and it really was a treat to squirm into a sports jacket, shirt, and tie. We made it downtown without very much time to spare but were in time for the Ballet Folklorico at the Palace of Fine Arts. Onstage the principal curtain was Tiffany glass depicting the mountains, plains, and seas of Mexico.

As the orchestra played the overture, various coloured floodlights would play over the areas of that glass screen in such a way as to take the audience from pre-dawn to sunrise and the heat of the day to sunset and dusk and darkness. It was done magnificently. Then the stage exploded with an extraordinary series of folkdances from all areas and cultures of Mexico. The passion, raw energy, and visual and audio delights went from peak to peak.

Overall I can't remember enjoying a performance so much. It was not flawless, but then that was not the point. There was a special exuberance and joy in the performers that was quickly conveyed to the audience. It was a wonderful way to delve deeper into the Mexican temperament and to finish off our orientation. Afterwards we stood around in the square outside for a while simply enjoying the atmosphere and the people. On the way home we passed the square in front of the Cathedral and the Presidential Palace. They were beautifully illuminated and provided still another wonderful goodnight to us all.

Back at our residences after a Coke and some singing, Sue, Ellen, Kathy, Henn, and I packed the medicines and other communal supplies for all the individual project sites. It lasted until 4 a.m. and you can get rather giddy when you're doing anything with people like that and it doesn't really matter what it is or how tired you get because somehow you just know that it is very good.

May 16, 1966: They almost forgot to wake me up this morning. I ended up with only about fifteen minutes to do everything, including almost all my packing. My suitcase ended up being a mess but that was probably the best way to pack it anyway. Yesterday I had managed to pick up a bottle of Mass wine. As we headed downtown there were nine of us plus baggage in that one cab. What a twisted mass of humanity, and even when we arrived we had to wait only half an hour for the bus taking us north. Once on that bus I slept for the first hour or so.

My diarrhea was still bothering me as Montezuma had struck again. Even so I was able to perk up as the scenery began to explode all around us as we worked our way up into the hills and mountains. These bus drivers have to be good, and they are. It took at least half an hour to make our way around one gorge that was only a couple of hundred yards across. The mood was very good, with Bernie telling all kinds of jokes.

About four hours later we got off at Jacala. Mike Cassidy and Kathy Gillespie, the co-leaders of the San Nicolas grouping, were to have gone on ahead of us with the group heading for Pisaflores so they could be there before us. It didn't work out that way, and, since we landed here in Jacala in the middle of siesta, the telephones, post office, and so on were all closed. We put in the time by wandering around town, buying fresh orange juice, talking with the people, playing with some children, and getting traveller's cheques changed into pesos. I started to feel Hidalgo's heat and for protection bought myself the largest straw hat I could find, even though it was still too small.

The Pisaflores bus finally arrived and after some hasty reunions and fresh farewells we hired three 1942-vintage cabs to take us out to San Nicolas. It was a wild ride on a very weakly defined road. Fortunately, the scenery was a welcome distraction from the driving, about which we could do nothing. When we were still almost three kilometres from town we were met by a large group of schoolchildren who had run out along that rocky road in their bare feet to greet us. I was inclined to dismiss it as sentimental but had to admit that I still found it quite moving. Once in town we talked farther with a young doctor from Jacala, who had come with us to endorse our presence even though several of our students had spent the previous summer in this same posting. The local schoolteachers had vacated their homes and offered them to us for accommodation. The boys moved into Santiago's and the girls into Coca's. It turns out that we even have showers. Then it was supper by candlelight, a *cerveza*, a singsong with the *niños*, and off to bed. We had actually made it to Sunny San Nick.

May 17, 1966: The first thing I learned after waking up was that the boys had killed a scorpion beside my bed while I was still sleeping. They attempted to reassure me that "it was only a black one." Last night before we went to bed, Mike and Kathy had a long conference with what amounted to the local Chamber of Commerce. They talked about possible projects like continuing to improve the road, opening up the *ranchos*, teaching reading and writing both to the children and the adults who wanted it, a dispensary focusing on preventive medicine, and finding ways to get more government aid. Coca, the schoolteacher, seemed to an outsider like myself to have the men almost too much under her thumb, but it certainly was interesting to watch the show.

It was mainly a day for rest and reading. It took a while to get the chapel ready, but we ended up having our first Eucharist at 5 p.m. The church was apparently originally built by Junipero Sierra and it even has a small separate chapel that no one can remember ever having been used. In the body of the church there are several notable statues, including a couple made of papier mâché with all the appropriate bloody joints, etc. Doctrinally these people are apparently quite unsophisticated, but that is no small wonder, given the weakness of their school system and the fact that the priest from Jacala manages to get to this town perhaps only once a year.

Because we're not fully set up yet, we had all our meals today at Santiago Olivia's store. At noon we had cooked sardines, but tonight we settled for soda crackers and coffee. Santiago talked to us about the history of San Nicolas. There are currently about 350 families here, comprising about 1200 people. After supper we sat out under the stars for a singsong surrounded by a crowd of curious children and teenagers.

May 18 to 31, 1966: I've just returned from my second trip to the *rancho* of La Palma. If I don't make a general entry I am liable to stop making any entries at all. These have been a very strange two weeks filled with many reflections, impressions, and just plain quiet moments. On the whole I've been very much in low key, and even Brother Rat has not been as ferocious as usual.

[That was the final entry in this "lost journal." The entries resurfaced only this spring, in 1999. I have no memory of deciding to stop making entries, and I wonder now what a wealth of detail is now lost forever. I am allowing the existing entries to stand on their own. The rest of this text will include my 1995 attempts at recreation, along with further memories whose recording was set aside because of time pressures. Those stories have continued to press me for fuller recognition and I am finally incorporating them into this May 1999 revision. The following will be of necessity primarily thematic and episodic in approach rather than chronological.]

I was first sent with the group to be centred at San Nicolas, a sleepy backwater about seventeen kilometres off the main highway. There was one of Junípero Serra's original Mission Churches still in use in this little community, but it was in considerable disrepair. The students who had been here in the previous summer had concentrated on teaching reading and writing both to children and adults as well as general hygiene and helping to construct a road from San Nicolas out to the main highway, thereby hoping an increase in commercial contacts would alleviate at least some of the sources of despair.

Those students had to endure unexplained gunshots in the middle of the night and being called upon to tend to the wounded and bury the dead that resulted from a very intense Hatfield-and-McCoy-style family rivalry. This particular dimension of San Nicolas had quieted down by the time our group arrived. On the other hand, it was never clear when that type of violence might erupt again.

During our sojourn there in 1966, one of our registered nurses set up a small clinic and soon won the confidence of the village. Her greatest single "miracle drug" was Aspirin, but she was usually reluctant to hand it out because of the risk that people might become too dependent on it and unable to raise the funds to buy it after we left. Her most memorable case was a *campesino* who worked daily in the fields. Though he was probably in his eighties, no one, including himself, was certain of his age. Shyly he informed our nurse that what was bothering him most was a case of impotence, which had appeared for the first time during recent months. In attempting to identify the full scope of the problem, our nurse finally learned that what impotence meant for this gentleman was that he was now for the first time in his life having difficulty making love the second and third time each night.

Out of San Nicolas the one major *rancho* we opened was at La Palma with four of our students. The rest of the students remained in San Nicolas and expanded on the educational and road-construction projects of the previous year. One day, while trudging back up through the mountain pass that would take us back from La Palma to the town of San Nicolas, my student companion, Michael Cassidy, suddenly shouted, "My God, what is that?" I had been concentrating simply on where to step next, but when I looked at where he was pointing I had difficulty believing what I was seeing. There on the other side of the same gulch that we were attempting to conquer, perched on the uppermost branches of a sturdy mountain pine, was what seemed initially to be an oversize mockup of something either preternatural or prehistorical and out of place. I suggested that we slow our pace but not stop so as not to disturb it.

As we continued this otherworldly creature took flight and sailed further up the pass to alight again and wait for us to catch up. It's when it flew that I realized what it must be. It resembled an eagle but seemed much larger than that, with an enormous wingspan that must have measured at least eight feet. I concluded that it must be a condor. I had heard of and seen pictures of so-called South American condors but had never heard of the existence of such magnificent creatures in Mexico. Upon reflection, I had to ask myself, Why wouldn't it be here? The Andes and both branches of the Sierra Madres were virtually contiguous mountain systems, birds are not known for keeping up their national visas, and since this creature was at least twice the size of any other vulture of the area, what else could it be?

I forgot my aching joints and blistering feet and kept moving steadily along the gulch so as not to unnecessarily alarm this visitor from another world or plane of existence. Or, much more probably, we were the ones invading its space. When it chose to fly, it was then at its peak of existence. It was like a spaceship that glided effortlessly, with a grace that would make ballet dancers envious. I found myself wishing it could tell me what it thought about flight and what it made of the things it saw from such a grand perspective. Then I became slightly more realistic and wondered why it was following us or keeping pace with us or perhaps even showing us the way up that mountain pass.

At that point I even wondered if because of the way we were dragging along perhaps it was waiting for at least one of us to drop and thereby give it an opportunity for a special treat for its dinner. After all, from what I could remember condors were known for being scavengers. But even that possibility had a dignity to it. I cannot recall from before or since ever having had such a close personal encounter with anything so magnificently wild and primitive.

In the evening of that same day I had an adventure of a different kind. I had been out at La Palma for several days and as usual ate what the students ate. That had been going on for a while and I was definitely missing my animal protein. The students who had remained at San Nicolas had prepared a special treat for me. They knew I would be late coming in from the trek, so they themselves had already eaten. They couldn't quite suppress their giggles, so I was alerted to watch for something that was not only special but probably also quite different. It was obviously being staged for my evening meal. When I sat down they plunked in front of me a small scotch, which was always a treat but not quite the protein I had been hoping for. A small pot of vegetable stew followed, but from their heightened expectations I realized that "it" had not yet arrived. There was never any electric light in San Nicolas, so as usual the candles had already been lit out of necessity. So I had a little difficulty in identifying what was on the plate they then placed before me.

As close as I could tell it looked and smelled somewhat like extra small chunks of ground beef that had been pan-fried. I did pause to ask what it was and they said, "Don't worry about it! Just eat up and enjoy!" It did seem like some type of protein, and my cravings overcame my hesitancy. I took a forkful, tasted, chewed, and swallowed. I could not remember ever having eaten anything like this. It wasn't particularly delicious, but it did seem to fall loosely into the category of protein, so I proceeded to polish off the rest of the plate. All during this exercise I had an audience of the half-dozen students resident at San Nicolas. Their general reaction to my behaviour was akin to that commercial where "the other kids" whisper to each other, "Mikey likes it!"

After I finished I pressed them for an identification of what I had just ingested. Finally they admitted that it was *guajolote*. I knew that was the Spanish word for "turkey" and that especially in the mountains of Mexico it was more available and far less scrawny than a chicken. I was tempted to jump to the conclusion that these students had pooled their resources and bought a turkey from a local *campesino*. But I had to press them further, because what I had eaten didn't taste like any turkey I had ever known. Finally, they admitted that to be exact they had served me turkey blood pudding. The *campesino* in question had stressed that the people of the mountains never wasted any part of any animal meat that they were fortunate enough to keep for themselves. So the students had followed his advice and decided to test out this particular application of the principle on me before they ate it themselves.

La Palma was the principal *rancho* in the San Nicolas network, which you approached after a long climb over the top of a mountain ridge. It was nestled in an oasis of lush emerald green on the gentle curve of a lazy river, which wrapped itself around the base of a steep mountainside. The soil was so rich there that several kinds of fruit trees were growing wild. Almost half of the *campesinos* owned their own land here and had small bank accounts in the nearby town. Despite this, the infant mortality rate was over fifty per cent. The students discovered that the main culprit was the river, which was used for everything but which was polluted by similar usage by three or four villages farther upstream. At the same time, mothers did not feed their babies the abundant fresh fruit, which usually ripened, dropped to the ground, and rotted or was cleaned up by the free-roaming pigs. Upon gentle questioning by the students, the mothers said that was simply the way they had always done things.

Ironically, there was also plenty of fresh water from nearby mountain springs that could easily have been pumped at very little cost down the mountainside and into the village through plastic tubing that could be simply laid on top of the ground. Even if the *campesinos* were not prepared to dip into their own cash reserves, the students had brought extra funds to subsidize small projects exactly like that. However, it is poor community development to interfere or impose. The students got a Mexican dentist from a nearby town, who had a crush on one of our students, to come and chair a village meeting devoted to the discussion of the *rancho*'s most pressing communal needs. The four students situated at this *rancho* waited outside as patiently as possible.

Inside the meeting hall the villagers became more and more animated. They apparently had never before had a meeting like this and they were enjoying it immensely. The students assumed that they would opt for the obvious and go for the new water line. After several hours the *campesinos* emerged and announced enthusiastically that they had agreed unanimously that their top priority was to finish cementing the basketball court. Furthermore, they would then move on and put a new thatch roof on the chapel. The students gulped, quickly recovered, and volunteered to help. That was the kind of facilitating they did, in the hope that people would discover the value of working together and eventually fine-tune their own sense of priorities.

Marriages in these mountains were a much valued sacrament, but their timing was according to the degree of wealth necessary to provide an appropriate ceremony and feast for one's extended family and friends. That was an "official" marriage. The "real" marriage took place when a young man had cleared a level patch for a thatched hut whose total building costs would not exceed forty to fifty dollars of our money. Upon receiving the consent of his beloved's father, they would simply move in together and begin raising their family.

There was a minor panic one morning in San Nicolas when the special priest from the big town, who was supposed to come and do an "official" marriage in the old mission church, suddenly took ill. A whole flock of excited dressed-up people came rushing down our side street. Their Spanish was too rapid for me, but one of the students soon informed me of the situation. They were begging me to do the ceremony, since the banquet and everything else were ready.

Did we ever scramble. I had not yet done a wedding in Spanish, so I quickly wrote out a brief homily in English while one of the students went up to the dusty sacristy and found the liturgy in a Spanish missal. Another student did a translation of my homily into Spanish, and yet another struggled with me over the phonetics. We arrived at the church soon afterwards, to everyone's relief. It was a wonderfully warm ceremony with Mexican touches like the groom's gift of a plate of polished copper coins. During the ceremony the bride's two oldest children were tugging at her new skirt and her youngest was placed quite unselfconsciously to the breast exactly in the middle of the exchange of vows.

The people of San Nicolas liked my homily so much they rushed up after the ceremony asking me to do all sorts of things. They had difficulty grasping why I didn't understand their Spanish, since for them I had just finished speaking it so well. All seven of our team who were currently in town were invited to the wedding banquet. We were seated on benches at tables made from old doors placed on trestles and covered with sheets. The food was sumptuous compared to what we had become accustomed to.

I seemed to provide the only snag when I inadvertently bit into a piece of cooked cabbage without noticing the tiniest of peppers that was lurking underneath that innocent-looking camouflage. In Mexico, when it comes to peppers, the smaller they are the spicier they are. In a very few seconds I was on fire and out of breath. All available liquids were offered to me, including *cervezas*, pulques, and *aguardientes*, amid general hilarity at this gringo's discomfort. I ended up with quite a headache, but I obviously survived.

After that day the villagers of San Nicolas abandoned all shyness, insisted that their children attend every class on anything, and even asked the students for suggestions on what they might do for themselves. San Nicolas had had Canadian CIASPers the previous year and would have another set of students the summer after us. It was a good example of why this approach would work so well. While the students were back home doing their academic year, these people would be vying with each other to see how much they could accomplish before the students returned. It was one way to cut down on the danger of the *campesinos* becoming too dependent on any form of outside help.

For the second half of my time with the project, I was assigned to work in and around the town of Pisaflores. This centre was about forty kilometres farther northwest into the higher mountains of the state of Hidalgo. That meant it was 332 kilometres north of Mexico City. As the crow flies it was only about five miles west of that old Pan-American Highway to Nuevo Laredo, but from the point where we left the highway it took up to three hours to follow the twisted and worn pathways called roads down into gulches and up around numerous turns as we worked our way into these mountains. Kathleen Gillespie along with Mike Cassidy, the project co-leader for the San Nicolas grouping, drove me over in a jeep that she borrowed from one of the local schoolteachers. Kathleen was from Stamford, Connecticut, and was in her second year with CIASP.

At one point after leaving the main highway and working our way down through the labyrinth of canyons and gulches, we had to cross a rapidly moving river. In the middle of the continuous rapids you could see the stumps of bridges that rushing flood water had previously wiped out. The trick was to take off the fan belt of this surplus army jeep and get a passing *campesino* to sit on the nose of the jeep's hood to yell directions as we drove across on a narrow band of gravel that snaked through the rapids a couple of feet below the water level.

Our guide would wave rather vigorously in whichever direction he wanted us to turn so as not to fall off that irregular ledge, which was completely invisible to the driver. By now the rushing water was coming in the open driver's side, pulling at our feet and legs and rushing out the passenger's open door. It was definitely interesting. We did make it across, thanked our faithful guide, reattached the fan belt, and continued down the two ruts through the heavy undergrowth that our guide assured us would eventually get us to Pisaflores.

After we slowly made our way down the rutted road into town we had to get directions to the local church and rectory where we were to meet the local team of Canadian students. No such structures were in sight, but when we inquired of three different *campesinos*, they all pointed in the same direction and said repeatedly, "Arriba! Arriba!" We knew that the word meant "higher up," so we concluded that there must be another level higher up the side of the hill.

The village's principal square was the size of a couple of football fields, but as we drove around its perimeter the only visible route up that hillside was a set of maybe thirty-five or forty irregular stone steps that were each approximately twelve feet wide. We checked with still another passing *campesino* and he confirmed in Spanish that "Yes, the church is up there!"

Kathleen was already quite experienced in operating this outdated yet still functional jeep, so we both shrugged and she dropped it into a lower gear and gunned it. With a mighty roar we charged up those stone steps as if we were intent on conquering Chapultepec Castle.

Kathleen knew we could not afford to hesitate or this old machine would stall and we could topple backwards down the steps. The few people on those steps plastered themselves against the buildings on either side and literally gaped in shock and wonder at what was happening. Kathleen maintained the pressure on the accelerator as we completed the last few steps and blasted into a very small square in front of the church and rectory. She then had to jam on the brakes and screech to a halt or we would have plowed into the buildings on the far side of this rather tiny church square.

As soon as we got out of the jeep we noticed that everyone within sight had become frozen with jaws dropped at what they had just witnessed. We were informed that no one had previously attempted, let alone succeeded, in driving any type of vehicle up those steps. We had obviously not come the right way and the *campesinos* giving us directions had simply showed us the way they themselves were accustomed to going to church, which of course was by foot and "up those steps." In all probability it never occurred to them that what we required were directions for driving to that same destination. Even Padre Zepeda shook his head in disbelief when he heard of the method of our notorious arrival. Apparently the story of this escapade entered into local folklore and was still being told several years later.

There was a resident priest in Pisaflores who had been responsible for getting the students to come there in the first place and whose word and reputation kept them safe in the *ranchos* of the surrounding mountains. His name was Padre Zepeda and he always travelled with a pearl-handled revolver on his hip. It was not an affectation and it was not only because of various snakes in the mountains. It was also because the local *caciques*, or large absentee landowners, had put a price on his head because of his efforts to organize a union for the *campesinos*.

In fact in recent months yet another of the *campesinos* active in the *campesino* union movement had been found dead one morning in the ditch beside the main road into Pisaflores. It had been a classic execution by a single bullet to the back of the head after severe beating and mutilation. This had happened several times and was always attributed by the local people to hit men who had been sent up from Mexico City by the *caciques* so as to slow down by means of terror any communal struggles for justice.

There was a small barracks on the main square for a dozen of the *federales*—soldiers from the central government, and their captain. They did semi-annual swings through the surrounding mountains but basically attempted not to see anything or do anything. One day I happened to see a middle-aged *campesino* staggering across the square directly past those indifferent, lounging soldiers. He was almost completely covered in blood from machete slashes to his body. I never learned if he survived, but apparently he was considered the winner in a duel with machetes over his wife's alleged infidelity.

A small cantina stocked, among other things, tins of large sardines from Norway, which for us became a major delicacy on our return from swings though the *ranchos*. In this same store there was a barrel of Mexican cigars that resembled pieces of twisted rope. You paid for them by the fist-ful, regardless of how many came out when you grabbed. I loved them. I had already run out of my own cigars and pipe tobacco, and when I later couldn't even find any Mexican cigarillos I finally began my cigarette-smoking days with this Mexican version, which, I must admit, amounted to little more than puffing and sucking on tiny tubes of liquid tar. For various reasons I was already into smoking almost anything that burned. These newly discovered Mexican cigarettes helped to fill my craving.

In the Pisaflores region most of the students were scattered in groups of three or four and billeted, always at their own expense, in one of the eleven *ranchos,* which were small mountain villages with clusters of 100 to 300 people. Those *ranchos* were from three to five hours by mule away from Pisaflores within a thirteen-mile radius from the town itself. Both in town and on the *ranchos* the students taught basic reading and writing to the children or worked on communal construction projects with the men. For example, they worked that summer on helping local people to set up a small canning factory so as to utilize more fully the natural fruit crops of the area. The town of Pisaflores itself was home for approximately two thousand people.

I was sent on circuits of these *ranchos* to dispense the sacraments where requested—which was almost everywhere, because the elderly, the women, and children often never saw a priest from one end of the year to the next. Besides dispensing the sacraments to the *campesinos* and their families, I would spend a night or two in each place acting as a news-bearer, informal counsellor, or morale-builder to the students. I saw many wonderful things and heard stories that have stayed with me over the years.

In all of these places we almost always ate exactly the same common fare. The staples were tortillas done on hot stone slabs in wooden shacks, pots of *frijoles cocidos,* which were a type of cooked beans, occasional ver-sions of scrambled eggs, and wonderful fresh coffee with *pilon,* which was crystallized unrefined brown cane sugar. If most of these people had chicken once a month and some beef semi-annually they considered themselves fortunate. A full day's labour of an experienced tenant farmer around Pisaflores earned him five pesos, which at that time was equivalent to forty cents in our currency.

Oh, and the work they had to do for that money. There were large hillsides of coffee bushes, but the main crop was corn. The difficulty was that the land around there was notorious for being almost exclusively straight up or straight down. When planting corn a *campesino* carried a six-inch iron or steel wedge in one pocket, a bag of seeds that hung from his rope-belt, and a primitive pickaxe type of tool whose shape resembled that of the sort used by professional mountain climbers.

Upon arriving at their planting row for that day, the *campesino* would first get his footing on the slope of up to seventy-five degrees. He needed one hand and the pickaxe literally to hold himself on the side of the hill while he used his other hand to grasp the wedge and dig a small hole in the rich but tough soil. He then tucked the wedge into his rope belt so he could reach back and get a seed from his pouch. He then tucked the seed into the hole and patted snugly. Then he carefully shifted his weight and used his pickaxe to find the next safe placements both for his pickaxe and his feet. He would repeat this process, which could proceed for up to ten hours, seven days a week, with few breaks. That was what work meant for most of the men in those mountains.

The CIASP project leader for Pisaflores and its surrounding *ranchos* and *ranchitos* was Annie Harris, from Rye in Westchester County, New York. Annie had been one of my TMS originals, as had Kathy Gillespie. Annie, next to Pat Uhl, had also been my most faithful guitarist during those crucial first two years and then her younger brother Basil became one of the mainstays of my guitar brigade at Newman. Kathy and Annie, along with Mike Cassidy from Montreal, were the co-leaders of CIASP that summer. I had even visited the young women and their parents in their homes while in New York City in the summers of 1964 and 1965. Because of our ongoing relationships it was a treat for me to "take orders" from them in this student-run movement.

The day after my arrival in Pisaflores, my other boss, Kathleen Gillespie, made her way back to San Nicolas without driving back down those now infamous steps, and Annie sent me out on my first swing through the *ranchos.* I continued to learn many things. For example, these people often went barefoot or, at most, used primitive rope sandals. That meant that while working in the fields, which ranged from overgrown mountaintops to tropical jungle gulches, they were in constant danger of being bitten by various kinds of snakes. At least some of the bites were potentially fatal. As a typical gringo I had always thought that the way you handled a snakebite was to lance the location of the bite, suck out as much of the venom as possible, and then if possible pour alcohol on it before binding it tightly.

"There were even a few compliments, if my memory still serves me"

✣

The materials reproduced on pages 123-137 are from Michael Quealey's personal papers.

Since November of 1963, a group of students on the St. Michael's College campus at the University of Toronto have been concentrating on the exploration of new methods for making the Eucharist as meaningful an action as possible. In any culture the nature of sign or sacrament has always been essential to any appreciation of the Mass. Just as Christ is the greatest sign of God's love for His people, and the Church is the greatest sign of Christ's presence among us, so to, the eucharistic assembly is the greatest sign of the Church's existence. In this service of worship God's people gather to listen to and be nourished by His Word.

The Fathers of the Church gathered at the Vatican Council have emphasized that Christ Himself gave us this sign of the Eucharist "in order to perpetuate the sacrifice of the Cross throughout the centuries until He should come again, and so to entrust to his beloved spouse, the Church, a memorial of his death and resurrection: a sacrament of love, a sign of unity, a bond of charity, a paschal banquet in which Christ is eaten, the mind is filled with grace and a pledge of future glory is given to us."

Recognizing the life giving force of the eucharistic action, and encouraged by the directives of the successors of the Apostles gathered in ecumenical council under the leadership of John XXIII and Paul VI, we have been seeking the most fitting means of participating in this the most significant action of the Christian assembly. This exploration has included a re-discovery of the timelessness of the ancient psalms, the richness of both familiar and neglected areas of sacred scripture, and the importance of true silence if we are to listen to Him. By becoming more deeply involved in such a celebration, we have encountered a renewed sense of the appropriateness of hymns and canticles to express our joy as His people. We have also come to realize the importance of expressing our individual and collective response to God's message and action not only by meaningful silence, but also with words and music appropriate to this generation of Christians.

ROMAN CATHOLICS HAVE NEW IMAGE OF OLD BOGEYMAN LUTHER

BY ALLEN SPRAGGETT
Star staff writer

SUBTLE, but apparently very real, rehabilitation of Martin Luther is taking place in the Roman Catholic Church.

An article in the current issue of The Ecumenist, published by the Centre for Ecumenical Studies at St. Michael's College, reflects this new Catholic viewpoint towards the Protestant reformer.

Titled "The Changing Image of Luther," the study, written by Toronto Basilian priest Rev. F. M. Quealey, scorns the traditional Catholic polemics which have made of Luther an impious upstart, at the best, and an incarnate devil, at the worst.

"In recent years Catholic historians have been seriously re-evaluating Martin Luther both as an historical figure and as a symbol," Father Quealey writes.

"The violence and religious strife that accompanied the Reformation precluded for many years any objective analysis of the person and role of Luther himself. As one of the great influences on the course of modern religious and secular history, Luther has been lauded as a liberator and castigated as a traitor."

'That Saxon pig'

Father Quealey contends that traditional Catholic portrayals of Luther have been caricatures, motivated by emotion, not by reason or objective scholarship. The reformer has been denounced by Catholic polemicists as "the son of the Devil," and "that Saxon pig."

On the other hand, suggests Father Quealey, Luther's partisans have tended to rush to his defence and drench him in whitewash, sometimes with an equal disregard for the facts. Luther's friend Melancthon called him "the dove of the Holy Spirit," and another Protestant godmaker hailed him as the angel of the Apocalypse prophesied by St. John in the Bible.

"By the turn of the 20th century," Father Quealey writes, "historical oversimplification was the great crime of both sides, as Protestants and Catholics searching for an identity sought out and cited sources to substantiate their preconceived hypotheses."

Some fairly modern Catholic scholars have tended to run down Luther, Father Quealey said, "discrediting him even as an original heretic and castigating him as a friar who elaborated the doctrine of salvation by faith alone into an apology for his own weakness and inability to fulfill his religious vows."

Kinder light

Increasingly, however, Catholic historians are looking at Luther in a different, kinder light. Some are concerned to point out that the decadent state of the church in Luther's day invited a reform movement such as his. Abuses among the clergy, both higher and lower, abounded.

"The overwhelming fact," allows Father Quealey, "is that despite the acknowledged need for sweeping corporate reform, the episcopate and the papacy in the century before Luther could not or did not reform."

Father Quealey urges Catholic researchers, especially in English-speaking countries, to get behind the myths to the true flesh-and-blood man, Luther, as the "more advanced theological circles in Germany and France" are doing.

The new, "advanced" view of the Protestant reformer?

Says Father Quealey: "The new Catholic scholarship views Luther less as a villain bent on the violent disruption of Christ's body and more as one searching for religious conviction who became eventually a catalyst for real reform within the Church.

"For Bouyer (a Catholic scholar) Luther's concept of salvation is in perfect harmony with Catholic tradition, conciliar definition, and St. Thomas."

Father Quealey attributes the new, more sympathetic Catholic attitude towards Luther to "the phenomenon of ecumenism with its fruitful interchange of insight and understanding / . . At least some church historians and theologians have abandoned polemics and have become involved in the excitement of talking with one another concerning the manifold significance of Martin Luther."

125

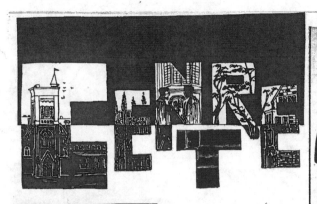

NEWMAN

TUESDAYS --- *'Christianity & Sex; Past & Future'*

'Topic of The Week/Symposium of Arts' **THURSDAYS** --

SUNDAYS --- *'Shake-up & Dance.'*

ALL AT 8:00 P.M.   89 St. George St.

Man, it was a ROUGH week. Monday I spoke to that STUDENT group on a Christian view of U.S. FOREIGN POLICY! Tuesday I lectured a WOMAN'S CLUB on MORALITY AND LSD!

Wednesday it was a TEACHER'S SEMINAR on FREE LOVE, BIRTH CONTROL AND THE BOMB! Thursday I gave a talk on SEX IN THE CINEMA to a steam-fitters convention

Friday was a DEBATE on NORMAN MAILER and the NEW LEFT down at the LEGION HALL. Then a TV inter-view on PAVLOV AND POP ART and then a guest DEE JAY stint at a teenage ROCK and ROLL bash!

Saturday was the usual PEACE demon-stration at the EMBASSY, a guest spot on this RADIO SHOW about PUBLIC HOUSING and a POETRY READING at a local JAZZ SPOT!

Sunday I'd just done this GROOVY sermon on LENNY BRUCE when this LITTLE OLD LADY grabs me in the vestry and wants to talk about TRINITY and SALVATION and stuff like THAT! Naturally I mumbled some EXCUSE and SPLIT fast!

I mean a guy in my POSITION can't AFFORD to get involved in controversial stuff like THAT!

Who the hell does she think I AM?

GORDON SINCLAIR?

OFF-BASE

*A STRANGER
IN CHURCH*

A Radiant Smile Of Welcome

By AUBREY WICE

"I was a stranger and ye took Me in." (Matt. 25:35)

THE street was quiet as I walked up the semi-circular drive to the new look-ing red brick building on St. Mary st. in the heart of the city.

Rev. F. M.
Quealey

Inside, a b u z z e r on t h e locked door waited to be press-e d. Within seconds after my finger touched it, the door swung open and I was in-side Loretto College, a girls' school.

A gracious greeting by Mother Olga made me feel welcome and with a radiant smile she guided me up the stairway.

I was in time for the 11 a.m. Mass, the one Sunday service males are permitted to attend in this all female atmospherer.

AIR OF INTIMACY

The chapel had the inti-macy of a family room and a fireplace would have not been out of place. Muted c o l o r s highlighted the warmth of the rich Ontario oak pews, ribbed paneling, altar rail and the pale blue carpeting.

From St. Michael's Col-lege across the way came Rev. F. M. Quealey, a Basi-lian father with the build of a football player.

In light colored silk vest-ments he stood at the front and told us of some changes from the normal Mass.

The bread for the Holy C o m m u n i o n was whole wheat, the kind they had originally, h e explained. The pieces were larger than usual and were meant to be chewed. Some churches, he added, were now using small buns.

At the first Lord's Sup-per, Father Quealey said, Jesus instructed His disci-ples to eat the Holy food. He said Jesus meant this literally.

FOLLOW TRADITION

Another link with the early days was the students picking up their own round piece of bread at the back and taking it to the altar before the service began.

After the consecration, they went forward to re-ceive it back as holy food. It was placed on their tongue as they stood at the rail. The normal way is to kneel.

This was mainly a Latin service, with a short part in Greek and a couple of lovely hymns sung softly and slowly in English with-out m u s i c a l accompani-ment.

I'm sure music would have spoiled it. Two of the students r e a d Scripture aloud from their places in the pews.

Father Quealey spoke of Mary and excesses of mixed up devotion in some coun-tries. Her main significance he said was that she was simply the mother of God.

128

Priest backs Lennon on Christianity view

A Roman Catholic priest said today that he found nothing shocking in Beatle John Lennon's belief that Christianity is dying.

"Lennon is merely stating what is becoming increasingly obvious today as far as the real relevance of Christianity to man," said Rev. Michael Quealey of the Roman Catholic Newman Centre at the University of Toronto.

The Beatles mean more to people than the type of Christianity provided today, he said.

Father Quealey said that in many ways, the Beatles are more genuinely Christian than some contemporary religious leaders.

Lennon's remarks didn't spark any "ban-the-Beatles" movement here where they appear Aug. 17.

Said Allan Slaight, program director of CHUM:

"Any artists' particular viewpoints don't have any bearing on their talents. I'm not really convinced that is what Lennon really said and, in any case, we're certainly not planning to ban Beatles' records."

Said Al Boliska, program manager of CHIN: "This is an obvious publicity stunt dreamed up by a couple of disc jockeys down there and nobody is taking it very seriously. I'm sure Lennon's comments were made with tongue in cheek."

Gordon Symons, program manager of CFGM, Richmond Hill, said:

"If Eddy Arnold had made this comment, there would be a great flap and to-do, but our type of listener isn't all that interested in the Beatles."

Bruce McGuiness, program manager for CHIC, thinks it is the Beatles, and not Christianity, that is dying.

130

MACLEAN'S REVIEWS

OCTOBER 1, 1966   VOLUME 79   NUMBER 19

At the same time it's easy to sympathize with the small Canadian production companies. When they do take a gamble and it comes off, the big foreign-owned producers often step in and take over. That is what happened to a fascinating folk album issued on Toronto's Markle label and called *Canticle Of The Gift*. The record, unique in the catalogues, features spiritual folk songs by liturgical beatniks (churchniks?) from the University of Toronto's St. Michael's College.

The American Capitol company immediately recognized the possibilities of the compositions, designed to accompany folk-style church services, and picked up the distribution rights as soon as the first small Markle printing was sold out. The original disc (M 15001) is fast becoming a collector's item.

ELMO CIPRIETTI

THE TABLET, THURSDAY, APRIL 28, 1966

'CANTICLE OF THE GIFT,' a recording produced under the auspices of the University of Toronto Newman Center, represents the effort of a group of St. Michael's College students, over a period of two years, to create liturgical music that would be meaningful for them. The songs are accompanied by guitar, flute and recorder and may be ordered from Newman Center, 89 St. George St., Toronto 5, Canada ($6). Rev. F. M. Quealy, C.S.B., director, stated that "the collection is offered not as a final answer to the problem of authentic religious music, but in a spirit of sharing with others what has proved helpful to us."

CANTICLE OF THE GIFT, a collection of spiritual folk songs by students at St. Michael's College in the University of Toronto. Markle M 15001. Mono-aural only, available from Newman Center, 89 St. George St. Toronto, 5. $6 per copy includes cost of mailing and handling.

By CHRIS WILSON

This is by far the best product to be born from the scriptural and liturgical renewal of the past decade. It eclipses all previous attempts at bringing the psalms and ordinary of the Mass alive in the vernacular.

The music is a spontaneous burst of creative energy and thoroughly idiomatic. There is nothing contrived or calculated, no phoney folklore. Nothing but joy unalloyed and pure delight in worship. The only problem at times will be to sit still in the pews.

The music has been evolved for use at student and community masses. The compositions are either original or arrangements by Miss Pat Uhl, Carole Giangrande, Jim Garvey and Louis di Rocco. About thirty students do the singing, much as the congregation would at one of these gatherings, with some solo parts.

The accompaniment is with one or two guitars, occasionally a recorder. One number is a cappella. In this way the disc has a varied texture and the pieces themselves are perfectly contrasted. The record never becomes monotonous and remains fresh after repeated hearings. The performances too are fresh and the sincerity of the singers is contagious.

There are arrangements of Kumbayah and Michael. But listen to the Canticle of the Three Children updated to ask that skipping ropes and subways bless the Lord. In Clap Your Hands All You People, the people do. Psalm 84, The Hills, is outstanding. The Canticle of the Gift conveys historically and vividly the true meaning of the Word as Flesh in the Eucharist.

These are songs which can be sung at Mass, on pilgrimage, at youth gatherings, anywhere. Recommended without reservations, even to the unconverted.

THE PILL:
THE POPE SAYS 'NO,'
CATHOLICS SAY 'SO WHAT?'

Rev. Michael Quealey, chaplain of the U. of T.'s Newman Centre, said the papal statement was too vague to be decisive.

"I have heard severe criticism of it as a good example of papal doubletalk," Father Quealey said.

"Within the Pope's statement, as I have read it, there seems to be more than enough ambivalence in his own mind.

"Behind this statement there still stands the spirit of the Vatican Council and of leading moral theologians who emphasize the privacy of the individual conscience, after that conscience has taken into consideration any and all declarations by church authority including whether these appear to be based on sufficient knowledge of the situation or not."

When men are animated by the charity of Christ, they feel united, and the needs, sufferings, and joys of others are felt as their own.

POPE JOHN XXIII

132

Everything is informal. It is a church they understand . . . where they are a part of the service. They compose their own music and the effect is melodious, intimate and devout.

A church for today

By DuBARRY CAMPAU
Telegram Staff Reporter

"Traffic lights and subways — Bless the Lord!

"Chewing gum and playgrounds — Bless the Lord!

"Lonely walks and crowded dances — Bless the Lord!

"All the works of the Lord — Praise Him, Exalt Him, forevermore!"

(From the Newman Centre Liturgy)

They come into the church laughing and chatting. It's 3.30 on a rainy Thursday afternoon and about 75 young men and women are going to take part in mass at St. Thomas Aquinas, the chapel of the Newman Centre, and next door to it.

They're dressed in sweaters, jeans, mini-skirts and jumpers — and most of them are wearing running shoes. Almost all of them greet the chaplain,

Father Michael Quealey, who wanders about talking, smiling and shaking hands. He, too, has on a bulky sweater and he looks very little older than his congregation.

Some of the group are putting out the mimeographed copies of the liturgy. A girl with long blonde hair is tuning her guitar. Two young men bring the altar, a simple, white covered table, down two steps to the floor.

DEVOUT

When everything seems ready, Father Quealey goes to the sacristy and returns wearing white vestments and the mass begins.

The service is entirely in English

and the congregation sings the responses, the psalms, the offertory, the Kyrie, the benedicte and the recessional to music most of which they have composed themselves and to a guitar accompaniment. The effect is melodious, intimate and devout.

For each of these services a theme is chosen. On this rainy Thursday, it is Silence. A young man in a tweed suit reads a poem by Leonard Cohen.

A beautiful girl in a blue knitted suit says: "Words can sometimes be used as an excuse to get to the silence. We want the silence more than the discussion." Others contribute their views on the topic — they speak spontaneously and informally.

KISS

A boy in suntans moves across the chapel to a dark-haired girl in red. They whisper for a moment and then come out in front of the altar. He says: "We think there is another medium in which we can express what we feel about silence." They perform a ritualistic, stylized dance, ending with clasped hands. Father Quealey himself speaks briefly on silence, suggesting that silence within oneself is vital.

Before communion the young people form a half circle before the altar. He takes the clasped hands of two or three persons within his own and they in turn give this "kiss of peace and joy" to another who gives it to some one else until everyone has received it.

This kind of service began when Father Quealey, already ordained, was doing graduate work at St. Michael's College.

"I don't believe in telling anyone what to do," he says, "but I do think we should help people wherever we are. As nearly as we can tell, only about 40 per cent of Catholics between their mid-twenties and early forties are attending mass regularly. Teenagers and younger university students are more religiously conservative — they have so many pressures and so much insecurity they tend to cling to the church automatically.

"But when they begin to feel more

sure of themselves they begin to question the church — or to think it's inadequate for them. Some of them get so hung up they feel guilty if they do go to mass.

"So, when some of the other graduate students came to me and said: 'Look, we're going to give the church one more chance if you'll help us,' I tried to."

He began saying what was really a private mass for this group in the basement chapel of St. Basil's church on the campus of St. Michael's.

"I wanted them to be participants, not spectators," he says. "There has to be a sense of involvement, if it is going to be meaningful at all."

Two years ago when he was appointed chaplain at St. Thomas Aquinas, he continued to emphasize the necessity for sharing in the mass at the services he conducts there.

"If there is a disagreement between the existing rules and the needs of people, I'm on the side of people," he insists.

133

Mike Quealey is chaplain of University of Toronto's Newman Club, where he is saying Mass at right in the chapel. He's on the same wave length as the young. But, he says, the institutionalized Church is not responding to them.

Religion And Rebellion In The Roman Catholic Church

These five priests say the conflict revolves around the existing rules and the needs of the people. If there is any disagreement, they are on the side of the people

By James Quig
Weekend Magazine

WEEKEND MAGAZINE assigned Staff Writer James Quig to find out why a number of priests have been leaving the Roman Catholic Church recently to get married — defections which had already been mentioned and discussed in Church publications. The five priests interviewed here certainly do not represent a majority opinion in the Church, but they are typical of younger elements who question many of the Church's old standards and values.

THESE FIVE MEN are priests, and for that reason their beliefs will alarm some Roman Catholics; I know, because I was raised to be a Catholic. But if their beliefs alarm you, they are not confessed here with that intent, for if these men are rebels they are rebels who share a deep sympathy for the traditionalists within their church. To them the parent who still finds it difficult to swallow meat on Fridays has a right to his way, his beliefs, his peace of mind. But these priests also share a concern for the parent's daughter, who swallows a little pill 20 days of every month, does not attend Mass on Sunday and believes priests should be free to marry. They believe she too has a right to her way, her beliefs, her peace of mind and above all, her God.

You don't have to be a Roman Catholic to know that the Church of Rome is a changing institution today. Birth control is the most critical issue. But a new issue has developed: clerical celibacy. Many priests are leaving their ministry to marry, and it was this fact that prompted this article. I set out to do a celibacy story, but immediately discovered that celibacy, for many, was not the real issue. I talked with

CANADIAN REGISTER, MAY 6TH, 1967 p 10

Newman Chaplain Relieved from Post

Father Michael Quealey, CSB, Chaplain of the Newman Centre at the University of Toronto, has announced that his appointment to that charge will be terminated this summer. Father Quealey has been chaplain for the past two years. During that time he has become widely-known for his experiments in adapting the liturgy to the needs of a special spectrum of the Catholic population.

He has also been an editor of the Basilian Teacher and an occasional contributor to The Canadian Register, dealing with the problems of modern University students.

Father Quealey attributed his removal from his charge to his convictions regarding the role of authority in priestly work and also to letters of complaint regarding his liturgical experiments.

"I was told that under no circumstances could I continue as Newman chaplain at any University, although there would still be teaching posts open to me," he said. "Under these conditions I don't feel I can continue to teach, in all honesty, wearing my collar. The students would come to me regardless, and in that case you still have a pastoral counselling situation. I don't understand why complainants did not approach me personally."

Father Quealey's removal was communicated to him by the superior general of the Basilians, Father J. C. Wey. He disclosed that he plans to take a position at York University as assistant professor of history and humanities.

Authorities have left the announcement of Father Quealey's plans to him, they told The Register. "He is at present a member in good standing of the Basilian Order," was Father Wey's only comment.

Catholic priest charges muzzling

By AUBREY WICE
Telegram Staff Reporter

Outspoken theologians attending an important conference here next week have been muzzled in advance by the church, a Roman Catholic priest charged yesterday.

Rev. Michael Quealey, York University lecturer and Newman Club director, made the charge at Mass yesterday.

The priest told an overflow crowd of more than 300 — mostly university students — that he had heard that outstanding theologians had been told to come and say only nice things, not anything new, because "the hierarchy is footing the bill."

A number of controversial modern theologians are scheduled to read papers at the International Theological Congress and Institute at the University of Toronto starting August 20.

Advance information is that they will speak about theological issues behind the sexual revolution, loss of faith, death of God, control of population, plight of authority in today's world and other matters.

Father Quealey said afterwards he had been wrong in his reference to the hierarchy paying the expenses. He said he later learned a lay group was putting up the money.

CFTO TV has bought television rights to the Congress as its centennial project.

The priest insisted, however, he was really fearful delegates would not speak their minds and the Congress would be "a dud."

"I've heard some really disturbing things this week but can't give you any details."

Standing by the altar in Saint Thomas A c q u i n a s chapel, Hoskin ave., the priest asked the people to pray for the success of the Congress.

"I think it would be tragic if these men do not speak openly, only in back rooms.

"People would come for a banquet and wind up getting Pablum."

Rev. L. K. Shook, of the Pontifical Institute of Medieval Studies, the organization directing the Congress, denied there would be any muzzling of the participants.

"No restrictions of any kind will be placed on the theologians," he said.

THE CANADIAN REGISTER
National Catholic Weekly

TH YEAR, NO. 23   AUGUST 6, 1966   KINGSTON, ONTARIO

Two Miles – Straight Up

Father Michael Quealey, CSB, is back in Toronto now but a few weeks ago he was making rounds by horseback in the Mexican interior as advisor to 86 Canadian university students working in 11 villages of the Pisaflores parish. Near the top of San Pedro Mountain, when he stopped for a breather after a two-hour climb, he met Don Julian of San Pedro village. Father Quealey's report on the student program is on page 2.

This summer 25 students from University of Toronto will work without pay in Mexico, to help promote the social and economic welfare of an under-developed community.

They work under the auspices of the Conference of Inter-American Student Projects (CIASP), an entirely student-run organization.

Their aim is to help the people become self-sufficient in social, educational and health measures, not to leave behind a beautiful model village.

The project was originally started in 1961 by a group of of eleven students who went to the small Mexican village of the outskirts of Mexico City.

The first Canadian contribution to CIASP was a group of eleven students who went to the small Mexican village of Pisaflores in 1963.

This year 250 students from 37 Canadian and American universities will be sent to the villages of Pisaflores, San Nicolas, Xochicuatlan and Tianguistengo in Mexico.

CIASP has made itself known as a Catholic group, but welcomes members of any faith or affiliation who are able to work smoothly within the goals of the movement.

The work which CIASP does depends on the individual's talents and the needs of the town or village. Some help the men harvest or plant crops while others can be found teaching a group of women and girls to knit or sew. Last year a veterinary student from Guelph spent her entire stay soliciting drugs from a Mexican firm and vaccinating 3000 chickens in the area.

Some CIASP'ers find themselves building latrines or pig stalls, while others busy themselves going to the poorest sections to work with the Indian women teaching the basic rules of hygiene and child care.

Still another group travelled with a local priest to nearby villages to conduct catechism classes. Some CIASP'ers could be found sitting in jail singing or playing cards with the prisoners, or perhaps at times having a religious discussion with them.

MUST DISPELL FEAR OF MODERN TECHNOLOGY

As the people are firmly set in traditional methods, a major objective of the project lies in dispelling the ignorance and fear of modern technology.

Only by gaining the confidence of the people can the students hope to have his ideas accepted. To this end, the student will often visit families or go down to the local cantine to chat with the men.

Perhaps he will casually say that honey is selling at a very good price in the main village. He will by this suggestion prompt the men to start collecting from their own hives. In a small way, the CIASP'er has helped to promote the village trade.

Yet there is more than work involved. The CIASP'er will often attend a variety of fiestas, have discussions or play dominos in a local cafe. He may go mountain climbing with a group of Mexicans or learn new dances from them.

The people don't want or expect a group of foreigners to come in for two months and tell them what to do. The CIASP'ers must, therefore, work through the local people and local organizations. They must find out what the people expect from them and respond accordingly.

Living conditions are at best novel and at worst almost unbearable. Once accustomed to the flies and mosquitos, however, the bed bugs and sagging rope mattress are nothing.

The lack of washing facilities won't be much of a trial for the hardened bohemian, but the prospect of taking a wary sponge bath in the woods won't be very exciting for the rest of us.

As there is no formal plan for the projects, the students try to put themselves at the disposal of the people. There is a project leader in the main village who does not direct the projects but helps with any specific problems which the students may have.

Well, these *campesinos* thought all of that was silly. What they did was the following. If possible they would first capture and kill the same snake that had bitten them. Then, using a knife or the ever-versatile machete, they would slit open the belly of that snake. They knew from experience where to find the small sac of liquid inside the snake that was its own antidote to the venom it was carrying in its system. The bitten person would then rip out that sac and swallow it. If the snake in question had escaped, the person would hurry back to the *rancho* and find the elder who was entrusted with a special vial containing the accumulated sacs of one particular kind of snake whose antidote seemed to work against snakebite. I have not yet been able to determine the medical validity of this custom, but I do not believe they were putting me on and I do believe that they were convinced it was the only sensible way to handle the situation.

Pisaflores was nestled in a small valley about eight kilometres from the main highway as the crow flies. In reality it took several hours one way to reach the outside world by twisting trails, rutted paths, and the unavoidable river ford that I described earlier. Incidentally, I learned later that that ford through the rapids had been known to kill the unwary, native or otherwise. Even crossing it in a large canoe dug out of a tree trunk and poled by an experienced riverman was not a sure thing.

On the other side of the town there was a mountain you had to climb every time you wanted to get at the rings of ridges and the *ranchos* and *ranchitos* nestled among the old Sierra Madre Oriental mountains, most of whose tops had been worn down by erosion and eventually overlain by rich soil. For this entire region Pisaflores was the regional parochial and economic centre. You had to climb that first mountain, whose official name was San Pedro, in order to get anywhere except back out to the main highway. It took up to three hours, and it was so steep and rocky in sections that you couldn't use horses or mules. I gave that mountain a nickname, which the locals found amusing because most of them simply regarded that climb as an everyday fact of life. I named it "El Bastardo," and even some of the natives came to use that term rather affectionately.

The relative ease with which the *campesinos* would carry backpacks and head loads of seemingly inhuman size and weight never ceased to amaze me. Their utilitarian sandals did not prevent them from developing massive calluses. They were stocky and definitely wiry, but I wondered how many of them survived very long. I did a lot more travelling in this area than I had managed back around San Nicolas.

Fortunately, no matter which direction I had to go in there was always a *campesino* or two who happened to be going that way. That was fortunate, because there were no markings along any of the trails and the seemingly endless turnoffs invited any stranger to get tangled up, turned around, and downright lost. Regardless of their age or gender, my companions on the trail always had to slow down to give me a chance to catch up. They didn't seem to mind and even seemed to enjoy how ignorant I was of the essentials of their survival. I was concentrating so hard on pacing my breathing and watching where I put each footfall that I was unable to use this opportunity for improving my Spanish. I learned later that several of my guides would regale their family and friends with accounts of their adventures with this strange gringo padre.

They seemed to accept that I was indeed a padre even if I wasn't one of theirs. The faith of many of the men was overlaid with, mixed with, or replaced by the secularism and cynicism they encountered out on the highway and in the larger towns where they had to go to sell any of their surplus crops. Padres of any kind were seen at the most about once a year, back there in *rancho* country, and once the women and children recovered from their shock at seeing their first real live white gringo and that this one happened also to be a padre, I was welcomed with a powerful, shy warmth that always made the effort of getting there well worth it.

This was true even in an area to the northwest that had been designated as bandit country until two years previous. That meant that even *los federales* did not enter those trails without explicit permission from the leaders of the bandits. Initially due to Padre Zepeda's insistence and then later when the *banditos* saw for themselves what the CIASP students were trying to do for their children and their villages, the moral code of the mountains came to include a major concern for the safety and well-being of our students. No incident involving any CIASP students ever occurred.

When I did my rounds I always carried a chalice, some altar wine, some wheat wafers, a lightweight alb and set of vestments, a Missal, my Divine Office, cruets, candles, and holy oils. All of this would be rolled up inside my sleeping bag and tied together by rope so I could carry it like a blanket roll behind my saddle. On the occasions when I was unable to get a horse or mule there always seemed to be a *campesino* around who was genuinely eager to shoulder that roll, especially when I was heading up the infamous El Bastardo.

I had worked out three brief homilies that the students most proficient in Spanish helped me to translate into appropriate phonetics. When I set out on a round of the *ranchos*, I never knew which if any of my services would be required. Masses, baptisms, confessions, anointing the dying, visiting the sick, and counselling were sprinkled through many of the days. Sometimes I needed a translator, but often enough my hand language, antics, and plenty of everyday phrases did the job for most things. Confessions were probably the trickiest, because after hearing the clarity of the phonetics in my homilies many people assumed I was proficient in Spanish. I mastered a few stock phrases, hoped I wasn't missing too much of the truly big stuff and counted on the Lord to do the follow-through. There were only a couple of primitive chapels outside of Pisaflores itself, but I would do a Eucharist at least for our students whenever and wherever it seemed most appropriate. I still believe that some of those Eucharists were among the most valid of any I did anywhere.

One of the things that seemed to amaze these people most of all was what would happen when we crested a mountain ridge and a lush valley or a rugged gorge would open up at our feet. At such moments most of our group, including myself, would respond involuntarily with a gasp of awe and stop and stare at what had unfolded before us. The *campesinos* accompanying us came to regard our reactions as a kind of entertainment. Because they knew the trail so well, they soon got to know what kinds of scenery would elicit our strongest reactions.

They would even go off the regular route to please us. Then, at the moment of arrival at such spots, they would step to the side partially so we could get an unobstructed view and also so they could concentrate on watching our excitement and wonder. They got a lot of obvious innocent pleasure out of this activity. As this continued it added a note of sadness to my reactions. This little drama seemed to confirm that even in such a dramatic physical setting human sensitivity can allow itself to become dulled by the familiar. It also indicated that their everyday hardships were so demanding that they ended up without the time or energy to draw on the wonders of nature either as sustenance or enhancement of their lifestyle.

Except for odd pockets like the *rancho* at El Rayo, the landscape around San Nicolas had been generally very dry and even austere. Here in the Pisaflores area, the landscape ranged from bare windswept mountaintops to deep gullies of tropical jungle where you would have to use your machete to cut open the trail into a *rancho*. Two days later, on the way out along that same trail, I would have to use the machete again to cut down the overhanging vines that had used the intervening time to reoccupy the tiny hole we had poked in their green universe.

There were two beauty spots that are among my favourite memories. The first was in one of the jungle gullies near the *rancho* of Gargantilia. The place was known to the local *campesinos* simply as Los Tres Puentes. It was named after three natural stone bridges under which ran a jungle stream of pure sparkling water. They took us there on a steaming hot day for a swim. We changed in the jungle undergrowth, which overhung the edges of the stream. Then we slipped into the exquisitely refreshing and murmuring waters of this swift spring-fed stretch of water. We swam slowly or floated languidly down under the first two bridges until we came to a broad pool. That pool really did appear to spread itself in homage before we entered under the third bridge and into a natural cave whose ceiling peaked at about fifteen feet above the water level. It was an almost perfect circle approximately thirty feet in diameter.

Brilliant sunshine shot in through the entrance and bounced diamonds of light off the surface of the water onto the roof of the cave and back down again. It was enormously peaceful and yet so very alive. The water was quite deep and the *campesinos* had warned us that it was bottomless because it was under that pool in that cave that the water drained down and on into an underground river whose destination had yet to be learned. When you allowed your feet to drift downwards they were tickled rather than tugged by the force of that downward draining. The atmosphere invited and even demanded silence and minimal movement. As we treaded water as long as possible we stopped all chatter because even glancing at each other seemed a distraction from each of us communing with nature in such a primitive yet inspiring form.

It was one of the most naturally mystical spaces I had encountered up to that point of time. There were five of us in there and without any given signal we all realized at once when we should leave. Was it because we could tolerate only so much of that quality of intensity? Or had we spent our allotted time in this gift of the universe? Still in silence we emerged back into the full sunlight and left the water to change back into our trekking duds. Three *campesinos* had guided us to this wondrous place. When we emerged from the cave they were obviously pleased that we had been so moved by this treasure of theirs that they had just shared with us.

They had done nothing to disturb our profound quiet, but I began to notice that they were nonetheless edgy about something. On the way back to the *rancho* for a small yet splendid fiesta prepared for us by its villagers, I used Betty Dwyer's translating skills and astounding sensitivity to the temperament of these people to push our guides as to what that edginess had been about. These particular *campesinos* did like us, but they truly trusted and loved Betty. With her gentle offhanded urging they eventually revealed that while they had very much wanted to share their treasure with us, at the same time they had taken a certain risk without letting us know what it was.

That risk-taking had led to their taking every possible precaution to protect us on the way down to the jungle stream and to stand guard while we were swimming and to do everything possible not to disturb our fullest possible enjoyment of that moment. Betty gently but in a style definitely her own quite firmly pressed them as to what exactly they were guarding us from. Eventually they revealed that less than two weeks before they had to kill a thirty-foot boa constrictor—a "killer snake" very close to the entrance of their cave of magic. Betty pressed further. Why were they still on the alert almost two weeks later? They reluctantly admitted that they were concerned that the mate of the original boa might be still in the neighbourhood searching for its missing mate.

As a footnote I must add that one of the reasons for the remarkable sparkle of this stream was the vibrancy of blue-green shades of the boulders, rocks, and pebbles covering the bottom of this stream. I collected about a dozen samples by which to remember this place and remind me lest I ever be tempted to block its eternal wonder. Two of those stones have been prominent in my backyard fountain since about 1984, and I have kept the rest in reserve for whenever I may need them.

My nomination for the second most splendiferous sight takes me back to my love–hate relationship with El Bastardo. One of the best aspects of doing a round of the *ranchos* was the sleeping accommodations. I came to dread getting back to the regional centres of San Nicolas and Pisaflores or even to the more prosperous *ranchos* simply because that meant I would be expected as an honour to sleep on sheets on a western mattress in a prosperous middle-class-style concrete block dwelling. I got so I would reflexively shudder when I realized that was what I would be facing for the night. The reason was quite simple. It was because of *las chinches*! You may well ask what in the world are *chinches*. The simplest answer is that they are Mexican bedbugs. Frankly, I consider that to be a gross understatement of reality! In Ontario their closest cousins might be the blackflies of northern Ontario. That is still inadequate, since blackflies are seasonal whereas *chinches* are downright eternal. Recovering from spending a night with them was like attempting to survive D-Day.

Fortunately there was an occasional alternative. That occurred when I had to spend the night as the guest of an ordinary *campesino* and his family amidst what many might regard as at best the primitive simplicity of their smoky, wood-slatted, and straw-thatched hut surrounded by small children, pigs, and mountain rats, all of whom shared the same space at various times of the day and night. For me it was a taste of paradise, whether at dawn, during the heat of the day, at twilight, or in the dead of night. The warmth and heartfeltness of the quiet unassuming hospitality was as rich as that in the finest of mansions and was often far more permeating and long-lasting.

The *pièce de résistance* of being a guest in these dwellings was the quality of the sleep available. The doors on these dwellings were ineffectual and the carefully placed slats of the walls provided the most successful natural air-conditioning I have ever encountered. And then there were those beds! Talk about primitive and sophisticated at the same time! They consisted of a sturdy wood frame with home-spun rope criss-crossing from each pair of sides covered by a palliasse, which was like a sackcloth pillow filled with straw. On top of this platform for a king I would spread my faithful companion sleeping bag with one of my temporarily extraneous articles of clothing scrunched up under my head as a pillow. I remember almost regretting having to fall to sleep at all because of what I would be missing of all that cacophonic orchestration of the jungle.

To return to El Bastardo! My single most favourite resting place, especially on a return swing from the *ranchos*, became a tiny little collection of huts too small even to have a collective name. They were nestled in the crook of a small gulch immediately over the crest of El Bastardo from Pisaflores. It was perfect for treks when I felt pushed for time but knew because of the reality factor in those mountains that I didn't have enough daylight and/or dusk left to make it all the way home to Pisaflores. It was then that I would stay with the Garcias high up there, just under the lip of the ridge. Incidentally, we had been told that ridge tipped off at between nine and ten thousand feet above sea level.

Aside from the profound pleasure of spending any time at all with this wonderful family, as well as the kind of restful sleep of the gods available in that setting, there remained the raw pleasure of waking to fresh coffee, with *pilon* of course, and then setting off on the final lap back to Pisaflores. That final lap consisted of several segments. First there was the approximately fifteen-minute climb to the top edge of the ridge of El Bastardo, or San Pedro, as he was known in more conventional circles. I would always insist on starting after dawn but before sunrise because of what I knew would be awaiting me at the peak of the trail.

Because of the height I had come to experience that both the *ranchito* of the Garcias and the lip of the San Pedro ridge itself were above the usual cloud line. That meant that under almost all conceivable weather conditions there was a predictable sunrise on that ridge approaching it from my non-Pisaflores side. I usually managed to arrive in time to witness that freshest moment of the rebirth of our world. It was perhaps the moment when I most felt I was able to identify somewhat with what it meant to be an Aztec, Mayan, Huastecan, or Modern Mexican. That sun and what it does as it rises to restore again one's individual and/or collective hope is much more than a mere metaphor in such a place.

As the subtle quiet of dawn yielded to the raw intensity of sunrise, my sense of where I was standing deepened. Whenever I was at that point at that time in the morning, the valleys below were covered in a slightly bumpy blanket of dense greyish-white cloud. I had to remind myself that I was on top of one of the largest mountains in the Sierra Madre Oriental Range. I had to do that because it seemed more like I was standing on a small central hill of an island in an endless archipelago.

In the near and far distance, other "islands" poked their rocky noses through that same sea of cloud, but there was no apparent evidence that any of these islands were connected to each other by anything solid like valleys, fields, towns, gulches, and people. Paintings of such scenes by early Chinese Buddhists had first been scoffed at by Westerners as flights of fancy. At the same time it all seemed somewhat like a giant Japanese formal garden, with the rocky noses representing the real islands in the Sea of Japan and in this case the carved clouds instead of the usual carved sand represented the endless sea that swirled out of sight yet still held all those rocky islands within an integrated circle ruled over by a sun that shines with its own peculiar brightness and crispness up here above the cloud line.

What was spread out at my feet was so magnificent that if anything it was almost too real to bear. It was still brisk with the freshness of mountain winds when I had crested that summit, but as I stood and stared or moved aimlessly around my little patch of bare rock the heat of the day began to match the rise of the sun into its heavens.

Finally, after an indeterminate pause I knew it was time to move down into the valleys to huddle down in the hollows of the ground along with most of the rest of my species. The next stage of this journey consisted of carefully picking my way down the main path leading down thousands of feet to the town of Pisaflores. This particular descent is possibly the most peculiar I have ever taken. Despite the twists and turns in the pathway it seemed to plummet almost straight downwards.

What seemed even much stranger was that down that trail was that massive cloud cover, which seemed ready to swallow me up even while I was still surrounded by the brilliance of a new sun. I had to use my reason quite deliberately to remind myself that my path did and would lead me into and through that cloud mass. It seemed much easier to accept that I was steadily walking into and under a massive and unknown sea. It took over half an hour to get down to the cloud line and begin feeling the upper wisps of that indifferent mass.

Then every step took me into denser banks of contending matter bumping each other to retain adequate airspace. I began exchanging my beads of sweat for droplets of fresh water sucked up from the tropical jungles that remained somewhere below. It was closer to a gentle Irish mist than a steady Ontario summer shower. More importantly, it was delightful and refreshing! It was darker than dusk but not as dense as night. I continued down my trail through those clouds for about an hour.

Finally, the air began to thin again and I gradually emerged into what seemed to be an entirely different world down there beneath the cloud cover. I slowed my pace on the lower reaches of San Pedro as I wanted desperately to savour endlessly the magical moments of that morning. I made that trip three times altogether, the last time completely by myself. It was amazing how the trip down El Bastardo contrasted so strongly with the arduous journey of climbing it upwards. At one stage I even wondered if it wasn't providing me with a concrete reversal of the Japanese proverb "Seven times down, eight times up."

That brings us to the animals. The ones we relied on the most, when they were available, were horses and mules. We were not in terrible physical condition, but even the best of us couldn't keep up on the trail with people of all ages and genders who drew on their generations of backbreaking toil. Horses helped. Not just any horses, mind you. The highly prized mountain horses were not the big, heavy, handsome ones but rather the small- to medium-sized wiry ones, who were much more sure-footed and panicked less easily.

Because of those features, mules were often the best of all. There was one particular mule in Pisaflores with whom I had a definite love–hate relationship. The owners had named him Hitler because of his mean disposition. If you were not firm with him he made mincemeat out of you. I'll swear that I saw him appearing to stand perfectly calm and contented until he would explode straight up with split-second timing and throw a would-be rider straight up and off before that person could get their foot into the second stirrup.

One sleepy morning I was saddling him up for a round of a set of *ranchos*. As I circled around behind him I got careless and cut the angle of my turn too close. He knew it and unleashed one of those two-hoofed kicks I thought happened only in Hollywood. I was extremely fortunate. As mules go he was very big and powerful. The hooves landed dead centre on each of my thighs. A little lower and I probably would have lost my kneecaps. A little higher and I probably would have had to deal with a ruptured stomach and broken ribs. A little to either side and he might have changed forever my views on optional celibacy. As it was, I went through the air and landed with a thud on my backside. My thighs throbbed and it took me a few moments to grab my breath. I immediately realized that, fear, rage, and wounded dignity aside, there were two other factors that seriously affected what I did next.

One was that this had happened in the town's main square and, while the townspeople did often see it as home-grown entertainment to watch what their Hitler might do to the uninitiated, I was not particularly the object of their scrutiny on that morning until this little incident occurred. It already seemed to me that in that mountain culture there could be a very fine line between false bravado or machismo and insisting on due respect. The other reality was that I needed this animal if I was going to be able to get to those *ranchos* that day.

I also realized that the next few moments would influence whatever else I was able to accomplish around Pisaflores. If I did not re-establish our relationship on suitable terms I could lose a lot more than a little dignity.

I was not particularly interested in finding out what Hitler had next on his agenda for me. I had not yelled at him because I simply couldn't. The square was approximately a hundred yards in each direction and everything had stopped as many, many eyes watched to see which way the fates would turn. Even Hitler maintained a dead calm, waiting for my next move.

I took my time getting back on my feet and then walked slowly but steadily to his mounting side. This time I kept the appropriate distance. I chose my mounting spot quite deliberately and when I reached it I stopped and remained completely immobile for a moment or two, staring at his massive throbbing side. Then, just as he peaked on one of his intakes of air I slammed my fist into his belly with all the force I could muster and then grabbed his cinch strap, which I yanked upwards as sharply as I could. While he was momentarily off-guard, I stepped quickly into the first stirrup, hoisted myself high and dropped onto his back with every ounce I could push. Next I anchored myself in the second stirrup, grabbed the reins, which were already draped over the pommel, and jerked back on them three times with that bit tearing at his mouth.

Then, for a moment, I went completely still while retaining a steady firm grip on the reins. He was so furious but so confused that he wasn't sure what he wanted to do. Even my freezing still for a moment seemed to confuse him, but I didn't see any point in giving him time to figure it out. I usually wore heavy steel-toed construction boots for my treks through the mountains, and now I used their heels to bang his ribs and jerk the reins to the direction that I, not he, was choosing. He tried his straight-up jumps a couple of times, but I was ready for him and I simply jerked harder on the reins and kicked harder with my heels.

In frustrated compliance he finally tore off across that square with me still on top and still in charge. By this time the people in the square didn't know whether to laugh, cry, or applaud, so they did all three simultaneously. From that day on they called me Padrecito Gringuito, which I was told was an affectionate diminutive. Hitler and I, meanwhile, went on to develop a relationship based on mutual respect, with neither of us for a single moment ever taking the other for granted.

In fairness I must include two other episodes in which I remain convinced Hitler did save my life. The first was on a drizzly day when he and I were alone on a long ride. At one point we encountered a not unusual rock slide that covered and obscured the best way up to the next level of the trail. I considered dismounting to increase our odds of navigating this mass of small stones and boulders whose degree of stability was difficult to judge. I knew he would let me know if he thought he couldn't do it, so I remained on board and slightly nudged him forward. Perhaps he was taken off guard by my unusual gentleness, but he began moving slowly ahead.

Almost immediately his hooves began to slip and slide on those chaotic stones. It was after we made a slight turn further upwards that it became critical. At that point my back was facing open air and a long drop down a mountainside. Hitler's hooves began to pick up speed in his scrambling as the rocks scattered in all directions from his pawing, but we were not in fact advancing upwards to ground any more solid. I knew it was far too late to try to get off, and at least my head told me that he knew a lot more about this kind of stuff than I did, so my best shot lay in giving him his head and trying to help him. I relaxed the reins and stood up straight in the stirrups, throwing my weight as far as possible forward up the mountain and over his head. It was one of those time warps in which I'll never be certain how much time actually elapsed.

It seemed like forever, as he redoubled the fury of his pawing for solid purchase on that mountainside. He may have preferred to be on his own without me on his back, but he seemed to realize that he was going to make it only if he took me with him. This was an animal with an enormously powerful life-drive. Even so, it seemed that he was very close to his last resources when finally he found the solid grip he was hunting for and lurched forward and upward so quickly that within a dozen strides we were back on an undamaged stretch of that ridge trail. I searched immediately for the first convenient stopping spot, dismounted, tied him to a solid tree and told him out loud, with some of my most complimentary crudity, just how proud I was of him and thankful too. It seemed to me that he glanced at me rather strangely, as if what was then happening was much more difficult for him to handle than a mere mountain slide.

There was one other time when Hitler seemed to give me back my life. This time it was late afternoon, going over the last ridge before El Bastardo. I was very damp and grungy and it had been a long, tiring day. Hitler and I met a section that was more rock slide than trail and going down it on an animal's back was much trickier than going up. I decided to dismount, but as first one foot and then the other hit open air, instead of solid ground, I realized in a flash that I had made a terrible judgment.

What had happened was that in glancing down before dismounting I thought I saw a thin strip of green border beside this admittedly narrow trail cut out of the side of a cliff. Because we were in that cliff's shadow the light was not very helpful. The basic fact was that I was tired and had become careless. What had appeared to me as a thin green border was in fact the top of branches and bushes that were at least ten feet tall growing out of the side of that mountain ridge and up beside the trail. What I was stepping into was really a clear drop. I wasn't sure exactly how far that drop went except I could tell that it was plenty far enough to finish me off.

What happened then came straight out of my primordial past. Whether it was because of genetics or the survival training of trying to grow up, I had, and still seem to have, unusually fast reflexes. My feet were both out of the stirrups and pawing at a mix of tree tops and thin air. My hands fortunately were still on the horn and rump of the saddle. Those hands went into reverse from their anticipated relaxation and grabbed both ends of that saddle because they knew that my life did depend on it. Hitler's reflexes were as quick and he froze rock solid without the slightest twinge. I do not believe that he had come to like me enough to save me, but I believe he did realize that if I were to go off that mountainside I might very well take him with me. I couldn't swing my feet far enough under his belly to get them on the trail itself and even that would not have got me out of this mess. I had to use my shoulders and arms to pull myself straight up until I could slowly slither and then lurch back into the saddle. I made it and I even ended up patting Hitler's neck after that one. He didn't even seem to mind being patted.

My next animal memories concern the ubiquitous pigs of the *ranchos*. To some extent the chickens but especially the pigs were the greatest concretization of hope for a *campesino* family. They were almost family pets, but they were also their investment strategy. Those animals were there to be used to bounce back from disasters, to finance new business ventures, or to pay for a child's future education, a few luxuries, or extras at the end of the harvest. I never saw a penned-up pig on any *rancho*. Pigs were expected to roam freely because they also embodied the *rancho*'s sanitation and recycling program. There was definitely never a garbage problem while they were around, and often they were the ones that vacuumed the smooth mud floors of the thatched huts.

My favourite "pig tale" concerns the *rancho* of La Palma, which was serving as home base for four of our students. Very soon after my arrival from San Nicolas the students considered it essential to introduce me to the mechanics of their "pigs-and-pebbles *bano.*" They showed me a stack of pebbles outside their own hut and explained that whenever I needed to use the two-holer outhouse on the village square I would have to take a handful of pebbles with me. It turned out that this was because this particular outhouse was a backsplit. In other words, its rear dropped down a gentle slope. The students were gurgling with great delight in showing me their local wonder. They asked me to look down into one of the holes. That was a surprise. I was old enough to have seen quite a few outhouses, but never one like this. When you looked down in this *bano,* instead of the expected standard stinking soup of you-know-what, you saw about four feet below the seat a cement floor that was spotlessly clean. You could also see light coming from somewhere behind the *bano.*

Next, the students took me around to show me that the light was coming from a semicircular opening over three feet high, level with the cement floor, and even with the ground outside. I was beginning to catch on, so the students spilled it. The pigs on that *rancho* had free access to whatever contents were deposited in that *bano* and they were the ones that kept everything so clean. I quickly replied: "That's all fine and wonderful, but what does all this have to do with pebbles?" When they could stop chuckling they took further delight in explaining that when you first entered the *bano* you had to check down the hole to see if the pigs were still cleaning up after the last customer. If so, then you had to throw enough pebbles at them to scare them away. If you did not do this there was a strong possibility that you would find yourself being licked and nuzzled where you might not want to be. Personally I have never heard a better pig story, which in itself makes it well worth the retelling.

I cannot leave the arena of animal life without a few comments on the mountain rats. While in Mexico, I never met a *campesino* who was afraid of them. Over the centuries they had found a way to live with them. Their method involved a considerable amount of wastage, but it did work. This is a corn culture. As such, corn is the people's main form of daily sustenance. After the corn is harvested it is stored in open bins on the rafters of their thatched huts. The nests of these mountain rats are always outside on the semi-tropical mountainsides. For example, at one *rancho* the students took me out to sit in a particular spot on the *rancho's* square. Typical of the area, it was actually the *rancho's* communal coffee-drying floor and the *rancho's* only levelled space. When the moon came up it shone straight down the main path leading into the *rancho*.

Sure enough, at first a few, then small groups, and then what seemed like hordes came like tumbling shadows that poured soundlessly onto the path and down into the *rancho*. As they hit the thatched huts they scattered to their favourite feeding bins and were long gone by sunrise. Occasionally a woman or young girl would wake up to discover that one of her magnificent black braids had been chewed off. But even that gave them something to talk about rather than something to be sad about. The *campesinos* had long been accustomed to losing approximately one-third of their corn harvests to the mountain rats. In return the rats kept down various other pests and predators. They were never known to attack people as long as there was enough food available for them.

I have two rather personal rat memories from those mountains. One morning, on the third day of a dysentery attack which had slowed me down but not entirely stopped me, I began stirring from sleep when I seemed to feel something moving around on my chest. Dimly I thought it was probably someone try to wake me and, because of my medication, I was deader than usual. So I made the effort to open my eyes and see what was going on. As my eyes focused I realized that I was eyeballing a rather large mountain rat that was sitting smack dab in the middle of my chest and staring right back at me. Well, the city slicker in me asserted itself and I jerked upright so suddenly that my friend the mountain rat was heaved ass over teakettle before he could get his legs under him and scamper out the open front doorway.

On another occasion, two students and I were trekking out to the main highway. We were not able to make it all the way on the first day, so we had to hunker down in our sleeping bags somewhere for the night. Because of the snakes, it was not sensible to sleep outside on the open ground in those mountains. We found an open communal storage shed in which we were allowed to stay overnight. One of the students had already spent a continuous year and a half in this area and she alerted the other student and myself to what we could expect to happen during the night. She pointed out that at the far end of the storage shed was a very large stack of burlap sacks that contained *pilon*, which meant chunks of unrefined brownish cane sugar.

This meant that it was completely predictable that the mountain rats would be in that night for a snack or feed. She explained that it didn't have to be a problem unless we interfered with them. All we had to do was set up our sleeping bags on top of the empty wooden skids at the other end of the shed and they would leave us alone. I was very tired and, despite some inbred misgivings, did fall asleep.

In the middle of the night the sheer volume of their scampering slowly woke me up and then I was very awake. It was true that they never touched us in any way, but, my goodness, what a scene that was. Enough moonlight made its way through the wooden slats that we could easily make out the endlessly tumbling shadows. It seemed to go on for hours and hours, but when we finally actually woke up nary a trace of them was to be found.

Some of the *ranchos* we visited were more isolated than others. In many of them the men of the *rancho* had been out to the nearest major highway or market town and had seen white people. That was not true of most of the women and children. They would stop dead in their tracks and stare and stare. We were so strange to them that they didn't even have any prejudices or predispositions one way or the other. When we encountered this, we never quite got used to feeling like Martians or throwbacks to the original conquistadores. In some *ranchos* Spanish was not even their primary language and I would sometimes need double translation.

In one *rancho* they asked me my name, and when I told them it was Quealey they all burst into uncontrollable laughter. It turned out that *quealey* in their native language of Huastecos was the same as *gusano* in Spanish, which means "worm" in English. Small wonder that they found it funny that the gringo Padre Worm had come to visit them.

In another *rancho* every hut I entered had an unusual small altar set up near the front door. The altar had a picture of the Virgin of Guadalupe, which of course was not unusual at all. In front of each such picture was a tiny vigil light or oil lamp. What was unusual was that immediately beside the Virgin and clearly receiving as much honour and respect was the statue of one of the old pre-Columbian native deities. In front of each of those statues was always a little pot that contained something with the consistency of paste or glue. I noticed that whenever a member of the family entered the hut they would first bow to the altar, perhaps place a small flower in front of the Virgin, and then would spit into the pot.

I tried not to be too intrusive and eventually learned that they sometimes also put bits and pieces of things from the jungles and swamps in the pot. I tried to discover why they did this. The closest I could understand was that by letting this pot be blessed at the feet of all the deities, and by keeping it moist with spittle, it would be ready when they needed to use it for bad cuts, sores, rashes, and infections. In still other areas of the mountains I witnessed kinds of healing that I would have previously thought impossible. These were supposed to be primitive people, and by many of our most familiar criteria they were indeed backward. Still, I came away from those mountains humbled at how much they had taught me about endurance and sensitivity, and how in awe I was at how much I still did not know about many, many things.

In this regard my single most puzzling story goes as follows. One morning as Betty Dwyer and I were leaving the Rancho Arena to cover a loop of *ranchos* on the very edge of the parish, Carol Prunier, a CIASP nurse who had been assigned to this *rancho*, asked us to do her a favour. She explained that two weeks earlier, while travelling on the trail we were about to take, she had been told of a *campesino* in his sixties who had just come out of a coma he had incurred when caught in an avalanche.

. His two companions at the time had been killed and he had lain in his hut for seven months in that coma being looked after as well as possible by his family. Especially in remote *ranchos* I cannot remember anyone who had spent time in a hospital and very few who had ever seen a doctor. They simply did their best and left the rest to a mix of fate and providence.

The man's name was Juan and he was quite willing to let our nurse give him a medical checkup. Even though at that time Juan was out of his coma for barely a week, he seemed in remarkably good health and spirits—that is, except for one thing. He was still rather uncomfortable from a massive bedsore that he had developed from lying so still on his back for all those months. Carol described it as at the base of his spine, inflamed, infected, approximately five inches in diameter, and at least two inches deep. At that time she had washed it, sterilized it, applied some antibiotic salve, and promised to return in five days to repeat the treatment.

Unfortunately Carol badly twisted her ankle a few days later. It had now been over two weeks since she had visited Juan, none of her teammates at the *rancho* was able to attend on her behalf, and she was increasingly worried about how much worse the wound had become. She had sent messages by the occasional *campesino* who was going that way to explain why she had not been able to keep her promise. She hoped that Betty's skills in Spanish and her acute sense of the sensibilities of these people, along with her marvellous sense of concern mixed with humour, might help remedy the situation. Carol gave us the necessary medical supplies and especially the antibiotic salve with its precise instructions. We agreed to try to help and set off in search of the Juan who had come out of a coma.

Confusion over directions took us down a few wrong paths through the jungle, but finally we found him. Carol had warned us that she had no idea of the shape in which we might find him, and by now he might even be feverish and hallucinating. She admitted that even with her professional training she had been quite frightened when she first saw that wound. Our first surprise was that Juan was standing, shy but jaunty, outside the front entrance of his hut. The word of our approach had gone ahead and he was quite moved that we were even trying to help. All he was wearing was a simple apron that covered most of his front. He had in fact received Carol's messages and was understanding of her inability to return as promised.

We explained that we had with us the same medicine that Carol had used before and that she had carefully instructed us in how to use it. He was quite willing to have another treatment and led us into his hut, where he unceremoniously stretched out face down on his rope bed. Five of his family members were spread out around that bed, curious about the operation that Betty and I were about to perform and willing to help out if necessary. It was cool but rather dim in there, but Betty and I quickly glanced at each other.

What we were looking at was not at all what we had expected to see. It was our second surprise so far. From Carol's description of the original wound and her prediction, based on her medical background, the wound was supposed to be much worse than two weeks before. Our shock came from the glaringly obvious fact that the wound was very much better.

Upon later reflection Betty and I realized that we had overlooked something when we first arrived. Carol had warned us to brace ourselves upon first meeting Juan, because the stench from his wound might by now be overpowering and we could well experience a strong urge to throw up. We had been so thrown off by how lively, fresh, and clean he looked when he first greeted us outside his hut that we missed the fact that there was no stench at all. As he lay stretched out before us he was downright gleeful about showing off his wound. It seemed to have become a badge of honour, and he indicated that because of his ordeal he had become somewhat of a local celebrity.

Who would have anticipated that such an ordinary *campesino* would have even been able to survive such a killer avalanche and then to

suddenly come out of his sleep of seven months? Now, to add to his glory
and respect, two more gringos had bothered to come all the way out here
to this land beyond time just to visit him and try to help him. And what
of the wound itself? Well, the most obvious fact was that it was completely
clean, with no sign of any infection, inflammation, or putrefaction of any
kind. The next surprise was that far from being significantly larger, as
Carol had expected, it was in fact significantly smaller. Indeed, clean or
not, it was still obviously a raw open wound.

But the previous diameter of five inches had shrunk to about three
inches, and the depth had decreased from about two inches to somewhere
under one inch. You could still see the outline of the original wound,
but inside that line was a ring of pink new flesh. Betty and I had to jolt
ourselves out of our state of shock to ask Juan and his family as gently as
possible what they had been doing to treat the wound. They were pleased
that we were pleased with the results of their ministrations but seemed
very vague about what they had been doing to get these results.

We asked Juan if he would still like us to use our medicine. He was
quite eager to co-operate. Carol had been very insistent that we begin
by washing the wound thoroughly. Even though it didn't look to us as
if this wound required any washing at all, we were determined to follow
her instructions. We asked the family if we could have some water. They
casually pointed to a dented, rather grimy aluminum bucket sitting on
the floor beside the bed. What was in that bucket was wet all right, but
there the resemblance to water vanished unless one included in that category various kinds of swamp water. Various pieces of leaf, bark, twig,
and unidentifiable gooey substances were clearly visible. Betty used her
gentlest tones to explain that what we meant by water was fresh boiled
water. The family seemed rather miffed that we should assume they didn't
know the difference between boiled and dirty water. But they made no
move to light the stove to boil the water and simply went on pointing to
that same bucket of what seemed to us filthy sludge.

Betty realized that we were missing something in this picture. We
paused at least to indicate that we were trying to take them seriously
and then with quiet deliberate wording Betty found the wisdom to ask
them, "What is in that water on the floor beside the bed?" The eldest
daughter, who was named Maria, replied, "Oh, just the usual stuff." Betty
concentrated on Maria and pressed her gently by then asking, "Well, can
you tell us what is so special about it?" Maria shrugged her shoulders and

answered, "I don't know except that everybody around here knows that it works." Betty responded with, "What do you mean 'it works'?" Almost defiantly, Maria replied, "Well, that's what we've been washing our father with three times a day since he came out of his coma." I'll swear that Moses on Mount Sinai couldn't have been more shocked when handed the Ten Commandments than Betty and I were at the simple yet profound wisdom of what was been revealed to us.

We realized immediately what we had to do. We stopped asking questions and bent down to use our hands to scoop up some of that swamp water and used it to bathe Juan's open wound. Then we added some disinfectant, mainly so Juan would feel that we were at least trying to do something for him. Finally we added the antibiotic salve, whose coolness caused Juan some pleasure. We stayed with Juan and his family for a while and accepted their offer of a soda pop each. Afterwards Juan walked us to the edge of his property and warmly thanked us for our efforts.

For quite a piece along that trail Betty and I respected each other's silence as we attempted to absorb the wonder of what we had witnessed. We suspected that what we had most given to Juan was another story to add to the lore of his family and *rancho* about the strange gringos who had emerged from the jungle one day just to visit him and that despite their silly questions really had been very well intentioned. A week later Carol was able to visit Juan again and reported back to us that he was continuing to improve dramatically.

I did not manage to develop individual relationships with many of the people in the mountains. Partly that was because I was never in one spot for more than a couple of days. Also, when I was on my swings though a series of *ranchos*, the primary needs in each stopping place would seem to be those of the students, because I was from the outside or home base and they would have huge gobs of stuff they wanted to talk about. In addition, my own ear problem has always made foreign languages a serious challenge and the need to talk in English with the students in each posting left me little time to concentrate on developing my own Spanish.

At the end of our tour all the three- and four-member teams from each *rancho* packed up, said their tearful goodbyes, and worked their way over the ridges and back down the mountain trails into our two main centres, San Nicolas and Pisaflores. At Pisaflores Padre Zepeda had arranged a parish fiesta for our leave-taking. There were games, lots of food, the singing of children, the dancing of adults, speeches from all sides, and, as their *pièce de résistance*, a full set of cockfights, which, as validly Mexican as they were, did do some damage to the stomachs of at least some of our students. Then we trekked out to the nearby old Inter-American highway in big groups and were picked up at Tamazunchale by our pre-arranged long-range tour buses.

On the outskirts of Tamazunchale I went to a locally renowned guitar maker. Annie Harris was with me, and she tested dozens of stringless wooden frames and then dozens of stringed versions for their timbre and tone. It was wonderful to watch her work at what she knew. From those we selected two or three possibles. Then I called in Manuel, a friend of ours from Pisaflores, who was renowned for his ability to bargain. I ended up with a handmade Mexican guitar for an agreed price of a little over eight dollars Canadian. I felt so guilty at joining the ranks of exploitative North American gringos that I immediately jumped my offer to all of ten dollars Canadian. The seller seemed more than pleased and I took my guitar back to Canada. I made innumerable promises to myself to learn how to play it, and never have, but still after more than thirty-five years cannot bear to part with it.

Once at Tamazunchale, everyone had a lot of intense experiences to exchange with their fellow students who had already been picked up by the buses. They had not seen each other for what seemed like endless weeks. As a footnote it was interesting that the crowdedness of their living conditions and the intense demands of the challenges they had embraced in recent weeks had resulted in not a single complaint about boredom or disgruntlement or evidence of a single summer romance.

In fact, I remember distinctly that while we were waiting for our buses some American tourists dropped by the same bus station to get some refreshments. In what they probably considered innocent asides they commented quite loudly on the primitiveness and crudeness of these stupid Mexican peasants. They definitely didn't bargain for what in fact happened. Our Canadian students lashed out at them with remarks such as "Aren't you the truly ignorant ones," "No wonder Mexicans and most of the world are inclined to see all Americans as 'ugly Americans,'" and "Did you ever ask how many American gringos are astoundingly stupid and indeed so stupid that they are even proud of it."

The students were spontaneously using the pronoun "we" to completely identify themselves with the Mexican people they had been living and working with for several weeks. They were also using the phase "you

gringos" to identify other white North Americans with whom these students were refusing to identify themselves. The feelings among those
eighty-six Canadian students were so intense and unanimous that I was
torn between being enormously proud of them and being aware of the
need to intervene before our students moved over the line from a ver-
bal to a physical lynch mob. Those Americans went into some kind of
shock and scrambled to get out of there as quickly as possible. I have
remained curious as to what they did or didn't take away with them from
that incident.

As a final treat, Betty Dwyer, who had graduated from St. Mike's in
1965, had gone with CIASP that summer and had remained in Mexico
during the intervening year as an advisor on various projects sponsored
by CIASP, arranged for all of us to spend overnight at Xilitla. This was a
small prosperous town in the mountains of the state of San Luis Potosi
where Betty had made strong friendships during the winter months. She
was especially close to a couple who had been engaged for years but whose
mutual feistiness had led to many postponements of an actual wedding.
Her name was Chave and she was one of the daughters of the leading
family in town. She was by then in her thirties and had earned a deep
respect from all segments of the community for a wide range of reasons.

Her *novio*'s name was Dante. His mother was Mexican and his father
was Italian. Dante had recently been appointed Chief of Police for the
city of San Luis Potosi, a city with a reputation spanning generations as
Mexico's capital of smuggling. It was claimed to be common knowledge
that Dante had been sought out and was appointed to the post because
he had proven himself to be the most successful smuggler of all. His being
asked to take on this job was supposedly a prime example of Mexico's
pragmatic politics, in this case honouring the principle "to catch a thief
you must hire one."

After returning to Toronto I continued to correspond with Chave, and
when she and Dante finally went through with their wedding the following
year I sent them a five-inch-high wood carving by a native Canadian of
two grizzly bears wrestling. It seemed an appropriate gesture as a gift for
a couple whom I had come to love. Approximately a year later I received
a package in the mail from Dante. A brief letter explained that they had
enjoyed receiving such an eloquent yet humorous comment on their relationship. He had been in the habit of keeping the little sculpture on his
desk at the jail in San Luis Potosi. One day, one of his long-term inmates

who had noticed the carving asked if he could borrow it as a model to help distract himself from his apparent fate.

Dante agreed, and some time later the inmate completed his version of the carving using wood from the local mountains. The prisoner gave his copy to Dante as a present after carving his initials and the place on its base. Dante in turn was sending that copy to me as a present he enclosed with this letter. He recognized that this copy in no way matched the artistry of the original, but he felt certain from what he knew of me that I would appreciate it as a memento of the story. He was absolutely correct. I wrote and thanked him for his kindness and promised to treasure it always. It remains in my principal memory cabinet to this day and I have retold the story often.

The road up into the mountains to Xilitla had been recently carved out of the side of a mountain ridge and was barely passable to anything, let alone buses. Crumbling edges, hairpin turns, rock slides, and sheer drops with nary a barrier in sight made for an interesting ride. The town itself had as a patron a rather crazed and/or eccentric English gentleman. Each year he would drop by with fresh architectural drawings and hire the villagers to construct these edifices on plots he had purchased. He always paid his bills, the villagers faithfully followed his plans while he was away, and their local economy was enriched. The results, however, gave the town an architectural look like nothing else I've ever seen in Mexico let alone elsewhere.

His structures were never ugly, only somewhat strange and usually devoid of any evident purpose. For example, close to the main square was one of his four-storey brick-and-concrete structures with no internal divisions but with a forest of fifteen-foot-high concrete arches on the roof. A stranger asked this patron one day what this structure was intended to be. He apparently replied quite matter-of-factly, "It is for the gorillas to play on." Someone had to attempt explaining to the *campesinos* what a gorilla was, since those mammals are not indigenous to Mexico, illustrated books were a rarity, and there were no zoos around.

At the same time other elaborate concrete structures enhanced a nearby mountain torrent to add pools for safer swimming for the children and adults of the village and rendered the torrent and especially its fifty-foot waterfall more accessible, viewable, and enjoyable. We Canadians spent a couple of wonderful hours that day swimming with, in, and through the results of this eccentric's supposed madness.

A large family of Betty's compadres who lived on the main square had prepared a Mexican fiesta in our honour. There were what seemed like tons of the Mexican food that most of us had come to love, simple yet obviously heartfelt speeches concerning what we had tried to do, splendid dancing and singing by children and adults of all ages from the hinterland of which Xilitla was the heart, our own participation, which was wondered at but definitely appreciated, three different bands of mariachis, fireworks, and lots of *abrazos* all around. It was deeply moving and memorable!

Perhaps it was the dancing of the elders from the *ranchitos* and the excitement and wonder in the eyes of the children, for most of whom we must have seemed like visitors from Mars, that embedded themselves most deeply in my memory. That night we bedded down inside the old stone church on that same square. We were still very excited at being together again and revved up by the singing, dancing, and drinking at the feast. We had spread our sleeping bags on the bare stone floors at the rear of the church and then began singing again. Oh, did we sing! On and on into the night about everything! That night, in that unlikely setting, I may have done my best rendition ever of "Old Man River."

The next morning we boarded our buses, headed carefully back down that mountain road to the main highway, and then turned north for the American border. We were a much hardier gang than we were on the way south. The Mexican buses that picked us up at four different spots, including Tamazunchale, had the usual washroom. That meant that we stopped only for three meals a day.

As on the way south, international regulations required that we switch from Mexican to Canadian buses at the American border. The drivers replaced each other on schedule, so we ended up driving three days and nights non-stop back to Toronto. The simple comfort of an ordinary bus seat was like nothing we had experienced for many weeks. Some students spelled each other off for the space in the overhead luggage racks, where they could stretch out and be rocked to sleep by the steady grind of the bus as it ate up the miles.

Most of us were so bonded by now that after we finished sharing most of our reactions to Mexico we began speaking much more personally with each other. This time the hours and days passed far more quickly than on the way south. Since our total group had been drawn from campuses throughout southern Ontario as well as Quebec, we began dropping off contingents at Windsor, London, Guelph, and Hamilton until we finally said goodbye at Union Station to those heading back to Halifax, Kingston, Ottawa, and Montreal. It was near midnight as I hitched a lift with one of the student's parents and finally crawled into a real bed back at Newman.

42. "Father Quealey Isn't in Mexico"

I did not notice it at first, but then it began to hit home. During those days immediately after my return from Mexico I began feeling more and more strange at the awkwardness of several people's reactions when I first re-encountered them. At first I really did think I was imagining things, or that it was an example of the infamous reverse culture shock. It really did seem to me that they behaved as if they had just seen the proverbial ghost. I took Stan Kutz aside and over a hefty hoist of my first scotch in weeks I described what seemed to be happening and asked him if he had any idea what it was all about. Stan was initially a little hesitant, but then he came out with it.

Apparently, while I was gone a very strong rumour circulated that I had not really gone to Mexico at all. The details varied according to the source, but there seemed to be a consensus that I had merely used CIASP as a cover and that what I had really done was head off and join up with a woman with whom I had been secretly carrying on for years and by whom, according to various estimates, I had already sired three to five children. Subsequently, I made some unsuccessful stabs at trying to get the name of this woman whom I supposedly had finally decided to honour, but I could never pry loose any identifications. There had been similar rumours for quite a while from many sources and for many reasons.

Perhaps the most significant feature of this episode was that so many of my closest friends and supporters had so automatically assumed them to be true. This situation was one of the main reasons why I almost immediately agreed to do an article and supply pictures to *The Canadian Register* on the activities of CIASP in Mexico. At the same time, if I had encountered this much smoke about someone I knew, I would have assumed there must be some fire somewhere. But where? I knew that my CIASP experience had been very clean indeed, and that all of it had been immensely valuable to me. Those convictions remained strong, but the tenor of my Toronto reception meant that I began my second year at Newman with an even heavier heart than I had before departing for Mexico.

One extremely sad note on our beloved CIASP phenomenon. During the 1966–1967 school year I continued to support it, spoke many times on its behalf, and again offered Newman's facilities to those students planning and training for the 1967 summer. In early June of that season I received almost unbelievable news from CIASP in Mexico. Eileen O'Connor, from St. Mike's, then in her third year with CIASP and one of my compadres from 1966, was on the staff at CIASP headquarters in Mexico City and called me directly. She had been alerted that a student named Lucie Mason, a recent graduate from McGill University in Montreal whom Eileen had met at the usual orientation sessions less than two weeks before, was being driven down to Mexico City.

Apparently Lucie had suddenly become ill and highly feverish at Rancho Nuevo, so she was brought back to Pisaflores with great difficulty from her *rancho*. The trip had taken at least three frantic hours on the trails, during which Lucie's condition worsened. Eileen quickly arranged for her admission and examination at a nearby hospital in Mexico City and was waiting there on June 2 when Lucie arrived. Lucie was diagnosed as having double pneumonia and brain fever with only a ten per cent possibility of survival. Eileen immediately arranged for Lucie's transfer to a world-renowned hospital in Mexico City, one of whose specializations was brain fever. Despite the finest efforts of that hospital. Lucie Mason died in Mexico City on June 4, 1967.

Father Tim Hogan from Windsor, a fellow Basilian and one of my long-term kindred spirits who had taken an assignment with CIASP that summer, conducted the body back to Montreal. To intensify the agony Lucie was the only daughter of a fourth-generation Afro-Canadian who was still a Pullman steward on the CPR. I had not known her personally but learned from many, many sources what a magnificent person she was, what she had already accomplished, and how eagerly she was being watched for the wonderful things she would be doing to life.

One of my last acts as a priest was to concelebrate at her funeral in a church in working-class Montreal. Afterwards, at the wake in the family home, I sat in her parents' kitchen, with no real words, able only to hold their hands. As far as I know, CIASP in Canada never fully recovered from that blow. Individuals like Eileen O'Connor continued to serve in various advisory and administrative capacities with the chapters and national organization of American CIASP. Changes in the patterns of student activism led to CIASP disbanding itself in 1970. It seems from the records that 1967 was the last summer for Canadian students to go in groups to Mexico under the CIASP umbrella.

[The contents of the 1967 paragraphs above result from a lengthy phone conversation I had on May 7, 1999, with Eileen O'Connor, who is currently a Professor of Biology at the University of Washington. Fortunately she has held on to her extensive records of CIASP. I am grateful for her help.]

43. "On Liturgical Aberrations," October 1966

The 1966–67 academic year began. It meant another session of doing seminar groups for the Department of History. The students at Newman were back on Thursdays and Sundays and, aside from the usual adjustments necessitated by graduations, transfers, etc., we made a very smooth transition into Newman's weekly rhythm. The intensity and success of the rumour over my CIASP absence led me to renew my efforts to have a talk with Pocock. During the spring I had attempted on three separate occasions to initiate discussions but was always put off by his secretary with stories of "the archbishop's busy schedule," etc. I renewed my efforts in September, because the degree of popular acceptance given to my not really having gone to Mexico convinced me that I should attempt to short-circuit or at least face whatever else might be crossing Pocock's desk. Once more I was blocked by his secretary.

Then a pastoral letter arrived from Pocock. It was dated October 4, 1966, was entitled "On Liturgical Aberrations," and was to be read from every pulpit in the archdiocese. The same day I also received a hand-delivered letter from Father Wey, my Superior General. Wey expressed the expectation that I would conform with the Archbishop's admonitions, especially with regard to the use of the vernacular in the Canon, and that I would do this with as much humility as I could muster. That Sunday I read Pocock's pastoral letter at the Newman liturgies in as flat a tone as I could muster and with no commentary before, during, or afterwards. I quickly fell into a quandary as to what to do. In March of 1995, when I began trying to recapitulate these events, I discovered that I still had the original of that pastoral letter. (See Appendix 1.) It is a document that deserves careful reading and rereading.

On the one hand it was the kind of letter I had been expecting from my first days with TMS. On the other hand it felt like a terribly unfair letter, considering the circumstances of my original appointment to New-man. I was unaware of any other priest in the archdiocese who was doing any, let alone all, of the listed aberrations except myself. One of its crucial statements was "It will be helpful for our priests to know that no autho-rization to experiment has been requested or given to any individual or group in the Archdiocese."

I found that particular remark to be two-faced at best. I had, for rea-sons explained earlier, deliberately not asked for prior authorization. At the same time, I had been doing what I was doing for three full years, almost to the day. Two of those years had been before my appointment to Newman and Pocock had deliberately appointed me to Newman based on my apparently successful "aberrations" with TMS. Even after he received a formal report from his own Liturgical Commission on my "aberrations" and before I actually assumed my responsibilities at Newman, he chose to do nothing to cancel or modify his mandate to me concerning Newman.

That same Liturgical Commission had clearly recommended that my "aberrations" not be stopped but that a method of "controlled experi-mentation and reporting" be established. That report had been submitted months before I began my appointment at Newman, and Pocock had obviously chosen neither to condemn my already existing "aberrations" nor to stop my taking over at Newman. At the same time he decided not to establish any method of "controlled experimentation and reporting" or to say anything to me personally one way or the other.

That initial Newman appointment could not be viewed as anything other than a de facto endorsement of my efforts at experimentation with TMS from 1963 to 1965. This present pastoral letter in effect denied the existence of those events and the obvious reasons for my appointment to Newman in March of 1965 to take effect in September of 1965. In the early 1990s I heard that the archives of the chancery showed in writing that Newman, as well as St. Dominic's parish in the city, had been formally declared to be "centres for experimentation." My source said that no date was given as to when that authorization had happened. I called the pastor of St. Dominic's. He confirmed that he had never been given such an authorization. Similarly, neither I nor any of the Basilians succeeding me at Newman ever received such an authorization.

That official record reportedly in the archdiocesan chancery nicely dodges what Pocock had been tolerating with full knowledge in the three years prior to this pastoral letter of 1966. If such a record actually exists, it had to have been inserted as a deliberate falsification of fact. I found this current letter of October 4, 1966, to be loaded with irony and soaked in hypocrisy. If I had only begun my "aberrations" after I had been appointed to Newman, then the contents of this letter would have made a lot more sense. As it was, I was now being condemned for very reasons I had been appointed to Newman. Father Wey's letter only added to the absurdity, neither suggesting nor allowing any recourse and thereby making me wonder why I was still trying to make it as a Basilian.

In the week following Pocock's letter, I tried once more to get to see him. This time I was given an appointment almost immediately. I wasn't very certain of what I hoped to accomplish with such a meeting, but I did know that at the very least I needed to clear the decks and get some direct clarification on what was going on, what that letter did and did not indicate about my present and future status.

When I entered Pocock's office he came around from behind his desk to greet me, and I was really taken aback by his opening remark: "Oh, Mike, I'm so glad to see you. I want you to know that that letter of mine did so much good. I now only get three or four letters a day against you, as opposed to the usual twelve to fifteen." He sat me down in one of his leather chairs, offered me a drink, and went on and on about how much pressure he had been under from priests and laymen who were having trouble dealing with the consequences of Vatican II. Never once did he refer, one way or the other, to exactly what I was or wasn't doing. The whole point of his case seemed to be that he had needed to send out that so-called pastoral letter so as to make life a little more livable for himself.

Depending on how this interview went, I was prepared to resign on the spot. In fact I was carrying a letter to that effect in my inside suit pocket. I was simply not interested in returning to a lock-step conformity to empty formalism where the specifics were determined by political pressures rather than any inherently liturgical sense of purpose. For example, this business of insisting on the Canon remaining in Latin at best perpetuated some unacceptable remnant of the clerical arcana. Even worse it meant that strict adherence to the timing of introducing the vernacular as a replacement for Latin was exclusively a matter of centralist control disguised as discipline.

It really did seem that John XXIII's hopes for responding to the legitimate needs of people had been successfully pushed off the value chart of every frightened centralist. If it was really wrong to use the vernacular, then what happened so soon afterwards that it became so very right? Pocock's timidity, ignorance, and de facto indifference concerning pastoral matters had enabled me to "do my thing" only as long as it made him look good. As soon as the negative feedback intensified, regardless of its inherent merit or lack of merit, he resorted to appearing to endorse rigid controls. Anything, so that he didn't have to be bothered. It seemed that I had become a liability instead of an asset in terms of his personal equanimity. If that was accurate, then I felt quite prepared to move out of his way.

That morning in Pocock's office I decided to focus and clarify the issue as sharply as possible. I asked him directly if what he was now telling me meant that he was not in fact expecting me to change the way I was already doing things. He nodded and said something to the effect that we could continue with that understanding. I then asked him if there was some reason I did not understand as to why he had not yet taken up my open invitation to come in person to see what we were and were not doing at Newman. He replied something to the effect that: "Oh, Mike, can't you see that if the word got around that I had done that, people would see it as my approving something that they see as a terrible threat? They would insist on seeing my visit that way, even though they had never witnessed your liturgy themselves."

I took it from that interview that he really didn't care what I was or was not doing at Newman and that he did not want to have to deal with the backlash. It was completely unreasonable for me to expect any stronger endorsement or encouragement. The winds of fashion had shifted and he was shifting with them. I left his office with the firm realization that I was completely expendable, that my days of official ministry were numbered, and that I might as well do some solid thinking about what I wanted to do next with my life.

44. Another Interview with Wey, February 1967

From October to February I basically did a repeat round of what we had done the previous year. I vaguely remember using Latin in the Canon for a few weeks and then, with no fanfare, returning to our previous practice. Nothing further was heard from the Chancery, but in February I was called in for another interview with my Superior General. This meeting was stiff, formal, and brief. Wey told me that he had to inform me of a decision that had been made by the General Council and that it was not open for discussion. As close as I can remember, he then stated: "This is to inform you that your appointment to Newman will not be renewed. Nor will you be given any appointment that has anything to do with people unless and until you take time off, go and live in an appropriate Basilian house, and take enough time to reverse all your opinions that have become so controversial and unacceptable."

After a chunk of silence, I asked if he could tell me how they had arrived at this decision. He said that it was not to be discussed. I asked then if this was because of pressure from the Chancery or from within the Basilian community. He replied that he had no comment on that. Finally, I asked him why he had chosen not to honour his promise to come to Newman personally to witness what we were and were not doing. He replied that that also was a "no-comment situation." I couldn't be sure to what extent he was being put up to this and to what extent he personally concurred in this decision, but he was obviously sticking to his guns to a degree I had never known him to be capable. Finally, I asked if I could have a week to think over my reply. He agreed that my request was reasonable, we set a time for the follow-up, and I left his office.

45. Jack Saywell, York, and Decisions, February 1967

I probably could have given Wey my response on the spot, but I decided that a little self-preservation might not hurt. I had been more shocked by Pocock in October than by Wey now. A combination of naïveté, arrogance, and concentration on what I loved to call "the sacrament of the present moment" had weakened my vision of the probably inevitable results of my attitudes and actions. It was now obviously far too late to rebuild those bridges. It was definitely time to be moving on. I have occasionally wondered if things would have been significantly better if I had chosen to handle matters differently. In answering that question I remain convinced that I might well have left the Basilians much earlier and in a far worse state of confusion and bitterness.

I had asked Wey for that week for one very clear purpose. I knew it would be a challenge to make this transition as smooth as possible for all concerned, including myself. In terms of what to do next it seemed most sensible to pursue something with my doctorate in History. I phoned York University and asked for an interview with Professor Jack Saywell, who was then the Dean of the Faculty of Arts. I did this because I had worked with him at the U of T and had done my big paper on Archbishop Walsh for him. I was certain that he liked me, that he would be my best contact in terms of knowing where there were openings in Canadian History in the then rapidly expanding Ontario university system, and that he would give me a solid recommendation for any appropriate position that might be available.

Well, I arrived at that interview and was only ten minutes into my story when Saywell interrupted and asked me if I would like to come to York and work for him. I had no difficulty in answering that I would like that very much. We quickly agreed that I would have a cross appointment, fifty per cent in History and fifty per cent in Humanities. Humanities was one of York's new interdisciplinary teaching units. I was to start with the next academic session, in September of 1967. About a week later I received a phone call from Saywell, asking me to send in a curriculum vitae so he could have "something for the files." It is not the way that university hiring is done these days, but I was glad it was available to me back in 1967.

46. The Final Interview with Wey, Late February 1967

I returned within the week to finish off my encounter with Wey. He asked me what I had decided. I asked him again if there was anything he could tell me about the process of their decision-making so that I might understand better what had happened. He said that there was not, and that he still had to refuse to discuss this with me. I then informed him that I had thought over his decision, and that while I did not respect it I obviously had to accept it. I went on to point out that the business of my taking time off and rethinking my positions was completely unrealistic.

I pointed out too that I had been moving steadily and unambivalently for several years now in very obvious directions. Long before I was ordained it had become increasingly clear both to myself and others where I stood on virtually every current issue affecting the Basilians. My

Basilian Teacher article entitled "Quo Vadimus?" (see Appendix IV), back in October of 1962, while apparently a shock to some, was in fact a natural conclusion of my well-known positions up to that time. Since 1962 the bulk of my attitudes and actions seemed to me to be consistent developments from then. As a result, it was abundantly clear that the time had now come for me and the Basilians each to go our own way.

His jaw definitely dropped and he really was taken aback at my response. His response to my response did surprise me. If he had really expected me to accept his suggestion of a "monastic withdrawal" and my eventual "formal renunciation of my heretical positions," then it meant that he had never known me very well, if at all. That previous week I remember trying to think of a Basilian house I might be willing to retire to in order to do my rethinking. I had been completely unable to think of a single place.

I pushed on to point out that many different individuals and groups, especially the community at Newman, would be affected by this decision. I suggested that I be allowed to finish out my current appointment at Newman until its normal expiry on August 15. In that way I would have a better chance to smooth the transition at Newman and give the Curia more time to find an appropriate replacement. He immediately agreed to that proposal and I almost burst out laughing. If I was so destructive that I "would no longer be allowed to have anything to do with people," why on earth was he agreeing to allow me to go on damaging, confusing, and abusing the community at Newman, along with all my other contacts, for another full six months? Well, he did agree and that little interchange was the last time I saw him before my departure. I left Wey that day with my last shreds of respect for the institutional Church in total tatters. This conviction definitely included the leadership of the Basilians.

47. "Telling the Story," March to August 1967

I had already known several Basilian and non-Basilian priests who had left the priesthood. Generally they had used an "in the middle of the night" approach. I decided that that did not usually benefit themselves or others affected by their decision. I had long been convinced during the sixties that the challenge was not so much whether to stay or leave as it was how best to stay in well or to leave as well as possible. I decided to sit down

personally before August 15 and directly inform as many as possible. That
may have been a serious error on my part.

At the top of my list of those who would have difficulty with my decision was my mother. I went to her home before she could hear the news
from anyone else. She was by then a widow living alone in a bungalow
on Wilgar Road in the Kingsway. She and Dad had moved there in the
late fifties, so it had never been my own home. She sat ramrod straight
on the chesterfield while I settled in a Queen Anne–style chair about
three feet away. When I had arrived that day, she immediately said that
she knew something was up. She looked as grim and forbidding as I had
ever remembered her.

I still believe that she attempted to control the mood and the agenda
with her stony silence. I was not even offered the usual cup of tea. Nor
did I request it. I had not been looking forward to this dreaded necessity
and did not want to encourage any distractions that might weaken my
determination to perform it as well as possible. I spent about two hours
trying to give her at least enough of the background so as to make my
decision more understandable even if no more palatable. Throughout
my presentation she sat stern and tight-lipped with no interruptions. At
the end there was a long silence. I asked her if she had any questions. She
said that she had only one: "Who is she?"

I shouldn't have been surprised, but I was hurt and disappointed. My
stories had never been able to replace her preconceived agendas. I tried
to explain that there was no one woman in this picture but that I would
probably eventually want to explore that option. She did not argue. She
simply got up, walked to the door, opened it, and stood aside. Her expression never changed, and the last thing she said that day was "If it actually
happens, I hope I don't live to see the day." In spite of myself and my vivid
memories, I must have been hoping for a different kind of response. In
fact this incident confirmed me in my decision to move on with my life.
It also proved to be the definitive and final instance of my looking for her
to accept me as myself.

What I realized would be the most devastating aspect of all this for her
would be her sense of personal disgrace, shame, and loss of social prestige.
She had gained something from my brother Brian and I becoming priests
that had filled a hole in her that nothing else had. First my and then
within a few months my brother's actions she seemed able to interpret
only as betrayals that would reopen that personal hole.

In an attempt to do what was humanely possible to ease my mother through that, I did offer to go around and personally speak to each of her brothers and sisters and our closest family friends so that she didn't have to be the first to tell them. What I should have anticipated but did not was that she proceeded immediately to phone each of them herself and to enlist them in various schemes to make me change my mind.

I ended up finding one or two of my many aunts and uncles who were accepting but got myself blindsided by the rebels of that generation who were the harshest in their outright condemnation. In addition, a couple of days after I had told my mother she phoned Stan Kutz and asked him to come to see her. Stan did and her first question to him was "Who is she?" He replied that if there was someone specific he didn't know who it was. Secondly, she asked if Stan thought that what I really needed were some electric-shock treatments. Stan replied that he thought not.

My mother, then, after never, never coming to anything I had done at Newman, or anywhere else, even though she lived only a half-hour away by car, began suddenly to show up every Sunday at Newman. She would sit there prominently, front and centre, trying to spot who "she" was and to intimidate me with her usual demeanor into doing what I "should" be doing, which of course was whatever she wanted me to do. Our relationship never recovered from that period. She did not in fact die before I left and remained at least technically alive for another thirty-one years.

I sought out the Basilian colleagues who were closest to me, I made appointments with nuns I had worked with, I sat down with those students for whom I was more than a public figure, and I visited at least a dozen couples and their children who had remained strong supporters of our endeavours at Newman. That list included the Mateos, the Gallaghers, the Cunninghams, the Dumphys, the Duffys, the Pengullys, the Bolands, and the Newlands. In short, I tried very hard to speak personally and directly to those I felt would be most affected by this change. Some, like almost all of my relatives, with the exception of one brother, opposed what was happening either silently or vehemently.

Others, such as the head of U of T's Faculty Association and the Chairman of the Sir Robert Falconer Association, protested directly to Wey and Pocock. Recently, in exploring a bag of old correspondence, I rediscovered about a dozen letters of encouragement from various Basilians, many of whom I had not known well but who had bothered to write and thank me for what I had been trying to do. For many people the six months between February and August dragged on endlessly. In that sense it now seems like a mistake to have allowed it to go on and on.

Probably my greatest single error in judgment in this area was my decision to sign up for a final Basilian retreat at Pontiac, Michigan. Most of those attending were from my own peer range. I was aware when I signed up that all of them knew what I was intending to do on August 15. Despite this, or perhaps because of it, the entire time was awkward, unpleasant, and unsatisfying. I must have been hoping for too much. I was not looking for supporters or sympathizers, as far as I know.

What I thought I was looking for was an opportunity to tell my story, to give others a chance to ask questions, and to say a straightforward goodbye to colleagues with whom I had shared several intense years. I couldn't have known it then, but a high percentage of that group would themselves leave the Basilians over the next ten years. Meanwhile my much more recent colleagues on Admiral Road proved to be a far solider source of simple warmth, understanding, and encouragement.

48. Final Days and Transition

One of the factors whose power I underestimated during this final round of leave-taking was the state of persistent rumours concerning my supposed "real" agenda. For example, one young woman who had been a TMS original became pregnant in the late summer of 1966. She returned to campus for her graduating year and came to Stan and me for help. We arranged with a professor and his wife from the Newman community to take her into their family. She was thereby able to complete her school year and had a fine support system as she brought the baby to term and then chose to put it up for adoption. Then some kind of reaction set in, and I learned from friends that she was letting it be known that in truth I had fathered her child. It turned out that the chief propagator of this in Basilian circles had, for several years in the 1950s, been the fellow scholastic whom I considered my closest friend.

I sought the girl out, confronted her, and had her come with me to talk to my erstwhile Basilian friend, who appeared to have succumbed to that most virulent of Basilian viruses, gossiping. The girl admitted to the Basilian that she had been lying, but I was certain that he didn't accept her statement. By this time I had become quite discouraged. There were things on which I might have been validly confronted. The only things that ever did come back to me were not true. Whether or not actual truths were also part of the gossip soup I was never able to discover. But the overall scene had become increasingly contaminated and unworkable. Rightly or wrongly, I had indeed used up my credibility and it was time to move on.

On June 4, 1967, Doc Walsh died at Montauk. During the previous week I had been unable to get him off my mind. Finally I called Betty Dwyer, who had graduated with John's daughter, Katie, had been in Mexico for over a year with CIASP, and had become another close friend of the Doc. I told Betty that I was having one of my Irish attacks, which meant that I couldn't get Doc Walsh off my mind. It was the beginning of June and I was crowded for time, but I had decided to follow my urge and head to Montauk for a flying visit to see him. I asked Betty if she was interested and she was. Betty had been working for the previous year on community development projects in Rochester and had enough flexibility to take off like this. We called ahead and asked if we could come and he agreed immediately. I left Newman early in the morning and picked up Betty around nine. We drove straight through to Montauk and arrived in time for supper with the Doc.

As it happened, he had insisted that his wife, Jane, take a long-overdue holiday to the British Isles. He had been unable to go himself, partly because of some health problems. So he was alone at Montauk. We cooked him a meal and the three of us had a quiet, subdued evening that lacked none of the usual charm and delight. We went to bed early for his sake. In the morning Betty and I did breakfast for the Doc and then we lingered over our coffee. Finally, around noon, Betty and I had to leave to get back to our commitments. As he gave us his usual grand wave from the back porch, we thought he seemed somewhat under the weather but that it wasn't nearly enough to wipe that wonderfully mischievous grin off his face. Within twenty-four hours he had the heart attack that killed him.

None of his family had seen him as recently as Betty and I had. It was in shock that I drove back to New York City for the second time that week. Doc was buried from St. Ignatius Loyola Church at Park Avenue and East 84th Street, in the Manhattan neighbourhood where he had grown up. His brother officiated and I was one of the many concelebrants. I don't believe I have ever been in such a grand church that was so filled with genuine grief. From Supreme Court judges to the homeless of Manhattan, to graduate students galore and to the natives of Montauk, an amazing cross-section of humanity converged that morning to mourn his passing and to acknowledge that he had touched them and that they were the better for it. He was twenty-five years older than I, but we felt like peers. He had become perhaps my surest touchstone of reality. I would miss him for many, many reasons. I still do. As a footnote it was the very next week that I went to Montreal for the funeral of Lucie Mason, whom I have spoken of earlier.

At the beginning of August an expanded Catholic group from Admiral Road reserved a wing of Bigwin Inn in Muskoka for a week-long marathon. I had less than two weeks left at Newman, but I wanted to be at Bigwin. On one level it was a profound learning experience on the vagaries and commonalities that each of us inherits and that we then shape into our own uniquenesses. It's a case of blind faith in a possible collective unconscious until an individual has specific concrete realizations that defy any other explanation. Possibly everyone in our group at Bigwin, myself included, had such experiences during that pressure cooker of a week in an otherwise naturally idyllic setting. If there is something about being shaken to one's core, then that happened to me that week. As I drove back to Toronto, the final steps of withdrawing from Newman almost seemed like a distraction.

The final seventy-two hours were messy, largely because of my own doing. Around August 7 was the last actual Sunday liturgy that I did at Newman. It turned out that a reporter was present and I didn't realize it. My homily touched on true and false forms of liberation and kinds of conformity and repression. As an aside I mentioned the upcoming much-ballyhooed international theological convention scheduled to begin at St. Michael's on August 20. I tried to express some hopes that the changing times of reaction and backlash against Vatican II would not inhibit the theologians from grappling with the many leftover issues from Vatican II that still begged for serious attention. The reporter had a field day with that. The headline in *The Telegram* read: "Catholic Priest Charges Muzzling."

Pocock was understandably upset, but true to form he made no effort to contact me, directly at least, to check on my version of the incident. Instead, I was informed by registered mail that my diocesan faculties were cancelled as of August 12. Wey and I had previously agreed on the usual Basilian turnover date of August 15. Wey had a note dropped off, again with not even the courtesy of an enquiry, stating he expected me to abide by the archbishop's ruling. Almost all that remained was whether or not I would abide by these draconian precepts rather than our previous agreement.

Bob Madden also called on behalf of some my Basilian confreres at St. Michael's who were quite upset by the item in the newspaper. Several of them, and especially Bob himself, I had always regarded as friends and supporters. I agreed to come over to the lounge in Elmsley Hall for an informal gathering with the Basilians who would be hosting the conference referred to in the newspaper. Stan Kutz came with me. Fifteen or so Basilians attended. I apologized for my carelessness in bothering to say anything at all without considering that a reporter might be present. I apologized for any unproductive flack that they had to put up with, especially now that my faculties had been cancelled and I no longer had my usual forum for a retraction and/or denial. I then elaborated on what I have stated above, namely that I was concerned about the general atmosphere in which the conference was taking place but that I had never charged any muzzling had taken or would be taking place. That group calmed down very quickly and they even ended up wishing me well in my future endeavours.

There were two other factors that made those final hours especially important to me. The first was that on that Saturday two of my oldest and dearest TMS originals had made serious adjustments to their plans so that I would be available to officiate at their marriage in Newman Chapel before my departure. One of them had been to Mexico with me in CIASP. I considered asking Pocock to delay his decree for their sake but decided that all the evidence indicated that such an approach would be a fool's errand. I had never even heard a story from anyone anywhere of this particular bishop ever really caring about any individuals in his so-called flock. Instead, I asked Stan to step in for me, partially because I already knew that this same couple were also very fond of him. Stan agreed, did a very fine job under necessarily awkward circumstances, and I attended from the pews.

The second factor was that my final scheduled Sunday Liturgy fell after Pocock's cut-off point but before my earlier agreed-upon date of departure. Considerable pressure had already been mounting around what many expected to be my swan song. While I had spoken very extensively to individuals, couples, and families, I had in fact not made any full statement to the Newman community generally. I felt they had a right to such a statement and I was also counting on the occasion to thank them and to say goodbye. It was probably already going to be an overflow crowd and the events of the week would contaminate it with the added presence of reporters and the curious. I was very, very angry at this turn of events.

I ached to defy this nonsense and to deliver as devastating a broadside as possible on how Jesus simply did not deserve the disciples he usually ended up with. I have always tended to be a word-monger, and that week I was flooded with internal flashes, juicy one-liners, and unanswerable words of wisdom. But in order to go on living with myself, I had to ask what it was that I could hope to achieve by indulging such defiance. Did I really want to lead a righteous mob down Church Street to sack the Chancery? Well, I did and I did not. By that point in time, the truth was that I did not want to stay at Newman or in the Basilians.

I had become increasingly aware of my various ways of mishandling my anger. Even so, the temptation to spill my bucket of seemingly endless bile was very strong. For once I was also almost lost for words. I was having difficulty imagining how to say whatever there was to say in such a way that it would be more helpful than harmful to this community that I had come to love. I reminded myself that I would not be around to help pick up the pieces or help others with any possible fallout from my final remarks. Finally, I realized that I didn't trust myself enough to handle a public defiance well. I asked Stan to stand in, he did, and he handled it in his finest form. He gave them my thank-yous and my goodbyes. He added his own, quite properly, because he had been ordered back to St. Michael's for the coming year.

One aspect of the transition that went very, very well was our contacts with our designated replacement, Father Peter Sheehan. He was in one of the first ordination classes after I was appointed to the Seminary as an undergraduate. He directed some of the first Basilian choirs and glee clubs in which I participated. We had not had close contact over the years, but I liked him and was certain he would serve the people at Newman well. He took the initiative several times for informal talks with Stan and me. They always went well.

I felt greatly relieved by this. I knew he was enough of his own person to carry on in his own style. I left Newman confident that he was at least one Basilian who knew and understood what we had been trying to accomplish. Later, I was pleasantly surprised to hear from ongoing members of the community that in fact Sheehan made no significant changes to the liturgy we had crafted and began rather to build on it. A few years later I was quite saddened to hear of his untimely death.

I asked T.A. if I might take the big red leather chair in my office with me. It had so many stories to tell. He agreed and the only other things I took with me from Newman were two old unused wooden chairs from the basement. T.A. and I exchanged a gruff goodbye. Wey had made no suggestion of any financial support to help me through the transition, even though I was later to learn that by then it was standard practice with other Basilians who had left the community. He didn't even bother to say goodbye. Whatever vestiges of respect that I had for him and what he represented dissolved completely that week.

I had found a wonderful bachelor apartment on the twelfth storey of a high-rise in the second block above Bloor Street on Walmer Road. The building was cruciform, with curved balconies connecting the extremities. Residents of the Annex have long referred to this building as "the Wedding Cake" because of its general appearance. Apparently some around town had been taking bets as to which woman I would finally move in with. No one collected on any of the bets because, despite the profound certainties that only gossips can muster, no single woman was part of this resolution. Stan helped me to move. We borrowed a panel truck. I had been invited to move into one of the group houses on Admiral Road to which several priests and nuns had already moved. I said no because I wanted some time to myself and because I was convinced that Admiral Road would not benefit from having my notoriety dumped in its lap at that stage in its development. My mother also had invited me to come and live with her. I was very certain that I did not want to do that.

I loved that apartment. I had a wonderful wraparound view of the city. It was more spacious than most bachelors and I began cramming every nook and cranny with stuff I wanted to live with. One of the great luxuries was not having to answer the phone or the doorbell if I didn't want to. I learned some primitive cooking and thoroughly enjoyed my concoctions. I began to entertain a little when I wanted and with whom I wanted. Above all I relaxed and spent hours in a balcony chair looking out over a world where life and death took so many different forms. Within days I experienced waves of relief as I realized just how much pressure I had been under while attempting, as much as possible, to stand for an institution in which I had long lost faith. Within a couple of weeks classes at York University had begun and I entered that new world with a lot of applicable skills already in hand.

The Admiral Road crowd had collectively purchased their first farm property near Mono Mills and gained possession on Labour Day, 1967. It was in completing the legal arrangements for this property that the term Therafields was invented to describe these farm fields that were going to be used for therapy. The name also stuck in popular usage and came to cover all the varied activities that began to blossom with that movement. From there on I spent most weekends until Christmas on volunteer work crews that transformed an equipment shed into a comfortable group room, an old barn into cooking, eating, and sleeping quarters, and a farmhouse into suitable living quarters for both part-time and long-term residents. It was usually very satisfying work. The crews numbered around thirty at a time, and an entirely fresh kind of bonding began to occur.

Roughly a month after leaving Newman I began my cross-appointment in History and Humanities at York University. For the History department I did a package of lectures and took three tutorial groups in "Problems in Canadian History." In the interdisciplinary Division of Humanities I took several tutorial groups and did a handful of lectures in a wonderful grab bag of a course focused on the theme "Modern Man in Search of Understanding." It was team-taught, with weekly course meetings in which we discussed each other's lectures before and after their delivery. It was my introduction to an increasingly fascinating group of committed professors and to a form of teaching that was fresh and remarkably honest. I was also soon asked to do committee work of various types. As of 1995 I had been teaching at York for twenty-eight years. As of May 1999 I am now preparing my syllabus for my thirty-third year.

Meanwhile, on weeknights I used the isolation of my apartment to put the final push on my thesis. I defended it in November of 1967 and was awarded my doctorate in Modern History from the U of T in the spring convocation. In May of 1968 I was invited again to move in with one of the house groups on Admiral Road and this time I accepted. I spent June helping out at the farm and early in July set out for England, Eastern Europe, Russia, and Finland as SCM's national representative at three world conferences of university students.

I returned late in August to live at 59 Admiral Road. In 1969 I moved to 63 Admiral, and then in 1972 to 61 Admiral. In 1974, Mary Lou and I became involved. We had first met when she was a sister-in-training at

Loretto College, where I was doing occasional chaplaincy duties in 1964. We met again in Therafields. By then she had left the convent, married, adopted a girl, and had a son. She and I were in the central group responsible for this roughly 800-strong therapeutic commune movement.

When the children were two and four her marriage ended. I had three significant affairs in the intervening years, but it was not until February of 1974 that Mary Lou and I realized that there was a great deal more happening between us than we were acknowledging adequately. That was when we became involved; her children, Jennifer and David, were five and seven at the time, and I became their stepfather. In 1976 we moved together to Brunswick Avenue and as of 1995 we have been here for nineteen years. As of 1999 we have been together for twenty-five years. Now how's that for a transition?

49. Reflections

To whom is all of this being written? My most immediate answer is that I am writing it to myself. Over the years I have often told one or another of the above stories, but I've never tried to string them together in a continuous narrative. There is Alzheimer's on both sides of my family, so I can't count on any, let alone many, years of retirement in which to commit all of this to paper. The specific timing was triggered when in 1994 I was finishing off a sabbatical from York and at the same time a Basilian, the first ever to do so, happened to ask me about the story of my years at Newman. The initial writing of this document was done in a rush. Finally, in the spring of 1999 I faced the fact that it was overdue for a revision and hence the present update, completed this May 9, 1999.

Beginning in 1994, then, I took the challenge to articulate that story so that it said what I could be satisfied with. That meant transposing and/or translating my oral tales into written form. I have some intention of reading at least certain sections to friends and colleagues from the 1960s and since. Fantasies of putting a copy in a time capsule have also occurred to me. Above all, I do have hopes that someday my children and my children's children might become curious enough to want to know what I thought my 1960s were all about and that this writing along with the scrapbook illustrations might help them to understand.

In format it is probably closest to a memoir, although it is also a collage and an apologia in the classical sense. It is a memoir because it represents my current remembrances of a very intense period in my life. In that sense it is like a war veteran's writing about his experiences in wartime, not so as to glorify war but simply because he seldom if ever experienced life with such intensity as during those years.

It is also a collage because I have interspersed photocopies of newspaper clippings, snapshots, and crucial documents so as to give fuller substance to the stories. Video did not exist in the sixties, that's how ancient that period has become. However, I might still figure out a way to add a soundtrack that includes the Beatles, Buffy Saint-Marie, Leonard Cohen, newsreel sounds from Vietnam, the voices of Walter Cronkite, John F. Kennedy, and Eric Sevareid, as well as excerpts from *The Canticle of the Gift*.

Finally, it is indeed an apologia in the classical sense. That means several things. It is much more sophisticated than saying "I'm sorry," although it does include that. I still remember how disappointed I was on how few and far between were the details of exactly what St. Augustine was confessing. I have indicated above how intrusive the gossip mill could and did become. As far as my liturgical practices were concerned, the religious authorities clearly revealed that they chose to base their convictions and decisions on gossip rather than on the Church's approved forms of canonical visitation.

After the pastoral letter "On Liturgical Aberrations" of October 1966, I successfully resisted the temptation to send out my own pastoral letter. I could have included a copy of the Liturgical Commission's Report of May 1965 and asked the pastors of the archdiocese for assistance. Why had I been formally appointed to Newman despite such clear foreknowledge of what I had already been doing and clearly intended to continue doing? Why was I now being scapegoated by the same religious authorities who refused to take any responsibility for having appointed such a known quantity in the first place?

Why had Pocock, Wey, and Kelly asked me to go to Newman? In traditional terms I was definitely a loose cannon. But they knew that and appointed me anyway. Even after the Liturgical Commission Report, there was no hint of their changing their minds. I had not sought the Newman appointment. At TMS I had been responding to a perceived need in a different manner that might help demonstrate a more productive way of doing things. Had I been set up for a fall? Or had they underestimated the backlash to Vatican II and been attempting to look good by sending a known radical to fix Newman? Whatever their original purposes, they fulfilled none of the commitments they made to me at that meeting in March 1965. In the end, without either a visitation or a hearing or a private consultation, they fired me for doing exactly what they had sent me to Newman to do.

If the gossip concerning my alleged affairs influenced those same authorities, then they never acknowledged it to me, one way or the other, with the possible exception of Wey and his one half-hearted comment on the area. That area of gossip around my personal and/or social behaviour did seem to engage many. Since none of those who bothered to come to me directly presented anything grounded in reality, I see no point in commenting on other possibilities. In the meantime, this current apologia attempts to explain, and not apologize for, the very public acts of liturgy that I did perform.

Using an overall perspective, this is the story of a major transitional period in my life. It happened to coincide with major transitional periods both in the Catholic Church and in North American culture. It was both a very exciting and a very threatening period to live through, especially if you happened to be in the Catholic Church and the Director of the Newman Centre. I believe that I experienced those years of 1961 to 1967 as a triple cultural crisis. Personally, I have always been convinced that I would have died one way or another if I had not joined the Basilians in 1951 at the age of seventeen. Ten years later I was ordained, and in the next six years my life as a Basilian grew, peaked, and disintegrated.

Later, I again became convinced that I would have died if I had not followed my path and left the Basilians when I did, in 1967, at the age of thirty-three. In those same years Vatican II, the council called by "the peasant pope" to "open windows" and concretize new forms and attitudes, flourished and then fizzled, especially after the death of John XXIII. In North America, the last of the heroes—the Kennedy boys, Malcolm X, and Martin Luther King—were assassinated and were succeeded by Vietnam, Watergate, Tricky Dick, and Ronnie Reagan.

Since 1967 my dominant attitude towards the Basilians has been one of gratitude. They did allow me to take advantage of various opportunities whereby I could discover and explore myself. At the same time I never understood why those same superiors were so unwilling to challenge those of my confreres who seemed interested only in hunkering down more securely in their various clerical country clubs. In more recent years, the Basilian Human Development Grants, the Reunions with Former Basilians, the range of acceptable living situations, fresh structures for formation, and the establishment of new foundations in Colombia all attest to an ongoing vitality in at least some sectors of the community.

These signs of recent life seem a long way from the systemic elitism of the priest-teacher ideology of the fifties and sixties, which treated those on the missions, in the parishes, or even those interested in pastoral concerns as second-stringers, has-beens, closet secularists, or enemies of community life. I'm still not clear how the metamorphosis from 1967 to 1995 occurred, because while I applaud the above features of the current scene, my memory can dig up few prototypes from its previous incarnation.

I do not feel I left the Basilians and the priesthood so much as I passed through them. At least for me, they were things I left behind like moulted skins from previous seasons. I did lose my faith and trust in the institutional Church, and that has been reinforced almost every time I witness the passionless sadism of most clerics when conducting what passes for acceptable weddings and funerals, let alone most regular Sunday parish liturgies. I still do believe in the Church as mystical body, but that has little to do with the regulatory manipulations of Roman Curialists.

By 1967 my faith in the dignity and value of each individual based on the radical uniqueness of their derivation was balanced more strongly than ever by my belief in the richness of a community based on diversity and communion. In many ways I did not leave Newman at all. I stopped using most of the formal religious language, but there have not been many days in the thirty-two intervening years when I have not wrestled with the movements of the Spirit and the impact of the powers of darkness both within myself and in those I encounter.

So many from Newman also chose to continue the journey through its Therafields phase that I probably did not experience the sense of loss and grief that was common for many others leaving the priesthood at that time. Therafields proved to be a liberating and enriching adventure until the late 1970s, when it too completed its natural life cycle and dissolved from within. Of course, therein doth lie another tale or two, but not for the telling today. This September of 1999 I return for my thirty-third year of teaching at York University. There too, in both my teaching and my administrative work, I have continued to hold to the same principles as at

TMS and Newman in terms of humanizing the learning atmosphere and blunting the brutality of yet another juggernaut system.

The July 10, 1994, issue of *The New York Times* had an article by Andrew Greeley on why apparently intelligent Catholics still remain associated with the Church despite its abysmal record of recent decades. His answer was embodied in the title, "Because of the Stories." Because of that article I married Mary Lou for the fourth time. The first time was in February 1974, when, by becoming involved, we were truly married. In mid-May of 1979 we went to Toronto's City Hall and were married for the second time. A week later, at Therafields Centre on Dupont Street, we invited over a hundred friends, including several former priests and nuns, to a full marriage ceremony that we had written and arranged ourselves. That was the third marriage.

By 1993 we had decided that we wanted to be buried from a Catholic Church, in the absence of an adequate substitute. Greeley's article provided me with a way to do it with some real integrity. We wanted that marriage to be without any fuss or fanfare, but we wanted it to happen in the sanctuary of St. Basil's because of the important personal events that had occurred in that space dating back to the 1860s. An old Basilian friend of mine, Father Bob Madden, helped us with the paperwork and officiated at that fourth marriage on the first Saturday in September, 1994. After meeting Tom Rosica in March, we have been attending Newman with some definite regularity. Life sure can do some strange spirals.

Afterword

Michael Quealey left the priesthood in 1967. He found other ways to live a life of engagement, service, witness, and commitment and ways to continue his quest for authenticity.

The three decades after 1967 were busy ones. Michael joined York University's faculty just after the events he describes in this memoir. He was in the process of finishing his doctorate in Canadian history and went to one of his mentors, John Saywell, for advice on pursuing a career in the academy. Saywell, in his late thirties at the time and already one of his generation's most prominent Canadian historians, had recently moved from the University of Toronto to York, and was York's first Dean of the Faculty of Arts and Science. Michael recalled that Saywell suggested he join the faculty of the new university, a small place that was growing and that would in Michael's time become the third-largest university in the country. And a new career began.

At York, Michael's appointment was a joint one, in both the Department of History and the Division of Humanities. He initially taught courses in Canadian history and in interdisciplinary general education in Humanities. As time went on, Michael moved his full appointment to Humanities, for he found that his wide interests and unusual training in both theology and history were better suited to the thematic courses offered there.

At the time he joined York, and for a number of years thereafter, most courses in Humanities were taught in team fashion, by groups of instructors who collaborated to design a course and share the lectures, each taking at least one small tutorial as well. In the first few decades, Michael taught with, among others, Ron Bloore, Eli Mandel, Arthur Haberman, William Whitla, Carole Carpenter and Jan Rehner.

For Michael, those were exciting times intellectually, for he and his colleagues met regularly, usually weekly, to discuss what was happening in the course, to critique one another's lectures in an open and collegial manner, to design assignments, and to tweak the syllabus. For him and others, it was an exercise in the joys of collaboration and the value of intellectual discourse.

In the 1970s Michael inaugurated a course in Humanities called "Modes of Fantasy," originally part of the first-year required general-education program. The title was an inside joke, the kind Michael liked. York had had a required course from its beginnings in the early '60s called "Modes of Reasoning," designed to introduce students to philosophy and logic. It ran into trouble immediately because it was not well taught, and students found it arcane and too embedded in disciplinary language and concerns. By the 1970s it was dropped as a required course. Michael decided that a new mode might work better.

It did work well and a "field" inside the Division of Humanities was born, one that prompted other instructors to join with Michael to offer a range of courses. After a few years, Michael moved out of "Modes," which became two courses, one at the first-year level and another at the second-year level entitled "Forms of Fantasy," and for some time he taught courses in the field at the third-year level ("Fantasy in the Modern World") and at the fourth-year ("Madness and Culture"). The fantasy courses, in their time, became some of the most popular ones in the Faculty of Arts. As well, Michael continued to work and teach in the field of Canadian culture.

Given his own history before coming to York, it was no surprise that Michael got engaged in many aspects of university life. He mentored a number of young faculty members, and was especially kind to and supportive of several part-time faculty members who were splendid teachers but unable to get full-time work because of the narrowing of the university job situation after 1972. In Humanities, he helped to build and shape the community of teachers and scholars and for a time was its Undergraduate Director.

Michael's engagement in the wider Toronto counterculture scene continued as well. He had begun his involvement in a new endeavour, a communal movement called Therafields, in 1964 or1965, even before he left the priesthood. Therafields, founded and guided by a charismatic lay therapist, Lea Hindley-Smith, was several things in one as it developed.

It was a communal living society, a counselling centre, and a psychiatric endeavour all at once.

A group of Catholic priests and lay people were attracted to Therafields as a way of exploring their own inner lives and growing within a defined community during the 1960s. Michael was among the leaders of this group. In the late 1960s Michael lived in Therafield communal houses on Admiral Road and Brunswick Avenue in the Annex, a neighbourhood close to the University of Toronto, where he had been involved as a priest in the Newman Centre and as a graduate student. He and others found Hindley-Smith, in his word, "brilliant." He stated: "Lea always said she was attempting to deliver people to themselves and she meant it" (Grant Goodbrand, *Therafields*, p. 61).

Later, writing a reflective essay about his life in 1999, Michael recalled seeing Therafields as a continuation of the quest that drew him to the priesthood.

> I carried forward into my "belief" or "faith" in Lea Hindley-Smith and her approach to delivering individuals to themselves by helping them to journey successfully inwards so as to deal with accumulated disturbances and to liberate the strengths and creativity of their uniqueness. By extension I believed fervently in Therafields as a collective or communal or community expression for our support of each other's struggles, as a mechanism for exploring wider and wider possibilities for psychoanalysis and for making it available to more and more of those who need it most, and as a tool for learning how to push forward to create and explore new forms of individuality and community. ("In This I Believe," p. 17)

The Catholic group, which came to include a number of former priests and nuns in addition to lay people, came to live together in houses owned by Therafields. They were one of several mini-communities in the movement and included students who often started as private clients of Hindley-Smith and members and associates of Hindley-Smith's family.

By the mid-1970s Therafields owned a number of houses in the Annex and several farms north of Toronto. It developed a number of projects that explored new types of therapy, organic farming, and the raising of grain-fed cattle; sponsored many cultural festivals of music, theatre, and dance; initiated several writing and publishing ventures; and even opened a private primary school for about thirty children. Therafields is judged to have been in its time, with 900 members and a variety of groups, among the largest communes, if not the largest, in North America, an important outgrowth of the counterculture movement of the 1960s, just as the Newman Centre was at the University of Toronto under Michael and Stan Kutz.

Michael worked tirelessly at Therafields for some years and engaged in therapy, organizing, and being part of the community. For a time, from the fall of 1967 to the end of 1968, he was second in command of the organization, described by his good friend Grant Goodbrand, also part of the Catholic group, as "effectively Lea Hindley-Smith's right-hand man" (p. 86).

Eventually, as Therafields grew, Michael and others began to wonder what it was they had joined. Hindley-Smith's marriage dissolved and she entered into a relationship with someone who was given authority despite his lack of skills. He was disliked by most of the community. Michael thought him pompous and empty. He said that he had been prepared "to give him a chance but there was nothing to this guy. There [was] no substance."

Conflicts began to arise, normal in any group, but the atmosphere changed. Michael never did like the idea of the farms, which he called "a fantasyland.... It was Lea's fantasy life about the quaint little village she always wanted" (p. 136). Eventually, about 1977, Michael and several friends in the community took action and directly opposed Hindley-Smith, her power over others, and the direction in which she had taken Therafields. In essence, Michael was no longer a member.

Reflecting on his work at Therafields, he stated that he believed in its goals so deeply that it took him a decade to realize that it "was but one more human endeavour that could and did become corrupted by power, self-delusion and nepotism" ("In This I Believe," p. 18).

Michael continued to do some counselling after leaving Therafields, not wanting to abandon those people he had been helping. Whether as a priest, counsellor, or professor, he was always ready to listen, though he was careful to keep a professional distance.

Michael may have left the priesthood, but he did not leave the Catholic community. He continued to be close to those who were part of his life before 1967, some of whom had left the priesthood also and others who remained. He made new friends, including Fr. Tom Rosica, C.S.B., who helped to draw Michael back to the Newman Centre after his retirement.

Every two years a number of former Basilians gathered for a long weekend on Strawberry Island, in Lake Simcoe, an hour north of Toronto, a
place used as a retreat by the Basilian Order. They were joined by friends
still active in the Church, and as many as seventy-five people attended
the reunion. The weekend would include a bonfire and songs, a visit by
the Superior General, some serious discussions, and much camaraderie.

As well, Michael attended mass on occasion, usually small masses
conducted in community, and sometimes took communion. He was by
temperament something of a heretic, though of the variety that thought
of itself as upholding the true values of the institution against which it was
thought to be rebelling, whether at York, in Therafields, or in the Church.

In 1974 Michael entered into a relationship with Mary Lou Dill, the
love of his life, who was also associated with Therafields. Mary Lou was
a former nun. A good friend described their getting together as a marriage made in heaven. Mary Lou had a young son, David, whom Michael
adopted and who took the name Quealey. In 1976 Michael and Mary
Lou purchased a house of their own on Brunswick Avenue, in the Annex.
After his retirement from York they moved in 2000 to Alliston, eighty-nine
kilometres north of Toronto, where they were close to family.

In his retirement Michael and Mary Lou were again drawn to the
Newman Centre at the University of Toronto, finding there a community where they could share their values and interests. Being sedentary
and isolated was not possible for Michael if life were to be richly lived.
Michael always believed in what he called "the miracle of friendship," a
commitment to others.

At his retirement party at York University a close friend and colleague
spoke about Michael and his contributions to York and said that Michael
was "the most oxymoronic man I know." He went on to describe Michael
as "sweetly stubborn, rigidly open-minded, obsessively free-ranging, dis-
ciplined in his unpredictability, and often rebellious in his loyalties."
Michael accepted the characterization; indeed he rather liked it, and
included it in a reflective essay he wrote in retirement ("In This I Believe,"
p. 21).

Michael was never exceptionally healthy, and in his later years had
many ailments and limitations. His life in Alliston grew quieter as the
years went on, though he was actively engaged with friends and family,
including his grandchildren, to the end. He died in September 2013, in
his eightieth year. The last words should be his, from his 1999 essay:

"I believe that 'valid belief' either in the supernatural or the natural, let alone in both, cannot be a 'fixed position.' From the nature of
its subject matter alone it must remain fluid, flexible and responsive to
change.... I believe that both for ourselves and others our goal should be
to live life with as much integrity as possible for as long as possible"("In
This I Believe," pp. 25, 29).

– *Arthur Haberman and Jan Rehner*

Works Cited

Goodbrand, Grant. *Therafields: The Rise and Fall of Lea Hindley-Smith's Psycho-
    analytic Commune.* Toronto: ECW Press, 2010.
Quealey, Michael. "In This I Believe." 17 March 1999. Unpublished document
    from the author's personal papers.

Appendices

Appendix I

Archdiocese of Toronto
Chancery Office

55 Gould Street
Toronto 2. Canada
Oct. 4, 1966

On Liturgical Aberrations

Reverend and dear Fathers:

With sincere gratitude I wish to acknowledge the sound leadership
and zeal of our Archdiocesan Liturgical Commission in guiding
and encouraging liturgical renewal in conformity with the norms of
Vatican Council II and the directives of the Consilium, the Canadian
Conference of Bishops and of the Ordinary.

To our clergy and people I also express my thanks for the vast
improvement that has taken place in communal participation. Many
of our priests have truly "become thoroughly penetrated with the spirit
and power of the liturgy, and become masters of it" (Constitution on
the Sacred Liturgy, n. 14). Certainly the majority of our pastoral clergy
are trying to fulfill the admonition of the Constitution "to promote with
zeal and patience the liturgical instruction of the faithful, and also their
active participation in the liturgy both internally and externally" (loc.
cit. n. 19).

Some have found it difficult to adapt to the spirit and the forms
so earnestly recommended by the Fathers of the Council and a few
through negligence or conviction have failed to provide any leadership
or enthusiasm in guiding their flocks along the path of renewal.

Their resistance is being encouraged by a smaller group of zealots
who in good faith, I believe, has undertaken unauthorized experiments

in liturgical change. The so-called traditionalists are inclined to identify these aberrations with authentic renewal, and so while rightfully opposing the deformation, feel justified in their hesitation [?] to undertake the liturgical formation of their people.

Number 22 of the Sacred Constitution on the Liturgy states three precepts which I draw to your attention:

(1) Regulation of the sacred liturgy depends solely on the authority of the Church, that is, on the Apostolic See and, as laws may determine, on the bishop.

(2) In virtue of power conceded by the law, the regulation of the liturgy within certain defined limits belongs also to various kinds of territorial bodies of bishops legitimately established.

(3) Therefore, no other person, not even a priest, may add, remove or change anything in the liturgy on his own authority.

It will be helpful for our priests to know that no authorization to experiment has been requested or given to any individual or group in the Archdiocese.

No fault should be found with those priests devoted to the youth apostolate who in order to engage young people in the liturgy gather them together occasionally in a Eucharistic celebration during which hymns with an appeal to youth are sung in a dignified manner to the accompaniment of guitars. I would, however, hope that every effort be made at these gatherings to influence the taste of our teenagers so that they will in time come to appreciate the better and more inspiring forms of artistic liturgical expression. The singing of these hymns at low Masses and the informal arrangement of the participants is not a violation of liturgical norms.

However, the omission of parts of the Mass and the addition of others, arbitrary tampering with the rubrics, and especially the recitation of the Canon in the vernacular are aberrations forbidden by the Vatican Council and by replies from the Consilium and cannot be tolerated.

What is legitimate for one is legitimate for all. Surely all priests of mature judgment can clearly see that unless the authority of the Church is recognized, if each priest is free to do as he pleases, liturgical chaos will result.

A Liturgical Commission is at present meeting in Rome. With the help of the most competent liturgists available to the Church, for the most part those responsible for the progress already made, the liturgy of the Eucharist and the Sacraments is again under study. With patience and filial loyalty let us await the guidance that will be forthcoming.

Finally, I wish to reaffirm my confidence in the loyalty of all our priests. Perhaps my own hopeful silence is in part responsible for the slowness of some and the undue haste of others. May this appeal for normalcy on the part of all be heeded so that we may move forward on the road to mature and authentic liturgical renewal.

Yours devotedly in the Lord,
[signature stamp] † Philip F. Pocock
Coadjutor Archbishop of Toronto

Will Superiors of houses kindly see to it that this letter is read by all priests and students in the house.

Appendix II

Université d'Ottawa
Avenue Laurier Est

University of Ottawa
Laurier Avenue East

March 20th, 1967

Dear Michael,

It was a great pleasure to receive you and your gang for a weekend in Orleans. I was amazed to see you arrive with such a numerous group. Of course, you could convince any number of kids to go with you for a weekend to the moon. It strikes me that our weekend was a big achievement. Who would have thought, two years ago, that a large delegation of the Christian Community from U of T would come to Ottawa and at the end of the encounter ... animate the FRENCH Mass. I liked very much each and everyone [*sic*] of your group. Please tell them that their visit left very good memories here.

The weekend was easy going, relaxed, with many highlights such as the Friday night discussion, the Saturday Mass, the kitchen ware orchestra, the Sunday Mass, the lunch at the Del Rio and many other moments. But more intensely important than all of this, for me, was the talk we had together at 4:30 upon your arrival.

I am gratefull [*sic*] that you have told me of your plans for the near future. I may not have measured in our few encounters of the past two years, the tensions imposed upon you by the lack of understanding from people who had given you a job to do without backing you up. Of course you were formulating a type of christianity [*sic*] that could attract the university generation while scandalysing [*sic*] the previous generation. But, believe me, what you have done in Toronto has been an inspiration for many of us. As I was watching you function in Toronto, it was always clear to me that you had very lucidly decided to stick your neck out for the pastoral approach you believed in, accepting all consequences in advance. However, I was amazed to see how peacefully you have reacted to the recent decisions of your bishop and general. In front of the recent fait accompli it was only logical that you waste no strength waging a war, but that you rather look for a job where you will really produce with a team who will not spend all its time watching if you toe the party line. These kids at York will be lucky to have you.

I, as a witness, appreciate the value of your new incarnation but deplore the loss of one of the best Newman Chaplains I have known. Will our Church need to see many hundreds of its priests decide that their road must be outside of the usual priestly functions, and will we suffer enough from that humiliation to discover that She must renew herself completely [*sic*]. Nothing here is written to influence you. I am sure that the Spirit is with you and that you are sincerely looking for your way to bring about the realm of Christ. I am only telling you that sharing your plans for the future is also sharing your ~~your~~ [*sic*] hope and your joy and also … the weight on your shoulders.

May the joy of Easter be fully yours,
[hand-written] Louis Raby

[hand-written postscript] Best regards to Father Kutz. Please write when you have time. I will be gratefull [*sic*] if we can keep contact.

The Post-Controversial Generation

F. Michael Quealey, C.S.B.
The Basilian Teacher, April 1967

There is now present on university campuses a new mutation of students. They are to be found chiefly in freshmen and sophomore classes and they manifest a new set of characteristics which identify them as distinct from any of their predecessors. The student activists of even two years ago are dismayed at this new mutation. Seniors and graduate students who until recently were in the vanguard of student movements for free speech, greater participation in university policy making, and some form of course control are now looking over their shoulders only to realize that the interests and commitments of younger students lie elsewhere. These older students are experiencing a process of aging, far more profound than any traditional freshman-senior gap. In this case, it is the seniors, not the freshman, who tend to feel alienated or out of touch with campus moods.

Given the present rate of cultural change some sociologists claim that someone turning thirteen this year must expect at least three major cultural changes before they are out of their teenage years. This means that a person can be obsolete by the time they are fifteen unless somehow they are equipped to handle such cultural adaptation. If they do achieve a certain personal stability and emotional maturity then there will be a continuity of growth manifested in various ways. It seems that such students are arriving on campuses in increasing numbers and are shaping new kinds of responses to the realities they find there. This does not apply necessarily to the majority of any one class but then the majorities, whether on campuses or in any other sector of our society, are not the primary determinants of cultural change. Rather, it is the creative minority who shape the direction of change. In this sense the university is probably an increasingly significant decision-making focus for our society. Yet even here the peer-group has become the strongest dynamic, largely because of the rigidity, irrelevance, or confusion on the part of various groups of elders.

Perhaps the most significant difference between the creative, committed students in freshman and senior years is their attitude towards institutions. In recent years the main thrust of student effort has been against the debilitating, depersonalizing impact of any and all institutions. This attitude bore strong resemblances to classical anarchism with its insistence on the unique dignity of each person, the dynamics of individual freedom and the need for various forms of participatory democracy and parallel communities. However, in reacting so strongly against existing structures student movements of the radical left tended to bog down in their own newly created structures. Such students often became doctrinaire, formalistic, and rigid as any of the most traditional institutions of Church or State.

The "post-controversial" generation, on the other hand, have a different attitude to structures and institutions. They have been disillusioned with marches, protests, and demonstrations, in general, yet they can, and do, involve themselves for specific movements both for and against a wide range of existing institutions. Their commitment, however, is always of an "ad hoc" nature. If and when a specific movement is generated to protest a specific injustice, when they feel there is a real hope for attainment of realistic goals by the judicious use of pressure, and when there are no long-term strings attached to their commitment they will assemble, work, and create with remarkable intensity and astuteness and then disperse. They are especially reluctant to assume executive positions in any organization as they seek for a self-identity rather than identification with any specific institution.

Even in "ad hoc" groupings they behave differently. They dislike being lumped into large groups and will not tolerate being talked at endlessly. They will acknowledge their own relative lack of experience but will respect and listen only to those of their elders who show signs of having understood and grown through their accumulated experience. They prefer to talk interminably in two's and three's. Perhaps all of this is because they are exposed, at least vicariously, to such varied experience or because the educational system really is working better these days. Whatever the specific causality, this generation has already worked through the old controversies about law and freedom, faith and science, conscience and authority. It is in this sense especially that they can be termed "post-controversial." They have achieved a far greater measure of peace than graduate students who may have come late to this kind of questioning and find themselves encumbered by more complicated defense mechanisms.

These younger students are also not as resentful of the absoluteness of standards previously dictated to them by parents or authority figures. They themselves quickly pass beyond externally imposed systems of any kind and accept the difficulty of working out a personal scale of values. At the same time, they can and do respect the value systems of others, whether of their peers or their elders, provided that such systems enable the individuals concerned to be free, vital, sensitive, and able to respond well.

So too in discussion groups or on experimental weekends, these students tend to be far more deeply respectful of other individuals. There is not nearly the same impatience or intolerance whereby a student passing through a phase of radicalism might protest vehemently his love for humanity, while ignoring the specific needs and stages of development or regression in his fellow students and associates.

Culturally these new mutants are increasingly transnational. While accepting and enjoying the specific cultural tradition in which they have been raised, they proceed to develop multiple cultural identities. This process is accelerated on campuses located in metropolitan centers possessing multiple cultural diversity. Such centers tend to have far more in common with ocher cosmopolitan centers around the world than with other urban, let alone rural, areas within their same nation.

While the signs of this process may be seen in everything from their eating habits to their political concepts, it is perhaps best reflected in their music. The songs of the freedom marches are simply not being sung now by these younger students. Rather they are responding to everything from Turkish army songs and South African chants to classical Indian melodies. Within the area of contemporary folk music itself, they are listening to those singers who are talking about social problems in sophisticated satirical terms. The relevance of the individual rather than the group seems paramount. Even Vietnam as an issue in music or discussion is seen not so much as something taking place in Asia as it is triggering something deep in each person. Hence it is the roots of violence, war, and the breakdown of civilization within the individual person which are the main focus in their concern for Vietnam. When they sing together in groups there is more spontaneity and individual performing than previously. The current popularity of the jug-band music is perhaps the best sign of their new mood.

For several years now university students have been avoiding social or academic functions that have any exclusively denominational character. They accept the validity of a religious viewpoint, but only in an open forum where there is a genuine encounter with other convictions. Their search for a deeper relevance for their own faith is not predetermined but genuinely open-ended. They have enough confidence in their own convictions that they want to share them and yet remain open to the possible viability of alternate positions. As far as liturgy is concerned, their attendance is more sporadic and selective, yet apparently more sincere. They do want to celebrate their experience of community and they are more likely to criticize specific forms of worship as irrelevant for their needs rather than reject wholesale the possibility of genuine participation in this area.

The so called "crisis of faith" which has always affected large numbers of university students is not taking on new tones. Students tend to feel that they are passing through, rather than losing, that faith inculcated in them from their earliest years. Most of them want to retain some real link with the institutional Church, if at all possible. They often sense rather acutely, however, that there is an increasing gap between the institutional Church and the real life of the Church. They feel that their needs are being neglected by bishops whose primary concern is with regular big-city parishes, rather than the specific demands of any Christian presence on a campus.

These new mutants are remarkably tolerant of the difficulties faced by any bishops today. Even so in most cases they are no longer joining religious communities or the priesthood because they feel there are far better ways to be Christian today than get involved unnecessarily with mounds of irrelevant paraphernalia. They feel a kind of confidence in their understanding of Christ's basic message of a healing and liberating service. If there is no room for them to give and share their talents, energy, sensitivity, and creativity within the framework of the existing institution, then they feel free and able to live their lives more abundantly outside the context of any recognizable Church. Increasing numbers of these students are moving in such a direction. This process should be understood not so much as an opting out of the Church, as an opting for a fuller, more relevant, and hence truly Christian life.

Appendix IV

✣

Quo Vadimus?

The following meanderings might be termed "a view from below." As such, they are intended as a series of reflections and queries by a young Basilian finishing his formal training and about to return to the educational apostolate of our community. Despite the fervent phrasing of some of these reflections, I must admit at the outset that many of them have been only partially tested by experience. They are intended more as stimuli to further discussion than as concrete solutions. Some, in fact, are simply gropings into the magnetic unknown where there must lie at least some of the solutions to some of the problems now confronting not only the young Basilian educator but also the entire community's commitment to this form of the apostolate.

Just how apostolic is our present apostolate to Christian education? I feel that this is as good a starting place as any to add my chips to the existing pile of reflections on that rather amorphous animal, "the priest-religious-teacher." There have already been a great deal of "fuss and feathers" raised over this point and it is questionable how much is to be gained by stimulating frayed nervous systems. As far as younger Basilians are concerned, this has been a problem of serious discussion for well over a decade now. In 1954 the scholastics presented a strong appeal to our General Chapter for positive encouragement and direction from older and more competent confreres so as to investigate the possibilities or realities of a so-called "Basilian philosophy and theology of education." Both then and since, juridical nods of approval have been registered, but, for various reasons, little, if anything, has been realized along these lines. As a result the problem has germinated in many directions. Private conversations, letters to chapters, local theological conferences, and even articles in this periodical testify to its persistent recurrence as a spur or prod in our community consciousness....

If there is a built-in conflict in the vocation of the "priest-religious-teacher," and I believe there is, then it is not so much between the demands of scholarship and the structure of regular religious existence as it is between the nature of the priesthood and our commitment to the classroom. Even this "conflict," however, arises not from the tension of irreconcilables but from the dynamism of complementary stimuli. The intellectual life, as well as the primary ends of the religious life, are basically self-centered. Priests, on the other hand, are selected from among men and ordained for others, not for themselves. The priesthood is not an extra graduate degree or a special academic gown which qualifies an already recognized scientist, teacher, or scholar as a super-educator or a super-intellectual. Rather, it involves a modal change in one's existence which gives new relevance to all of our existing activities. Because of this, the "priest-teacher" is committed to a built-in conflict which amounts to the challenge of reconciling, harmonizing, and balancing the horizontal and vertical lines of personal salvation and co-redemptive activity.

The working out of this "conflict" is a deeply personal problem and is studded with many dangers. Some religious, for instance, abandoning the adventure of a scholarly-religious existence will choose to neglect regular religious exercises on the grounds of the demands of their teaching apostolate. So too, others will deviate from the challenge by using their religious commitment as an excusing cause for poor scholarship and careless teaching. By the same token, the priest-educator may use his classroom merely as a time-filler or as a contact point for outside counselling and fringe benefits. On the other hand, a priest's pedagogy or personal scholarship may so absorb and delude him that he will become unapproachable to students seeking the solace and strength of his priesthood. All of these positions, while common enough, are really extremes, deviations, and abnegations of a responsible commitment to the role of the priest-religious-educator.

Historically speaking, the experience of the Church as well as of our own community manifests a justifiable commitment of ordained priests to the continuance of Christ's redemptive activity in the realms of education and scholarship. At the same time history has also witnessed a considerable evolution in the priestly apostolate. The criterion has always been the needs of the Church and over the years almost every conceivable activity consonant with those needs has been entered into by priests and sanctioned by the Church. The end is always "instaurare omnia in Christo," but to that end priests, over the centuries, have not only performed at the altar but have also gone into dungeons, council chambers, hospitals, classrooms, and factories.

In a society in which change seems the only constant, we fail at times to realize that it is the speed of that change which has become so bewildering rather than what is changing. The tendency is to become so absorbed in reacting to existing problems that we cease to find solutions or invent, plan, and shape our future. Again, historically speaking, the Basilians, as a religious community of priest-teachers, were founded in the adverse atmosphere of the French Revolution in response to the need to train and educate priests. Many subsequent Basilian foundations were responses to the real needs of particular periods, areas, and peoples. The Church has learned from bitter experience that such responses must be both timely and appropriate. The Church has also learned that its commitment to any one response whether it be political involvement, great landed estates, or established education institutions must be terminated when the need ceases or shifts. Otherwise, a genuine anti-clericalism may be the legitimate response to a very real clericalism.

Drawing then on the Church's experience, on our own neglected Basilian "spirit" (i.e., as opposed to "customs"), and on my own somewhat chaotic imagination I would like to present the following reflections for consideration or disposal. As a community, we are now experiencing a breathing spell, a period of much-needed consolidation. This should also be a period of concerted, cooperative, intensive analysis of our roots, our meaning, and our mission. Contemporary sociological analysts are unanimous on the panoramic possibilities of the age we are just entering. Our problem is how we as Basilians, as priest-religious-educators, can best fulfill our apostolate amidst these shifting perspectives. Will we rest on the laurels of previous generations of Basilians or will we have the courage to discard the paraphernalia and proceed with the mission of Christian education according to the present mind and the present needs of the Church?

The decisions which Basilians took only a few decades ago were often taken with courage and in response to real needs. Today those very decisions are often subjected to rather intensive criticism not so much because of their original appropriateness but because of the uneasiness engendered by their continued application. Are we not now facing new needs which demand new instruments, new inventions, new improvisations? Criticism in itself, however, is not enough. What can we propose as replacements for established, even though increasingly uncertain, prototypes and institutions.

Assuming that God's plan calls for the Basilians to remain, grow, and flourish, then a later historian of our community may well look back on the stage we are now passing through and consider it as a providential hiatus following upon a period expansion which was characterized by compulsive duplication. Such an historian may see the early 1960s as a period when we consolidated our strength, intensified our training program, examined the meaning of our existence, and prepared for a distinctively new period of expansion. Those same early sixties might then be seen as years characterized by an experimental probing of the spiritual market so as to discover where our precious resources of "priest-religious-teachers" could best be invested. If the above hypothesis has any validity at all, is it not possible to speculate as to which directions might be taken by such investments?

An evolving religious community must always be concerned about "spreading itself too thin." Yet, in many cases is this not a fear more than a danger? Granted that such thinking has providentially becalmed us long enough to permit some overdue reflection, but just what do we mean by "too thin"? Are our present attempts to "beef up" the staffs of our existing institutions being motivated primarily by financial considerations, and if so is this not a tragic waste of the talents and training of our priest-teachers? What of our entire hypothesis of a school staffed almost entirely by priest-religious-teachers? Is this merely a hangover from a period when the Church found it necessary to establish entire school systems so as to preserve the faith? In that same period clerics and religious were the only ones capable of pioneering such inventions but do those same contingencies still dominate the situation? Is not the danger that in many areas such institutions have long ceased to be "inventions" and have tended rather to become vested interests?

The present educational apostolate is disturbed by two further factors. In the first place, we are witnessing, for the first time on this continent, a surge of Catholic lay educators on all levels of learning. Once before in history, during the Renaissance, qualified Catholic laymen were prepared to assume the burdens of Christian education. Unfortunately, the universities then were controlled not by the Church but by clerics. As a result those laymen set up their own universities and the [*illegible*] have been trying to catch up ever since. Secondly, a factor which has been blissfully assumed, and then almost completely neglected, has been the tremendous fund of good-will and cooperation generated by North American pluralism. It would seem that the Church in general, and the religious communities in particular, have scarcely begun to exploit the freedom engendered by our lack of state interference. With these factors in mind, it might be high time for us to pull our priest-teachers out of the classrooms, or at least out of certain classrooms.

We come now to a ticklish problem. Despite the occasional hassle it now seems a community-wide consensus that a priest appointed to teach mathematics, French, history, physical training, classics, science, manual training, or literature is truly exercising his priesthood in so far as he teaches his subject matter to the best of his ability. Incidentally, it should be noted that I am taking for granted here, as elsewhere, that our priest-religious-teachers are properly qualified and trained in their subject matter and in their pedagogical techniques. Constant insistence and sheer necessity have inspired personal and group movements which indicate that we are well along to the solution of that preliminary problem of the priest-religious-teacher. Rather, the danger has become, in at least some of our schools, that our academic standards are all too readily accepted by our secular counterparts. This can lead to a dangerous complacency. Such a school, or a religious community made up of such schools, filled with good-living, hard-working, scholarly priest-religious-teachers, could be guilty of a terrible squandering of their real resources.

I am not disputing the fact that a priest can and does exercise his priesthood regardless of the subject matter he is teaching. There have been more than enough apologias, and even rationalizations, for such a commitment. What I am challenging is whether or not, today, in view of the needs of the Church and society for priest-religious-teachers, our men are being properly marshalled and committed at the really decisive points of action.

Traditionally, for example, we have adopted the format of a single well-staffed secondary school as the best means of performing our service to a particular area. There was a time when such a gesture would satisfy the needs of a given community for Christian secondary education. Today, such a gesture is an acceptance of futility. Even worse, have we not, perhaps unintentionally, turned many such schools into intellectual ghettoes? By running that one school as well and as traditionally as possible are we thereby absolving ourselves of any responsibility to the remainder of those same truthless, priestless, Christless areas? Can we afford to concentrate 15, 20, or 30 priest-teachers in a single school catering to a very small segment of a population clamouring for Catholic education? Are we justified in perpetuating such a system, once appropriate and realistic but now tragically archaic, on the grounds that we must accept the inevitable and be content with educating only the best, or only the wealthiest? What could or might be done? How could the talents, training, and energies of our priest-teachers be *better* spent in the apostolate of Christian education?

I recently met a Catholic layman who is principal of a large public secondary school here in Ontario. This principal had over 600 Catholic students in his school. He was quite aware of a law allowing for one hour a week of religious instruction in public schools according to the faith of the individual student. Despite such a law, this layman had to take the initiative and repeatedly and vigorously request the cooperation of local priests to help him implement even a simple program of religious instruction for his Catholic students. After three and a half years a priest finally entered that school for the first time. In the many Ontario centers in which we now maintain schools are there not neighbouring collegiate, commercial, technical, and district high schools in which sizeable proportions of the student bodies are Catholic? Are not these same Catholic students being bypassed and could not the same law indicated above be utilized to ensure their continued instruction in the faith?

Is it merely a dream to envisage a house or hostel of, say, a dozen wandering priest-teachers? These men would lead a community life as Basilians yet each one would go out each day to various collegiates or public schools. In such an arrangement, each priest-teacher would be responsible for the entire religious instruction of the Catholics in one or two such schools. Even though it meant only seeing various classes for one hour a week it would seem with the various pedagogical aids now available and his own background as a Basilian that such a priest-teacher could provide a highly respectable course in high school theology. By performing such a task this priest-teacher would also be helping literally hundreds of

Catholic students gain a deeper understanding and appreciation of their faith. This not an "extra." This is a real need. These are the very Catholic students who outnumber those in our contentedly complacent classrooms by as much as four to one. These are the same Catholic students who succumb so quickly to the secularist tendencies of our society. These are the same Catholic students of whom an almost insignificant fraction attend parochial instruction classes. These are the same Catholic students who lose all contact with the Church and who, despite their numbers and because of the Church's apparent lack of concern for their welfare, are simply not rushing to fill the ranks of the lay apostolate let alone entering the seminaries and convents. To perform such a task is doubtless more complicated than I have indicated. On the other hand, it simply cannot be denied that this is a very real, concrete, immediate, and neglected need of the Catholics in our present society. Both our theological background and our training as educators would appear to have admirably equipped Basilians for such a challenge.

The problem of Catholic youth in non-Catholic institutions is only one direction which could be explored for a more sensible commitment of the abilities and energies of our priest-teachers. Let us examine for a moment our present structure of secondary education. Assuming that a locker-room atmosphere and attitude have not permeated the classrooms and the business of learning, even so, have we begun to exploit our resources and facilities? Another glaring need of our society is for adult education programs, and more specifically, for practical courses in theology for ordinary laymen.

Many will shudder at such a prospect and cries of inadequacy may be heard on the speculative level and sighs of exhaustion on the practical level by already over-burdened priest-teachers. Well, on the speculative level, all Basilians now filling the ranks of our houses have been exposed to an increasingly refined theological training. Granted, they are not likely to provide any stunning commentaries, but the extent and depth of their theological understanding after four years of varying degrees of exposure is often underestimated both by themselves and by others. Besides, Catholic professional men and lay apostles, despite their craving for something beyond the normal Sunday sermon, are, at the same time, amazingly illiterate when it comes to an understanding of their faith. They are now admitting their need for guidance and instruction if they are to render meaningful their own co-creative activity. For us to feign incompetency when faced with such an obvious need is both false modestly and a rejection of our mandate as "priest-teachers."

The argument of lack of time and energy is far more pervasive and compelling. Here the problem hardens to individual situations. Yet, is it a question so much of lack of time and energy as that our time and energy are often being expended on activities not ideally suited to our apostolate as priest-teachers? It is all too obvious that if an individual priest-teacher is willing to take on, say, one or two night classes of lay theology, then he cannot continue to teach mathematics for six or seven periods during the day, coach a team after school, and then help set up for a school dance in the gym. Something has to give. Again, I insist that a priest-teacher can be exercising his priesthood in each of the above activities. On the comparative basis, however, once the needs of society for his abilities have been assessed it would seem there is little choice between whether a priest-teacher spends his evenings teaching a course in lay theology or preparing equipment for the next day's hockey or baseball practice.

One of the most promising indications that Providence is steering the Church into a dynamic renaissance of redemptive activity has been the emergence on the intellectual level of enthusiastic, scriptural, liturgical, and theological studies and the appearance on the practical level of energetic, competent Catholic laymen. For us, as Basilians, to reject the implications of these phenomena would be rather ridiculous if not pathetically clericalist. With the emergence of competent, dedicated Catholic lay scholars and educators we are being given the opportunity to "disengage," if necessary, from many of our present activities so as to devote ourselves to new, more pressing demands to which a priest-teacher is more peculiarly suited. Aside from that omni-present bug-bear of finances, is there any reason why the dedicated Catholic lay teacher, who is such a refreshing creation of this generation, is there any reason why he could not, and indeed *should* not, take over an increasing proportion of the teaching load, the coaching load, the disciplinary load, yes, even the administrative load so that we can be freed for [*illegible*] dedication to the even more demanding functions of a modern priest-teacher?

I have mentioned the possibility of each of our schools conducting evening classes in theology for laymen. From here it is only a step to the point where we can use our existing facilities for instruction classes for those interested in the faith, for workshops and public panels on current sociological problems, for study groups and classes geared to a deeper

understanding of the arts and their meaning for Christian life and worship, and for social action groups in which as priest-teachers we could
cooperate in the formation and training of effective lay apostles. Another
area which we have barely begun to exploit as priest-teachers is the use
of mass media. The personnel of TV stations, for example, are being
subjected to increasing pressure for more public service programming.
They are literally begging for our cooperation and assistance. Publication
is still another area virtually foreign to our experience yet which holds
almost limitless vistas.

I have concentrated thus far on our high schools because that is the
area in which we are most deeply committed as a teaching community.
This is not to say that the same principles are not applicable to all levels
of Christian education. On certain levels, for example, it might be demon-
strated that the talents of some of our members, as priest-teachers, could
best serve the Church's needs by an involvement in "Boys Towns," or in
rehabilitation centers, or in course and counselling work in reformatories.

On a different level these same principles might determine a radical
shift in our approach to higher education. How, for instance, should we
react to the challenge to our teaching apostolate being posed by those
gigantic state colleges and universities where literally thousands of Catholic students are not being serviced? Our commitment on such a level
might take the form of an exploitation of the Newman Club framework
accompanied by stringent measures to ensure a theologically oriented
atmosphere while at the same time using and not being dominated by
the social fluff. Even in our exiting colleges and universities it would seem
that a meaningless duplication of specialists could be obviated by greater
recourse to the interchange of professors on a term to term basis. The
establishment of genuine graduate schools of philosophy and theology
would also appear as a much more realistic commitment for our man-
power than the mere mimicking of secular liberal arts colleges.

The ramifications of these same principles are magnificently manifold.
For instance, the financial involvement and appendages of many of the
above approaches would be relatively minor. To embrace these types of
activity would also enable capable Basilians to move into areas of need, to
establish centers, to train others to take them over, and then to move on
to new areas of the apostolate to be found in the eagerness with which a
religious community or individual Christian founds, builds, trains, and
then moves on and on to new areas of need? Whether he was establishing

a parish or making tents, Paul never seems to have settled very long in any one place. Are the proximate or remote needs of our society, either at home or abroad, any the less real or demanding? Or, are we more interested in carving out our own little kingdoms than in working for the realization of His?

In at least certain areas of the community there is a rising concern over many aspects of the above problems. There is alarm at our complacent contentment at the state of our cozy cocoons. Some confreres fear that in the coming months and years we are liable to immerse ourselves in the time-consuming task of dividing the spoils into provinces or in quibbling over the jots and tittles of our constitutions and rules. If so, then we may well confuse activity with action, may miss entirely the real problems and opportunities, and may well lose what little there still remains of that spirit of adventurous realism which supposedly characterized our founding fathers. In the present context, however, the basic question which each of us, and which the community as a whole, must answer is, are our existing commitments and activities appropriate to our apostolic mandate as priest-teachers, are their greater needs for our apostolate in other directions, and, if so, how quickly can the switch be made?

Simply because we profess to be "priest-teachers" we should be driven out of some classrooms and driven into others. Such a re-channelling of our energies would not only satisfy the real needs of our society for priest-teachers, and provide the proper encouragement for qualified laymen to fill the positions we have thus far *had* to fill, but it would also provide several "kick-backs" as far as we as a religious community of priests are concerned. By imbibing the enthusiasm which first instituted the Basilians, by applying a true Basilian sensitivity to the needs of apostolate as priest-teachers, and by adapting, disengaging, inventing, and exploring as did our founders and those great Basilians of the 1850s and 1920s, then we might even achieve a dynamic maturity and a purposeful existence which could go a long way towards healing fratricidal conflict and petty particularism.

More specifically, if, as priest-teachers, we were prepared to implement practical courses in lay theology, then theology as such would cease to be relegated to seminary professors or to a frantic night of cramming before junior clergy exams. The challenging possibilities of such a re-evaluation might also give new verve and meaning to the existence of an individual priest-teacher who, despite his dedication and knowledge, is simply running out of steam after ten or fifteen years of grinding out six or seven classes a day on subject matter which is essentially secular. This new focus might also alleviate the dangers of boredom. It is not difficult to find interesting things to do either within ourselves or outside the community. In this context it should be noted that even our so-called teaching or so-called scholarship can easily become mere escapes from our real commitment to the Church's apostolate as priest-teachers. The stimulus of such new vistas might also shift the emphasis of common life from "recreation in common" to "Christian education in common" or "redemption in common." Perhaps, even our normal conversation might become less sweat-soaked and more meaningfully and eternally relevant.

The greatest objection to any of the foregoing reflections will doubt-less be on the question of finances. I cannot help but feel that the entire financial question is largely a straw man of our own contrivance. Granted that the implementation of many of the above suggestions would involve additional expenditure, or rather a reduction in our present capital invest-ments. Granted too that the serious integration of Catholic laymen into our work will skyrocket costs if we even attempt to approximate the salary scales of comparable secular institutions. Even here, however, if we are really intent on the apostolate of Christian education, then we should not be satisfied with merely aping the slow adjustment of our society as to the proper financial status of its educators. If Catholic institutions were truly "Catholic," or even more so truly "Christian," then it would seem that their wages would be sufficient to attract the finest minds and teachers to join us in this form of the apostolate. It is rather a sad situation if a Catholic school is known for the smartness of its athletic equipment or the elaborateness of its dance decorations rather than high salaries paid to competent laymen.

All this is very nice, you may say, but where is the money going to come from? In North America we are living in the midst of a society in which there is no shortage of money. If we are not receiving sufficient financial support, could it be because we are no longer satisfying the real needs of that society? Are not many people reluctant to dispose of funds in areas where they presently have no confidence that such funds will be well used? Suppose we were to appeal for financial support to enable us to hire more first-class Catholic laymen so as to free our priest-teachers to conduct courses in theology or to take convert classes? Would we not be much better received that if these same people were to receive the impression that their money was being earmarked for a fancier staff residence or another set of golf clubs?

There is still another indication of a static, unimaginative approach to the financial side of the apostolate of Christian education. That is our almost blind adherence to traditional structures of education which commit our energies during crucial years to the establishment, maintenance, and expansion of huge physical plants. Not only does this create a juicy vested interest which must be maintained regardless of its shifting value but, more important, it deprives a religious community of its fantastic freedom of movement, flexibility, and adaptability. Once there has been a heavy expenditure of money, time, and personnel on a particular institution, we tend to canonize its work as traditional and, lacking the courage to disengage when we are no longer *needed*, we perpetuate and perpetrate one more vestige of genuine clericalism.

How many of our institutions have simply become big businesses mesmerized by an aura of sanctimonious, yet amazingly non-productive, scholarship? How many of our most valuable priest-teachers are now kept "busy" as executives or administrators of institutions which we have established, and established well, mind you, yet which we should now pass on to other hands so as to free us for new needs? Then too, while granting the existence of our present institutions and their current expenditures, even so, it is difficult to see how running raffles, commercializing athletics, or following the cocktail trail can be anything but bizarre when compared with the needs of our society for the unique services of priest-teachers. Finally, are we not succumbing to the very secularism and materialism we have sworn to fight if we consider new buildings, balanced budgets, championships, or even scholarships as the basic barometers of our apostolate as priest-teachers? Are we not simply counting the cost and thereby being found wanting?

If we could only come to a much deeper appreciation of our function in the Church as priest-teachers then perhaps we would appreciate much more the question of vocations. Is not much of our present concern over vocations simply because we are worried that perhaps not enough capable young men are coming along to fill the gaps or to continue our present commitments? Strangely enough, scarcely anyone seems to ask the logical question of whether or not such present commitments are worth continuing. How many sacred cows are being supported by Basilians?

There is no lack of generosity in today's youth and if we are not attracting enough of them, or the best of them, then it may be because they do not see anything in many of our present commitments to which they could dedicate their lives.

Imaginative growth has always provided a far greater attraction and stimulant than mere preservation at any costs. There are dangerous liabilities from being committed to one very particular form or expression of the apostolate of Christian education. For example, instead of utilizing to the full the entire spectrum of personalities and talents within a religious community, you are liable to push, bend, or break someone in your frantic efforts to perpetuate the archaic. Here again, the very lack of change or interest in certain phases of our existing apostolate may be one more indication that disengagement should be seriously considered and new avenues of employment sought.

If the demands of perpetuating existing institutions, regardless of their continued worth, can blind us to the very real needs for priest-teachers in our own localities, then all the more understandable, if terribly tragic, is our prevailing reluctance to become seriously engaged as priest-teachers in mission areas. Historians of the next century may look back on the 1960s and marvel. They will see our decade as the period when the Pope himself issued a clarion call for labourers to work in the unharvested mission fields of South America, Africa, and Asia. In view of such a clear designation of the mind of the Church as to the areas of greatest need, those same historians may marvel that there was so little response. They may point to North America where those supposedly loyal sons and daughters of Her religious communities busied themselves with their "Commitments" and were content with contributing mere pittances as their "gestures" towards spreading him to "the uttermost parts of the world."

Why did the Peace Corps have to be a secular phenomenon and, even so, how quickly, or how well, have Catholic institutions followed its inspiration? How many Tom Dooleys have been produced or encouraged by our schools and colleges? All witnesses testify to the hardships, toil, and abundant fruit of work in these areas. If technicians, lay apostles, and missionaries of all shapes and sizes are so clearly needed, then what could not even a handful of priest-teachers accomplish along the lines of the apostolate of Christian education? In many ways Basilians would seem to be ideally qualified for a heavy involvement in this area.

The critics of such a commitment, and incidentally of the Church's clear call to such a commitment, demolish the hopes and desires of young men and young religious by branding it all as mere romanticism. Well, there is something deeply romantic in all of us, and the problem is rather where we will focus that romance. Will it be selfishly turned in upon ourselves, will it desperately seek a relevance in non-community activities, or will it find its meaning in a constantly rejuvenated Basilianness? Perhaps again, we, like other religious communities, have obscured, obstructed, or even lost our apostolic flavour? Perhaps young men are scanning our ranks for the impetuous Peters and the ubiquitous Pauls and finding neither are going elsewhere to make their commitments and swear their allegiances.

In the sixteenth and seventeenth centuries certain European religious communities refused the challenge of the New World. Instead they stayed at home and minded their institutions. They gradually dwindled and died. Those that answered the challenge flourished both at home and abroad. Not since those centuries has there been a similar race against time nor such a clear command from the Holy See as to the most important areas of the apostolate. Will we, as priest-teachers, be on these boats or will we be "too busy?"

November 1963

Books in the Life Writing Series
Published by Wilfrid Laurier University Press

Haven't Any News: Ruby's Letters from the Fifties edited by Edna Staebler with an Afterword by Marlene Kadar • 1995 / x + 165 pp. / ISBN 0-88920-248-6

"I Want to Join Your Club": Letters from Rural Children, 1900–1920 edited by Norah L. Lewis with a Preface by Neil Sutherland • 1996 / xii + 250 pp. (30 b&w photos) / ISBN 0-88920-260-5

And Peace Never Came by Elisabeth M. Raab with Historical Notes by Marlene Kadar • 1996 / x + 196 pp. (12 b&w photos, map) / ISBN 0-88920-281-8

Dear Editor and Friends: Letters from Rural Women of the North-West, 1900–1920 edited by Norah L. Lewis • 1998 / xvi + 166 pp. (20 b&w photos) / ISBN 0-88920-287-7

The Surprise of My Life: An Autobiography by Claire Drainie Taylor with a Foreword by Marlene Kadar • 1998 / xii + 268 pp. (8 colour photos and 92 b&w photos) / ISBN 0-88920-302-4

Memoirs from Away: A New Found Land Girlhood by Helen M. Buss / Margaret Clarke • 1998 / xvi + 153 pp. / ISBN 0-88920-350-4

The Life and Letters of Annie Leake Tuttle: Working for the Best by Marilyn Färdig Whiteley • 1999 / xviii + 150 pp. / ISBN 0-88920-330-x

Marian Engel's Notebooks: "Ah, mon cahier, écoute" edited by Christl Verduyn • 1999 / viii + 576 pp. / ISBN 0-88920-333-4 cloth / ISBN 0-88920-349-0 paper

Be Good Sweet Maid: The Trials of Dorothy Joudrie by Audrey Andrews • 1999 / vi + 276 pp. / ISBN 0-88920-334-2

Working in Women's Archives: Researching Women's Private Literature and Archival Documents edited by Helen M. Buss and Marlene Kadar • 2001 / vi + 120 pp. / ISBN 0-88920-341-5

Repossessing the World: Reading Memoirs by Contemporary Women by Helen M. Buss • 2002 / xxvi + 206 pp. / ISBN 0-88920-408-x cloth / ISBN 0-88920-410-1 paper

Chasing the Comet: A Scottish-Canadian Life by Patricia Koretchuk • 2002 / xx + 244 pp. / ISBN 0-88920-407-1

The Queen of Peace Room by Magie Dominic • 2002 / xii + 115 pp. / ISBN 0-88920-417-9

China Diary: The Life of Mary Austin Endicott by Shirley Jane Endicott • 2002 / xvi + 251 pp. / ISBN 0-88920-412-8

The Curtain: Witness and Memory in Wartime Holland by Henry G. Schogt • 2003 / xii + 132 pp. / ISBN 0-88920-396-2

Teaching Places by Audrey J. Whitson • 2003 / xiii + 178 pp. / ISBN 0-88920-425-x

Through the Hitler Line by Laurence F. Wilmot, M.C. • 2003 / xvi + 152 pp. / ISBN 0-88920-448-9

Where I Come From by Vijay Agnew • 2003 / xiv + 298 pp. / ISBN 0-88920-414-4

The Water Lily Pond by Han Z. Li • 2004 / x + 254 pp. / ISBN 0-88920-431-4

The Life Writings of Mary Baker McQuesten: Victorian Matriarch edited by Mary J. Anderson • 2004 / xxii + 338 pp. / ISBN 0-88920-437-3

Seven Eggs Today: The Diaries of Mary Armstrong, 1859 and 1869 edited by Jackson W. Armstrong • 2004 / xvi + 228 pp. / ISBN 0-88920-440-3

Love and War in London: A Woman's Diary 1939–1942 by Olivia Cockett; edited by Robert W. Malcolmson • 2005 / xvi + 208 pp. / ISBN 0-88920-458-6

Incorrigible by Velma Demerson • 2004 / vi + 178 pp. / ISBN 0-88920-444-6

Auto/biography in Canada: Critical Directions edited by Julie Rak • 2005 / viii + 264 pp. / ISBN 0-88920-478-0

Tracing the Autobiographical edited by Marlene Kadar, Linda Warley, Jeanne Perreault, and Susanna Egan • 2005 / viii + 280 pp. / ISBN 0-88920-476-4

Must Write: Edna Staebler's Diaries edited by Christl Verduyn • 2005 / viii + 304 pp. / ISBN 0-88920-481-0

Pursuing Giraffe: A 1950s Adventure by Anne Innis Dagg • 2006 / xvi + 284 pp. (photos, 2 maps) / 978-0-88920-463-8

Food That Really Schmecks by Edna Staebler • 2007 / xxiv + 334 pp. / ISBN 978-0-88920-521-5

163256: A Memoir of Resistance by Michael Englishman • 2007 / xvi + 112 pp. (14 b&w photos) / ISBN 978-1-55458-009-5

The Wartime Letters of Leslie and Cecil Frost, 1915–1919 edited by R.B. Fleming • 2007 / xxxvi + 384 pp. (49 b&w photos, 5 maps) / ISBN 978-1-55458-000-2

Johanna Krause Twice Persecuted: Surviving in Nazi Germany and Communist East Germany by Carolyn Gammon and Christiane Hemker • 2007 / x + 170 pp. (58 b&w photos, 2 maps) / ISBN 978-1-55458-006-4

Watermelon Syrup: A Novel by Annie Jacobsen with Jane Finlay-Young and Di Brandt • 2007 / x + 268 pp. / ISBN 978-1-55458-005-7

Broad Is the Way: Stories from Mayerthorpe by Margaret Norquay • 2008 / x + 106 pp. (6 b&w photos) / ISBN 978-1-55458-020-0

Becoming My Mother's Daughter: A Story of Survival and Renewal by Erika Gottlieb • 2008 / x + 178 pp. (36 b&w illus., 17 colour) / ISBN 978-1-55458-030-9

Leaving Fundamentalism: Personal Stories edited by G. Elijah Dann • 2008 / xii + 234 pp. / ISBN 978-1-55458-026-2

Bearing Witness: Living with Ovarian Cancer edited by Kathryn Carter and Lauri Elit • 2009 / viii + 94 pp. / ISBN 978-1-55458-055-2

Dead Woman Pickney: A Memoir of Childhood in Jamaica by Yvonne Shorter Brown • 2010 / viii + 202 pp. / ISBN 978-1-55458-189-4

I Have a Story to Tell You by Seemah C. Berson • 2010 / xx + 288 pp. (24 b&w photos) / ISBN 978-1-55458-219-8

We All Giggled: A Bourgeois Family Memoir by Thomas O. Hueglin • 2010 / xiv + 232 pp. (20 b&w photos) / ISBN 978-1-55458-262-4

Just a Larger Family: Letters of Marie Williamson from the Canadian Home Front, 1940–1944 edited by Mary F. Williamson and Tom Sharp • 2011 / xxiv + 378 pp. (16 b&w photos) / ISBN 978-1-55458-323-2

Burdens of Proof: Faith, Doubt, and Identity in Autobiography by Susanna Egan • 2011 / x + 200 pp. / ISBN 978-1-55458-333-1

Accident of Fate: A Personal Account 1938–1945 by Imre Rochlitz with Joseph Rochlitz • 2011 / xiv + 226 pp. (50 b&w photos, 5 maps) / ISBN 978-1-55458-267-9

The Green Sofa by Natascha Würzbach, translated by Raleigh Whitinger • 2012 / xiv + 240 pp. (5 b&w photos) / ISBN 978-1-55458-334-8

Unheard Of: Memoirs of a Canadian Composer by John Beckwith • 2012 / x + 393 pp. (74 illus., 8 musical examples) / ISBN 978-1-55458-358-4

Borrowed Tongues: Life Writing, Migration, and Translation by Eva C. Karpinski • 2012 / viii + 274 pp. / ISBN 978-1-55458-357-7

Basements and Attics, Closets and Cyberspace: Explorations in Canadian Women's Archives edited by Linda M. Morra and Jessica Schagerl • 2012 / x + 338 pp. / ISBN 978-1-55458-632-5

The Memory of Water by Allen Smutylo • 2013 / x + 262 pp. (65 colour illus.) / ISBN 978-1-55458-842-8

The Unwritten Diary of Israel Unger, Revised Edition by Carolyn Gammon and Israel Unger • 2013 / ix + 230 pp. (b&w illus.) / ISBN 978-1-77112-011-1

Boom! Manufacturing Memoir for the Popular Market by Julie Rak • 2013 / viii + 249 pp. (b&w illus.) / ISBN 978-1-55458-939-5

Motherlode: A Mosaic of Dutch Wartime Experience by Carolyne Van Der Meer • 2014 / xiv + 132 pp. (b&w illus.) / ISBN 978-1-77112-005-0

Not the Whole Story: Challenging the Single Mother Narrative edited by Lea Caragata and Judit Alcalde • 2014 / x + 222 pp. / ISBN 978-1-55458-624-0

Street Angel by Magie Dominic • 2014 / vii + 154 pp. / ISBN 978-1-77112-026-5

In the Unlikeliest of Places: How Nachman Libeskind Survived the Nazis, Gulags, and Soviet Communism by Annette Libeskind Berkovits • 2014 / xiv + 282 pp. (6 colour illus.) / ISBN 978-1-77112-066-1

Kinds of Winter: Four Solo Journeys by Dogteam in Canada's Northwest Territories by Dave Olesen • 2014 / xii + 256 pp. (illus.) / ISBN 978-1-77112-118-7

Working Memory: Women and Work in World War II edited by Marlene Kadar and Jeanne Perreault • 2015 / vii + 243 pp. (illus.) / ISBN 978-1-77112—035-7

Wait Time: A Memoir of Cancer by Kenneth Sherman • 2016 / xiv + 138 pp. / ISBN 978-1-77112-188-0

Canadian Graphic: Picturing Life Narratives edited by Candida Rifkind and Linda Warley • 2016 / viii + 305 pp. (illus.) / ISBN 978-1-77112-179-8

Travels and Identities: Elizabeth and Adam Shortt in Europe, 1911 edited by Peter E. Paul Dembski • 2017 / xxii + 272 pp. (illus.) / ISBN 978-1-77112-225-2

Bird-Bent Grass: A Memoir, in Pieces by Kathleen Venema • 2018 • viii + 340 pp. / ISBN 978-1-77112-290-0

My Basilian Priesthood, 1961–1967 by Michael Quealey • 2019 • viii + 221 pp. (illus.) / ISBN 978-1-77112-242-9